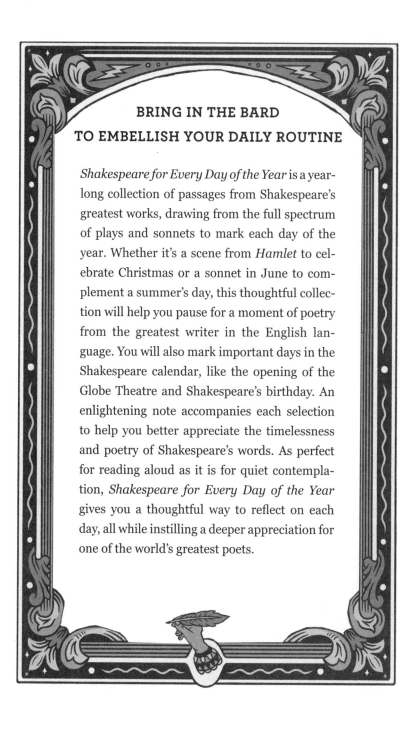

BRING IN THE BARD
TO EMBELLISH YOUR DAILY ROUTINE

Shakespeare for Every Day of the Year is a year-long collection of passages from Shakespeare's greatest works, drawing from the full spectrum of plays and sonnets to mark each day of the year. Whether it's a scene from *Hamlet* to celebrate Christmas or a sonnet in June to complement a summer's day, this thoughtful collection will help you pause for a moment of poetry from the greatest writer in the English language. You will also mark important days in the Shakespeare calendar, like the opening of the Globe Theatre and Shakespeare's birthday. An enlightening note accompanies each selection to help you better appreciate the timelessness and poetry of Shakespeare's words. As perfect for reading aloud as it is for quiet contemplation, *Shakespeare for Every Day of the Year* gives you a thoughtful way to reflect on each day, all while instilling a deeper appreciation for one of the world's greatest poets.

PENGUIN BOOKS

SHAKESPEARE FOR
EVERY DAY OF THE YEAR

Allie Esiri is a former English stage, film, and television actress and has been in numerous productions of Shakespeare's plays, including performances with the English Shakespeare Company. A lifelong lover of Shakespeare's poetry, she also studied Medieval and Modern English at Cambridge University.

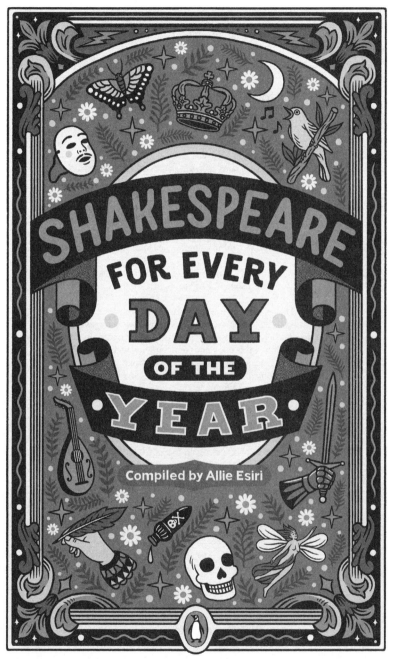

SHAKESPEARE
FOR EVERY
DAY
OF THE
YEAR

Compiled by Allie Esiri

PENGUIN BOOKS

for Eliza, Rosie and Jack
The love I dedicate . . . is without end

PENGUIN BOOKS
An imprint of Penguin Random House LLC
penguinrandomhouse.com

First published by Macmillan Children's Books, an imprint of Pan Macmillan, 2019
Published in Penguin Books 2020

LIBRARY OF CONGRESS CATALOGING-IN-PUBLICATION DATA
Names: Shakespeare, William, 1564–1616, author. | Esiri, Allie, 1967–editor.
Title: Shakespeare for every day of the year / edited by Allie Esiri.
Description: [New York, NY] : Penguin Books, 2020. | First published by
Macmillan Children's Books, an imprint of Pan Macmillan, 2019. |
Includes bibliographical references. |
Identifiers: LCCN 2019048000 (print) | LCCN 2019048001 (ebook) |
ISBN 9780143134374 (hardcover) | ISBN 9780525506218 (ebook)
Subjects: LCSH: Shakespeare, William, 1564–1616—Quotations.
Classification: LCC PR2892 .E85 2020 (print) |
LCC PR2892 (ebook) | DDC 822.3/3–dc23
LC record available at https://lccn.loc.gov/2019048000
LC ebook record available at https://lccn.loc.gov/2019048001

Printed in the United States of America
1   3   5   7   9   10   8   6   4   2

Set in Georgia Pro with Archer

Contents

February

April

July

August

October

December

Introduction

O God! Methinks it were a happy life
To be no better than a homely swain;
To sit upon a hill, as I do now;
To carve out dials quaintly, point by point,
Thereby to see the minutes how they run:
How many make the hour full complete,
How many hours bring about the day,
How many days will finish up the year,
How many years a mortal man may live.

Henry VI, Part 3, Act 2, Scene 5

There have been surprisingly few anthologies of Shakespeare's work curated in recent years. Ted Hughes compiled a volume in 1971, just over thirty years after Cambridge scholar George Rylands published his acclaimed collection. Rylands' anthology was such a success that it was performed on Broadway and recorded by John Gielgud, winning the legendary actor a Tony, a Grammy and an Emmy award. In his collection, Rylands points out that the early anthologist of Shakespeare's work, Dr William Dodd, was publicly executed (for forgery) in 1777 at Tyburn in London – I rather hope this book is received in better favour than Dodd was at the end of his life.

As these anthologizers have demonstrated, Shakespeare extracts stand alone as works of art in themselves. In the case of the sonnets, that is precisely what they are – they can be enjoyed on their own merits, freed from their original contexts. Even entire plays don't concern themselves with befores and afters, and in this sense these extracts are no different. What happened to King Lear before he divides up his kingdom? How are we to know that Beatrice and Benedick live happily ever after?

Questions like these need not trouble us here. Soliloquies give us a fully fleshed out moment of a life – Hamlet's crippling indecision over whether to be or not to be; Viola's farcical befuddlement when she is handed a ring that is not hers; the slow hardening of Macbeth's murderous resolve; and Iago's breathtaking dishonesty even to himself.

Over the course of the year, we have space for more than just the best-known and best-loved passages. Every play is featured, even the ones you might not know, and parts of poems which were bestsellers in Shakespeare's lifetime, but which you may never even have heard of, are also presented. You can read some aloud – but bear in mind what a great actor once advised: speak the thought, don't just regurgitate the verse. Or use Hamlet's advice to the players, 'Speak the speech, I pray you, as I pronounced it to you, trippingly on the tongue'. As Shakespeare himself was an actor, this might even mirror his own view. His writing leaves you space to inhabit each character and scope to interpret their words, synthesizing your life with theirs. Whoever plays Hamlet reinvents the part anew. This is why Shakespeare means something different to every generation, and why he is never out of place in any age.

Although Shakespeare writes of politics, he is not political; there is no side to an argument he has not taken and disrupted with equal brilliance. He did not merely record history; he created it.

There is no source for Richard III's murder of his nephews in the tower; King John was not poisoned by a disgruntled monk, but died, albeit less dramatically, of dysentery; Shakespeare's Charles IV of France is a formidable foe of Henry V, whereas in reality he was severely mentally incapacitated. Shakespeare's embellishments are often remembered as history. That is because he drives at the heart of who people are; not merely as monarchs and politicians, but as human beings, ambitious, indecisive, flawed.

Although there have been critics disdainful of his plays, for example Samuel Pepys, who said of *Romeo and Juliet*, 'it is a play of itself the worst that I ever heard in my life', and T.S. Eliot on *Titus Andronicus*, 'One of the stupidest and uninspired plays ever written', many immortal talents acknowledge their debt and admiration for Shakespeare. Romantic poet Keats is typical among them: 'Thank God I can read and perhaps understand his depths.' During the course of my research, I interviewed actors and scholars, consulted libraries and radio series and I hope all these have helped me provide something to help you through the selection. There was a particular moment when I felt I came close to understanding his depths. It was a woman's story I heard on a Folger Shakespeare Library podcast. She was a teenager at the Nazi concentration centre Theresienstadt, forced to dig a mass grave, and as she did so, a guard overheard her reciting Titania's words, in Czech. He pulled her aside and said that he recognized the Shakespeare. He then told her to run away that night with her mother, as they were due to be executed the next day. Pretending to scold her, he yelled at her to go back to work. She and her mother escaped. She did not and could not know, but thought it was Shakespeare's words that jolted his humanity.

William Shakespeare wrote at least thirty-seven plays, one hundred and fifty-four sonnets and a handful of longer poems. Two plays, *Love's Labour's Won* and *Cardenio,* appear to have been lost, and next to nothing is known about his life and personality – not unusual for a man of his era and social standing, but tantalizing considering his posthumous prestige. However, it might be better this way. As Charles Dickens expressed it: 'It is a great comfort, to my thinking, that so little is known concerning the poet. It is a fine mystery; and I tremble every day lest something should come out.'

Shakespeare's words sit neatly around a calendar, with the passing of time as one of his most common themes. After all, as he put it, 'Time's the king of men; / he's both their parent, and he is their grave, / and gives them what he will, not what they crave'. Seasons feature strongly too. Although he spent his working life in London, his rural Warwickshire roots show through in observations such as, 'daffodils, / That come before the swallow dares, and take / The winds of March with beauty'. What's more, this calendar style would be familiar to Shakespeare himself. Almanacs – which included a yearly calendar and the important dates in the year – were bought by one in three Elizabethan families every year and were the second-bestselling volumes, after the Bible. The passage of time and the turning of the seasons were felt more acutely, of course, in Shakespeare's day, as rural communities lived their lives so much more closely to nature than most of us do.

Of the 31,534 words we know Shakespeare wrote, many were coined by him, and half of them were used only once. Shakespeare's new-fangled words include, well, 'new-fangled' as well as 'bedazzled', 'birth-place', 'cold-blooded', 'cold-hearted', 'eyeball', 'fortune-teller', 'puppy-dog', 'shooting star', 'unreal' and 'well-read' to name but a few. Phrases attributed to him include 'Blinking idiot', 'Brave new world', 'Brevity is the soul of wit', 'In my heart of hearts', 'Jealousy is the green-eyed monster', 'Neither rhyme nor reason', 'Own flesh and blood', 'Too much of a good thing' and 'What's done is done'. Chances are you were quoting Shakespeare before you saw one of his plays, or opened this book.

Each page of *Shakespeare for Every Day of the Year* contains a piece matched to the date. The introductory paragraphs explore his work, his time, his legacy and what we know about his life. There's an entry around the date of the Oscars where we discover which of Shakespeare's plays have won Academy Awards and others where we explore his exceptional writing of female characters; learn about his only son Hamnet who died aged eleven; speculate as to why he left his wife his 'second best bed'; see how he became the first writer to amass a fortune; and how he practically never invented a plot. You can read it daily or dip in as you like. As his distinguished friend Ben Jonson observed, Shakespeare was not just the 'soul of the age' and 'the wonder of our stage', he was, and Jonson could see this even then, 'not of an age, but for all time'.

Allie Esiri

January

January 1 | Romeo and Juliet | Prologue

Very few of Shakespeare's plays have a prologue, but among
them is the following from *Romeo and Juliet*. It is one of
the most famous openings in the canon and a fitting start
for our year of Shakespeare. The Prologue tells us that these
original star-crossed lovers are going to die, which amounts
to something of a spoiler. Because of this, the audience knows
that despite the levity and love in the beginning of the play, this
couple is hurtling, unbeknownst to them, towards a tragic fate.

CHORUS
Two households, both alike in dignity
In fair Verona, where we lay our scene,
From ancient grudge break to new mutiny,
Where civil blood makes civil hands unclean.
From forth the fatal loins of these two foes
A pair of star-crossed lovers take their life;
Whose misadventured piteous overthrows
Doth with their death bury their parents' strife.
The fearful passage of their death-marked love,
And the continuance of their parents' rage,
Which, but their children's end, nought could remove,
Is now the two hours' traffic of our stage;
The which if you with patient ears attend,
What here shall miss, our toil shall strive to mend.

January 2 | Twelfth Night | Act 1 Scene 1

Shakespeare mentions food in all of his plays, and many of the associated phrases have become absorbed into modern English expressions; perhaps in your 'salad days', when 'the world is your oyster', you may find yourself 'in a pickle'. You may have fond memories of a 'feast fit for the Gods', though not in the same sense as Brutus meant it in *Julius Caesar*: for him, the feast is Caesar, whom Brutus hopes to 'carve up'. The opening line of *Twelfth Night* is one of Shakespeare's most well known. Here, the lovelorn Duke Orsino orders his court musicians to keep playing romantic tunes so that he might become sick of thinking about love, like a glutton unable to contemplate another mouthful.

ORSINO
If music be the food of love, play on,
Give me excess of it, that, surfeiting,
The appetite may sicken, and so die.
That strain again! It had a dying fall.
O, it came o'er my ear like the sweet sound,
That breathes upon a bank of violets,
Stealing and giving odour. Enough, no more!
'Tis not so sweet now as it was before.
O spirit of love, how quick and fresh art thou,
That, notwithstanding thy capacity
Receiveth as the sea, nought enters there,
Of what validity and pitch soe'er,
But falls into abatement and low price
Even in a minute. So full of shapes is fancy
That it alone is high fantastical.

January 3 | The Merchant of Venice | Act 5 Scene 1

Music is a poignant feature in many of Shakespeare's plays, just as it was important in the philosophy of his era. Pythagoras's view, which was entertained right up until the Renaissance, was that the celestial spheres on which the planets and stars move around must make a sound as they spin. He called this sound the Music of the Spheres, a principle of harmony which governs the whole universe. With this in mind, in *The Merchant of Venice* when Jessica says that she is 'never merry' when she hears 'sweet music', Lorenzo observes that she must be attentive to the harmony of the universe; by extension, anybody who claims to be entirely unmoved by music should be regarded with caution.

LORENZO
The reason is your spirits are attentive.
For do but note a wild and wanton herd
Or race of youthful and unhandled colts
Fetching mad bounds, bellowing and neighing loud,
Which is the hot condition of their blood,
If they but hear perchance a trumpet sound,
Or any air of music touch their ears,
You shall perceive them make a mutual stand,
Their savage eyes turned to a modest gaze
By the sweet power of music. Therefore the poet
Did feign that Orpheus drew trees, stones and floods,
Since nought so stockish, hard, and full of rage
But music for the time doth change his nature.
The man that hath no music in himself,
Nor is not moved with concord of sweet sounds,
Is fit for treasons, stratagems and spoils,
The motions of his spirit are dull as night,
And his affections dark as Erebus.
Let no such man be trusted. Mark the music.

Shakespeare's song lyrics use a different metrical structure from his poetry (trochaic trimeter, not iambic pentameter or tetrameter, for you poetry buffs), though most were not entirely of his own composition. Living between Stratford and London, Shakespeare absorbed the rural influences of his home town and fed them onto the stage in the city in the form of pastoral songs, usually adapted from pre-existing common ballads and folk songs. The melancholy Jaques contributes his own verse to Shakespeare's greenwood song, exposing the shallowness of the philosophy of this ditty: 'Ducdame' means absolutely nothing.

AMIENS
Under the greenwood tree,
Who loves to lie with me,
And turn his merry note
Unto the sweet bird's throat:
Come hither, come hither, come hither.
Here shall he see
No enemy
But winter and rough weather.
[. . .]

ALL
Who doth ambition shun,
And loves to live i'th'sun,
Seeking the food he eats,
And pleased with what he gets:
Come hither, come hither, come hither.
Here shall he see
No enemy
But winter and rough weather.

JAQUES
I'll give you a verse to this note, that I made
yesterday in despite of my invention.

AMIENS
And I'll sing it.

JAQUES
Thus it goes:
If it do come to pass
That any man turn ass,
Leaving his wealth and ease,
A stubborn will to please:
Ducdame, ducdame, ducdame.
Here shall he see
Gross fools as he,
An if he will come to me.

January is the beginning of our calendar year, named after
the Roman two-headed god Janus, who faces both towards
the future and back at the past. He is mentioned by Salerio in
the dialogue with the inexplicably sad Antonio that opens *The
Merchant of Venice*. Shakespeare's England was yet to embrace
January as the first month, as the beginning of the year was still
in the spring, on 25 March.

ANTONIO
In sooth I know not why I am so sad.
It wearies me, you say it wearies you;
But how I caught it, found it, or came by it,
What stuff 'tis made of, whereof it is born,
I am to learn;
And such a want-wit sadness makes of me
That I have much ado to know myself.
[. . .]

SALERIO
            I know, Antonio
Is sad to think upon his merchandise.

ANTONIO
Believe me, no. I thank my fortune for it
My ventures are not in one bottom trusted,
Nor to one place; nor is my whole estate
Upon the fortune of this present year.
Therefore my merchandise makes me not sad.

SALERIO
Why then you are in love.

ANTONIO
Fie, fie!

SALERIO
Not in love neither? Then let us say you are sad
Because you are not merry; and 'twere as easy
For you to laugh and leap, and say you are merry
Because you are not sad. Now, by two-headed Janus,
Nature hath framed strange fellows in her time:
Some that will evermore peep through their eyes
And laugh like parrots at a bagpiper,
And other is such vinegar aspect
That they'll not show their teeth in way of smile
Though Nestor swear the jest be laughable.

Twelfth Night was the culmination of twelve days of Christmas revelry: the tradition was that misrule reigned supreme and social conventions during this period were gleefully subverted. In the spirit of this, the vain and straight-laced steward Malvolio finds a forged letter, apparently written by the Countess Olivia, instructing him to dress in yellow stockings and smile out of his usual temper in the acknowledgement of her love. While we may urge on his humiliating epiphany, we sympathize with his happiness, savouring this moment of wondrous possibility before the world shatters his dreams.

MALVOLIO
[*Reads*]
'If this fall into thy hand, revolve. In my stars I
am above thee, but be not afraid of greatness. Some
are born great, some achieve greatness, and some
have greatness thrust upon 'em.'
[. . .]
Daylight and champain discovers not more! This is
open. I will be proud, I will read politic authors,
I will baffle Sir Toby, I will wash off gross
acquaintance, I will be point-devise the very man.
I do not now fool myself, to let imagination jade
me; for every reason excites to this, that my lady
loves me. She did commend my yellow stockings of
late, she did praise my leg being cross-gartered;
and in this she manifests herself to my love and
with a kind of injunction drives me to these habits
of her liking. I thank my stars, I am happy! I will
be strange, stout, in yellow stockings, and
cross-gartered, even with the swiftness of putting
on. Jove and my stars be praised! Here is yet a postscript.

[Reads]
'Thou canst not choose but know who I am. If thou entertainest my love, let it appear in thy smiling, thy smiles become thee well. Therefore in my presence still smile, dear my sweet, I prithee.'

Jove, I thank thee! I will smile. I will do everything that thou wilt have me!

January 7 | Henry IV, Part 1 | Act 1 Scene 2

The day after Twelfth Night was the first day back to work after the Christmas holiday. This was known as St Distaff's Day, named after a tool used for spinning which was traditionally associated with women's work. As a result, it is emasculating for Goneril's cowardly husband in *King Lear*, when she proposes 'I must change arms at home, and give the distaff / Into my husband's hands'. Elsewhere, more in the back-to-work spirit, the future King Henry V, who has been staying away from the responsibilities of court life at the Boar's Head Tavern in Eastcheap, describes the effect of holidaying too much. A similar logic underpins his plan to eventually cast off his rowdy companions and seem more noble and king-like for having done so.

PRINCE HAL
If all the year were playing holidays,
To sport would be as tedious as to work;
But when they seldom come, they wished-for come,
And nothing pleaseth but rare accidents.
So when this loose behavior I throw off,
And pay the debt I never promisèd,
By how much better than my word I am,
By so much shall I falsify men's hopes.
And like bright metal on a sullen ground,
My reformation, glittering o'er my fault,
Shall show more goodly, and attract more eyes
Than that which hath no foil to set it off.
I'll so offend, to make offense a skill,
Redeeming time when men think least I will.

Shakespeare's non-dramatic poetry is as rich and intriguing as the plays for which he is now most known. He wrote narrative poems and a collection of sonnets – poems of fourteen lines – which were a fashionable form of poetry in the 1590s. These were shared first in manuscript before they were published. Frances Meres, an early admirer, wrote in 1598, 'The witty soul of Ovid lives in mellifluous and honey-tongued Shakespeare, witness his Venus and Adonis, his Lucrece, his sugar'd sonnets among his private friends.' His sequence of 154 sonnets was not published until 1609, by which time the vogue for sonnets had passed, and for centuries these would be among Shakespeare's most neglected writings. Although sonnets had traditionally been about unrequited romantic love, Shakespeare incorporated some profound insights about marriage, death, poetry, race, religion, homosexuality and, perhaps most of all, the passing of time. In Sonnet 19, the poet finds refuge from the destructiveness of time in poetry.

Devouring Time, blunt thou the Lion's paws,
And make the earth devour her own sweet brood,
Pluck the keen teeth from the fierce Tiger's jaws,
And burn the long-liv'd Phoenix in her blood,
Make glad and sorry seasons as thou fleet'st,
And do whate'er thou wilt, swift-footed Time,
To the wide world and all her fading sweets:
But I forbid thee one more heinous crime,
O carve not with the hours my love's fair brow,
Nor draw no lines there with thine antique pen,
Him in thy course untainted do allow,
For beauty's pattern to succeeding men.
   Yet do thy worst, old Time, despite thy wrong,
   My love shall in my verse ever live young.

January 9 | A Midsummer Night's Dream | Act 5 Scene 1

Shakespeare's reflections on the value of poetry are not confined to his poems; the figure of the poet is mentioned (and even has a presence) in several of his plays. In *A Midsummer Night's Dream*, a play in which 'the course of true love never did run smooth', order is restored once everybody reconvenes at Theseus's palace. Noble characters in Renaissance comedies traditionally restore order at the close of the play, though Shakespeare cunningly credits himself in bringing that about on stage. The poet, like the madman and the lover, is a daydreamer, but it's only the former who can record and make sense of their wild imagination.

THESEUS
The lunatic, the lover and the poet
Are of imagination all compact.
One sees more devils than vast hell can hold.
That is the madman. The lover, all as frantic,
Sees Helen's beauty in a brow of Egypt.
The poet's eye, in a fine frenzy rolling,
Doth glance from heaven to earth, from earth to heaven.
And as imagination bodies forth
The forms of things unknown, the poet's pen
Turns them to shapes, and gives to airy nothing
A local habitation and a name.
Such tricks hath strong imagination,
That if it would but apprehend some joy,
It comprehends some bringer of that joy.
Or in the night, imagining some fear,
How easy is a bush supposed a bear?

King Lear, which plots the tragic mental decline of an aged and deluded king, contains some of the fiercest dialogue in all of Shakespeare. Here the King, left out in a storm after a furious row with his two elder daughters, urges the weather to do its worst, the perceived ingratitude of his daughters having already caused him as much grief as he can imagine. There would have been little scenery at Shakespeare's company's home venue, the Globe, but the ever-resourceful Elizabethan stagehands would roll a cannonball in the hollow wooden eaves above the stage, to make the sound of thunder.

KING LEAR
Blow, winds, and crack your cheeks! Rage! Blow!
You cataracts and hurricanoes, spout
Till you have drenched our steeples, drowned the cocks!
You sulphurous and thought-executing fires,
Vaunt-curriers of oak-cleaving thunderbolts,
Singe my white head! And thou all-shaking thunder,
Smite flat the thick rotundity o'the world,
Crack Nature's moulds, all germens spill at once
That make ingrateful man!
[. . .]
Rumble thy bellyful! Spit, fire! Spout, rain!
Nor rain, wind, thunder, fire, are my daughters.
I tax not you, you elements, with unkindness;
I never gave you kingdom, called you children.
You owe me no subscription; then let fall
Your horrible pleasure. Here I stand, your slave,
A poor, infirm, weak, and despised old man.
But yet I call you servile ministers,
That have with two pernicious daughters join
Your high engendered battles 'gainst a head
So old and white as this. O, ho! 'Tis foul!

On 11 January 1613, a 26ft (7.9m) apparently complete
human skeleton was dug up in France, within living memory
of an equally unbelievable 20ft (6.1m) skeleton unearthed
in Switzerland in 1577. Although, disappointingly, these are
more likely to have been elephant bones (perhaps left over
from Hannibal's crossing), giants have populated folklore and
the public imagination since time immemorial, sometimes as
benevolent, but often as cruel and merciless figures wielding
terrible and almighty strength. In *Measure for Measure* – a
play centrally concerned with proportionality – Isabella,
pleading against her brother Claudio's death sentence for
fornication, evokes the giant in a speech weighing strength
against mercy. Many of Shakespeare's women are powerful
petitioners, though not all are interested in moderation; they
challenge power as often as they abuse it, sometimes as fiercely
vengeful as they are mercifully kind.

ANGELO
I show it most of all when I show justice,
For then I pity those I do not know,
Which a dismissed offence would after gall,
And do him right that, answering one foul wrong,
Lives not to act another. Be satisfied
Your brother dies tomorrow. Be content.

ISABELLA
So you must be the first that gives this sentence,
And he, that suffers. O, it is excellent
To have a giant's strength, but it is tyrannous
To use it like a giant.

LUCIO
[*Aside to* ISABELLA] That's well said.

ISABELLA
Could great men thunder
As Jove himself does, Jove would never be quiet,
For every pelting, petty officer
Would use his heaven for thunder,
Nothing but thunder. Merciful heaven,
Thou rather with thy sharp and sulphurous bolt
Splits the unwedgeable and gnarlèd oak
Than the soft myrtle; but man, proud man,
Dressed in a little brief authority,
Most ignorant of what he's most assured,
His glassy essence, like an angry ape
Plays such fantastic tricks before high heaven
As make the angels weep; who, with our spleens,
Would all themselves laugh mortal.

January 12 | Henry IV, Part 2 | Act 4 Scene 4

Winter occurs metaphorically throughout Shakespeare's works.
Westmoreland's news of victory at the Battle of Shrewsbury
gladdens the ageing King, giving him hope of lasting peace. The
King's feelings turn from wintry foreboding to summer joy.

WESTMORELAND
Health to my sovereign, and new happiness
Added to that that I am to deliver!
Prince John your son doth kiss your grace's hand.
Mowbray, the Bishop Scroop, Hastings, and all
Are brought to the correction of your law.
There is not now a rebel's sword unsheathed,
But Peace puts forth her olive everywhere.
The manner how this action hath been borne
Here at more leisure may your highness read,
With every course in his particular.

KING HENRY IV
O Westmoreland, thou art a summer bird,
Which ever in the haunch of winter sings
The lifting up of day.

In January 1593, when London's theatres were closed due to
the plague, Shakespeare turned his hand to poetry. His erotic
narrative poem *Venus and Adonis* became his most successful
published work in his lifetime. Based on an Ovidian myth, the
poem describes the goddess Venus's passionate love for the
beautiful mortal Adonis, who in Shakespeare's version is more
interested in going hunting than in reciprocating her passion.
Much of the poem consists of Venus's eloquent but unsuccessful
attempts at seduction: in the following lines, however, one of
the few passages from this work to find its way into Victorian
dictionaries of quotations, the rather prudish Adonis rebukes her.

'Love comforteth like sunshine after rain,
But Lust's effect is tempest after sun;
Love's gentle spring doth always fresh remain,
Lust's winter comes ere summer half be done;
Love surfeits not, Lust like a glutton dies;
Love is all truth, Lust full of forgèd lies.

'More I could tell, but more I dare not say;
The text is old, the orator too green.
Therefore, in sadness, now I will away;
My face is full of shame, my heart of teen:
Mine ears that to your wanton talk attended
Do burn themselves for having so offended.'

With this, he breaketh from the sweet embrace
Of those fair arms which bound him to her breast,
And homeward through the dark laund runs apace;
Leaves Love upon her back deeply distressed.
Look how a bright star shooteth from the sky,
So glides he in the night from Venus' eye.

January is mentioned only twice in Shakespeare's work,
and then only figuratively. Winter could be severe for rural
communities in Elizabethan England, and 14 January was
traditionally the coldest day of the year. The first mention
comes in *Much Ado About Nothing*, where Beatrice reassures
her uncle that the chances of her 'running mad' are as likely as
a 'hot January'. The second frames the month as synonymous
with the cold harshness of reality, contrasting with the
whimsical dreams of a bountiful midsummer. *The Winter's Tale*
consistently stretches the credulity of its audience, climaxing
with the onstage transformation of a statue into the living figure
of a long-dead Queen. Here, Shakespeare has the supposed
shepherdess Perdita, distributing flowers to the guests at a
sheep-shearing feast, chide the middle-aged Camillo for his
elaborate courtly flattery.

PERDITA
Here's flowers for you:
Hot lavender, mints, savory, marjoram;
The marigold, that goes to bed with' sun
And with him rises weeping; these are flowers
Of middle summer, and I think they are given
To men of middle age. Y'are very welcome.

CAMILLO
 I should leave grazing, were I of your flock,
And only live by gazing.

PERDITA
Out, alas!
You'd be so lean that blasts of January
Would blow you through and through.

January 15 | The Merry Wives of Windsor | Act 1 Scene 1

Elizabeth I was crowned Queen in Westminster Abbey on 15 January 1559. She had been on the throne for five years before Shakespeare was born and reigned a further thirty-nine years until her death in 1603. Although in many ways she reigned like an old-fashioned medieval monarch, firm and uncompromising, her court embraced the relatively modern entertainments of masques and theatre, and saw Shakespeare's company perform at her request. *The Merry Wives of Windsor*, which sees the rotund buffoon John Falstaff clumsily navigating affairs of love, is rumoured to have been written at the Queen's request as a kind of spin-off, following the character's success in the *Henry IV* plays. Elizabeth certainly saw the play performed, as one published copy boasts: 'it hath been divers times Acted by the right Honorable my Lord Chamberlaines servants. Both before her Majestie, and elsewhere'. Falstaff's roguish charm and bawdy wit made him perhaps the most popular of Shakespeare's characters among his first, and many of his subsequent, audiences. In the first scene of *Merry Wives* he characteristically defies law and order, here personified by the rural Justice of the Peace, Shallow.

FALSTAFF
Now, Master Shallow, you'll complain of me to the King?

SHALLOW
Knight, you have beaten my men, killed my deer, and broke open my lodge.

FALSTAFF
But not kissed your keeper's daughter?

SHALLOW
Tut, a pin! This shall be answered.

FALSTAFF
I will answer it straight. I have done all this.
That is now answered.

January 16 | The Taming of the Shrew | Act 1 Scene 2

Shakespeare's towering genius is often disguised in the simplest expressions, which speak to us so instantly that they continue to nestle seamlessly into the fabric of the language we use today. In *The Taming of the Shrew*, he coins the phrase 'break the ice' to describe the loosening of a stilted social situation, here applied to Petruchio's plan to woo 'the shrew' Katherine, elder sister to the more popular Bianca. We might express this moment in the play with some other immortal phrases from the immortal bard: now that 'the game's afoot', 'come what come may', Petruchio's pursuit of Katherine could turn out to be a 'wild goose chase'.

PETRUCHIO
Sir, understand you this of me in sooth,
The youngest daughter whom you hearken for
Her father keeps from all access of suitors,
And will not promise her to any man
Until the elder sister first be wed.
The younger then is free, and not before.

TRANIO
If it be so, sir, that you are the man
Must stead us all – and me amongst the rest –
And if you break the ice and do this feat,
Achieve the elder, set the younger free
For our access – whose hap shall be to have her
Will not so graceless be to be ingrate.

January 17 | A Midsummer Night's Dream | Act 4 Scene 1

On 17 January 1604 at Hampton Court, the protestant King James I initiated the production of a new, official vernacular translation of the Bible. Produced by a team of leading academics and published in 1611, the King James Bible would become one of the most influential texts in the history of the English-speaking world. Like any other Englishman of his time, when church attendance was compulsory, Shakespeare was intimately familiar with the Bible, a book which clearly interested him outside services too, since he shows evidence of familiarity with several different translations. Though Shakespeare's works owe a great debt to biblical passages, he never once uses the word 'bible', and unlike contemporaries such as Thomas Dekker he tends to avoid dramatizing the theological controversies of the Reformation. One of the passages to which he alludes most often is I Corinthians 2:9, a preference that reflects his seeming reluctance to venture much about the nature of God in his work: 'Eye hath not seen, nor ear heard, nor entered into the heart of man what God has in store for those who love Him.' Mentioned four times over three plays, this verse must have been as familiar to Shakespeare as it was to his audience. They may have laughed knowingly when it is disastrously misquoted by Bottom, a loveably bumptious amateur thespian, who, left asleep after his magical encounter with the Queen of the Fairies, wakes in wonder. After first remembering the rehearsal in which he was involved before his meeting with the fairies, he attempts to make sense of what he can remember of his enchantment.

BOTTOM
[*Awaking*] When my cue comes, call me, and I will answer. My next is 'Most fair Pyramus'. Heigh-ho!

Peter Quince! Flute the bellows-mender! Snout the tinker! Starveling! God's my life – stolen hence and left me asleep! – I have had a most rare vision. I have had a dream past the wit of man to say what dream it was. Man is but an ass if he go about to expound this dream. Methought I was – there is no man can tell what. Methought I was – and methought I had – but man is but a patched fool if he will offer to say what methought I had. The eye of man hath not heard, the ear of man hath not seen, man's hand is not able to taste, his tongue to conceive, nor his heart to report what my dream was! I will get Peter Quince to write a ballad of this dream. It shall be called 'Bottom's Dream', because it hath no bottom; and I will sing it in the latter end of a play, before the Duke. Peradventure, to make it the more gracious, I shall sing it at her death.

Time takes on many manners in Shakespeare, sometimes moving infuriatingly slowly, at other times charging at a giddying pace. The rich heiress Portia's hand in marriage is tied, fairytale-like, to three caskets which prospective suitors must choose between. She wishes time would move more slowly with her preferred suitor, Bassanio, so the choice might be delayed: the outcome could bind or separate them for ever.

PORTIA
I pray you tarry, pause a day or two
Before you hazard, for in choosing wrong
I lose your company. Therefore forbear awhile.
There's something tells me, but it is not love,
I would not lose you; and you know yourself
Hate counsels not in such a quality.
But lest you should not understand me well –
And yet a maiden hath no tongue but thought –
I would detain you here some month or two
Before you venture for me. I could teach you
How to choose right, but I am then forsworn.
So will I never be. So may you miss me.
But if you do, you'll make me wish a sin,
That I had been forsworn. Beshrew your eyes!
They have o'erlooked me and divided me;
One half of me is yours, the other half yours,
Mine own, I would say; but if mine, then yours,
And so all yours. O these naughty times
Put bars between the owners and their rights.
And so, though yours, not yours. Prove it so,
Let fortune go to hell for it, not I.
I speak too long, but 'tis to piece the time,
To eke it and to draw it out in length,
To stay you from election.

In contrast to Portia, Juliet urges on the coming night and the consummation of her secret marriage to Romeo. The devastating speed, and Juliet's heady encouragement of time's ravishing pace, is no small part of her tragic whirlwind love affair: 'Never was a story of more woe / Than this of Juliet and her Romeo.'

JULIET
Gallop apace, you fiery-footed steeds,
Towards Phoebus' lodging! Such a waggoner
As Phaëton would whip you to the West
And bring in cloudy night immediately.
Spread thy close curtain, love-performing night,
That runaway's eyes may wink, and Romeo
Leap to these arms untalked of and unseen.
Lovers can see to do their amorous rites
By their own beauties; or, if love be blind,
It best agrees with night. Come, civil night,
Thou sober-suited matron, all in black,
And learn me how to lose a winning match,
Played for a pair of stainless maidenhoods.
Hood my unmanned blood, bating in my cheeks,
With thy black mantle till strange love grow bold,
Think true love acted simple modesty.
Come, night. Come, Romeo. Come, thou day in night;
For thou wilt lie upon the wings of night
Whiter than new snow on a raven's back.
Come, gentle night, come, loving, black-browed night.
Give me my Romeo. And when I shall die,
Take him and cut him out in little stars,
And he will make the face of heaven so fine
That all the world will be in love with night
And pay no worship to the garish sun.

O, I have bought the mansion of a love,
But not possessed it; and, though I am sold,
Not yet enjoyed. So tedious is this day
As is the night before some festival
To an impatient child that hath new robes
And may not wear them. O here comes my Nurse,
And she brings news; and every tongue that speaks
But Romeo's name speaks heavenly eloquence.

Cressida initially enjoys feigning indifference towards Troilus, despite harbouring strong affections for him. Here, in a scene where they declare their love for one another, she has been confronted by Troilus over her coyness towards him up until this point. Unusually for a heroine, she goes on to act unfaithfully with the Greek prince Diomedes. Cressida's flirtatiousness does not end well for her, though her romantic freedom has been appealing, particularly to feminist readers of the play. The radicalism of having such a sympathetic character behaving so immodestly did not sit well with John Dryden: in his 1679 adaptation of the play, Cressida remains faithful to Troilus.

CRESSIDA
Hard to seem won; but I was won, my lord,
With the first glance that ever – pardon me;
If I confess much, you will play the tyrant.
I love you now; but not till now so much
But I might master it. In faith, I lie;
My thoughts were like unbridled children, grown
Too headstrong for their mother – see, we fools!
Why have I blabbed? Who shall be true to us
When we are so unsecret to ourselves? –
But though I loved you well, I wooed you not;
And yet, good faith, I wished myself a man,
Or that we women had men's privilege
Of speaking first. Sweet, bid me hold my tongue,
For in this rapture I shall surely speak
The thing I shall repent. See, see, your silence,
Cunning in dumbness, from my weakness draws
My soul of counsel from me! – Stop my mouth.

January 21 | Macbeth | Act 2 Scene 2

On 21 January 1549, the first Act of Uniformity was passed which made the Book of Common Prayer the sole legal form of worship in England. Although it was repealed during the reign of the Catholic Mary I, Elizabeth reinstated it with new force in 1552, having the book revised slightly to bring together the diverse communities of the Anglican Church. James I continued these efforts in 1604, making revisions to appease the requests of the Puritans. Many phrases from the book have become entrenched into the English language alongside those of Shakespeare and the King James Bible; married life begins with 'till death do us part', and all life ends with 'ashes to ashes, dust to dust'. Treacherous Macbeth is prevented from taking comfort in prayer after killing his king, which is both a treasonous and un-Christian act.

MACBETH
[*Looking at his hands*]
This is a sorry sight.

LADY MACBETH
A foolish thought, to say a sorry sight.

MACBETH
There's one did laugh in's sleep, and one cried 'Murder!'
That they did wake each other. I stood and heard them.
But they did say their prayers and addressed them
Again to sleep.

LADY MACBETH
There are two lodged together.

MACBETH
One cried 'God bless us!' and 'Amen' the other,
As they had seen me with these hangman's hands.
Listening their fear I could not say 'Amen,'
When they did say 'God bless us.'

LADY MACBETH
Consider it not so deeply.

MACBETH
But wherefore could not I pronounce 'Amen'?
I had most need of blessing, and 'Amen'
Stuck in my throat.

LADY MACBETH
These deeds must not be thought
After these ways; so, it will make us mad.

Shakespeare is keenly aware of the illusory nature of time passing. Time has an uneven character across Shakespeare's works, moving at a different pace for different people according to their view on the world. Rosalind, disguised as a young man called Ganymede, teasingly infers Orlando's feelings for her by how he perceives the passage of time in *As You Like It*.

ROSALIND
I pray you, what is't o'clock?

ORLANDO
You should ask me what time o' day: there's no clock in the forest.

ROSALIND
Then there is no true lover in the forest, else sighing every minute and groaning every hour would detect the lazy foot of Time as well as a clock.

ORLANDO
And why not the swift foot of Time? had not that been as proper?

ROSALIND
By no means, sir: Time travels in divers paces with divers persons. I'll tell you who Time ambles withal, who Time trots withal, who Time gallops withal, and who he stands still withal.

ORLANDO
I prithee, who doth he trot withal?

ROSALIND
Marry, he trots hard with a young maid between the
contract of her marriage and the day it is
solemnized. If the interim be but a se'nnight,
Time's pace is so hard that it seems the length of
seven year.

ORLANDO
Who ambles Time withal?

ROSALIND
With a priest that lacks Latin, and a rich man that
hath not the gout: for the one sleeps easily because
he cannot study, and the other lives merrily because
he feels no pain, the one lacking the burden of lean
and wasteful learning, the other knowing no burden
of heavy tedious penury. These Time ambles withal.

ORLANDO
Who doth he gallop withal?

ROSALIND
With a thief to the gallows: for though he go as
softly as foot can fall, he thinks himself too soon there.

ORLANDO
Who stays it still withal?

ROSALIND
With lawyers in the vacation: for they sleep between
term and term, and then they perceive not how Time
   moves.

Tamora, Queen of the Goths, is markedly less discreet than Rosalind in her addresses to her lover, Aaron the Moor, in Shakespeare's first and most violent tragedy. *Titus Andronicus* features villainy so barbaric that it would make Shakespeare's Richard III blush. Though less subtle than the plays he would go on to write, Shakespeare shows early signs of his delicate touch in characterization, for instance where he has the vengeful Tamora imploring her brutal lover to join her, basking in the contrasting beauty of the pastoral landscape.

TAMORA
My lovely Aaron, wherefore look'st thou sad,
When everything doth make a gleeful boast?
The birds chant melody on every bush,
The snake lies rollèd in the cheerful sun,
The green leaves quiver with the cooling wind
And make a chequered shadow on the ground.
Under their sweet shade, Aaron, let us sit,
And whilst the babbling echo mocks the hounds,
Replying shrilly to the well-tuned horns,
As if a double hunt were heard at once,
Let us sit down and mark their yelping noise.
And after conflict such as was supposed
The wand'ring prince and Dido once enjoyed,
When with a happy storm they were surprised
And curtained with a counsel-keeping cave,
We may, each wreathèd in the other's arms,
Our pastimes done, possess a golden slumber,
Whiles hounds and horns and sweet melodious birds
Be unto us as is a nurse's song
Of lullaby to bring her babe asleep.

The theatre patron Philip Henslowe recorded that *Titus Andronicus* was performed in his theatre, the Rose, on 24 January 1594. The play was a hit with Elizabethan crowds, who had an appetite for gore; after all, theatres were competing for audiences with public gallows and bear baiting. Marcus here speaks at length whereas his niece Lavinia is, of course, silent, as she no longer has a tongue (I said it was gory).

MARCUS
Who is this? My niece, that flies away so fast?
Cousin, a word. Where is your husband?
If I do dream, would all my wealth would wake me;
If I do wake, some planet strike me down
That I may slumber an eternal sleep.
Speak, gentle niece, what stern ungentle hands
Have lopped and hewed and made thy body bare
Of her two branches, those sweet ornaments,
Whose circling shadows kings have sought to sleep in,
And might not gain so great a happiness
As have thy love? Why dost not speak to me?
Alas, a crimson river of warm blood,
Like to a bubbling fountain stirred with wind,
Doth rise and fall between thy rosèd lips,
Coming and going with thy honey breath.
But sure some Tereus hath deflowered thee,
And, lest thou shouldst detect him, cut thy tongue.
Ah, now thou turn'st away thy face for shame,
And notwithstanding all this loss of blood,
As from a conduit with three issuing spouts,
Yet do thy cheeks look red as Titan's face
Blushing to be encountered with a cloud.
Shall I speak for thee? Shall I say 'tis so?

O that I knew thy heart, and knew the beast,
That I might rail at him to ease my mind!
Sorrow concealèd, like an oven stopped,
Doth burn the heart to cinders where it is.
Fair Philomela, she but lost her tongue
And in a tedious sampler sewed her mind;
But, lovely niece, that mean is cut from thee.
A craftier Tereus, cousin, hast thou met,
And he hath cut those pretty fingers off
That could have better sewed than Philomel.
O, had the monster seen those lily hands
Tremble like aspen leaves upon a lute
And make the silken strings delight to kiss them,
He would not then have touched them for his life.
Or had he heard the heavenly harmony
Which that sweet tongue hath made,
He would have dropped his knife and fell asleep,
As Cerberus at the Thracian poet's feet.
Come, let us go and make thy father blind,
For such a sight will blind a father's eye.
One hour's storm will drown the fragrant meads;
What will whole months of tears thy father's eyes?
Do not draw back, for we will mourn with thee.
O, could our mourning ease thy misery.

In Shakespeare's late great play, *King Lear*, silence is lent an articulacy as powerful as words themselves. Such maturing of the playwright's dramatic abilities has a precedent in *Othello*, when the devious Iago, asked for his motive, delivers his final line 'From this time forth I never will speak word,' leaving those on and off stage with the nagging injustice of having such a pivotal question unanswered. As the final battle between Cordelia's forces and those of her brothers-in-law nears, the blinded Gloucester, wearied with his ordeals, is hardly able to respond to his disguised son Edgar's imploring request that they should flee. In place of a fight scene, Shakespeare has this old man left on the stage alone, with no lines to speak while he awaits Edgar's return, and silence speaks his tragic despair.

EDGAR
Here, father, take the shadow of this tree
For your good host. Pray that the right may thrive.
If ever I return to you again
I'll bring you comfort.

GLOUCESTER
Grace go with you, sir!
[*Exit* EDGAR]
[*Alarum and retreat within. Re-enter* EDGAR]

EDGAR
Away, old man! Give me thy hand; away!
King Lear hath lost; he and his daughter ta'en.
Give me thy hand; come on.

GLOUCESTER
No farther, sir; a man may rot even here.

EDGAR
What, in ill thoughts again? Men must endure
Their going hence even as their coming hither;
Ripeness is all: Come on.

GLOUCESTER
And that's true too.
[*Exeunt*]

January 26 | A Midsummer Night's Dream | Act 5 Scene 1

On January 26 1595, William Stanley, 6th Earl of Derby, a prominent patron of Elizabethan actors, married Elizabeth de Vere. Although there is no evidence to suggest that *A Midsummer Night's Dream*, was ever performed at any aristocratic wedding, many commentators have liked to imagine that Oberon and Titania's blessings of the marriage of Theseus and Hippolyta within the play might have been shared with this real-life couple too.

OBERON
Now until the break of day
Through this house each fairy stray.
To the best bride bed will we,
Which by us shall blessèd be;
And the issue there create
Ever shall be fortunate.
So shall all the couples three
Ever true in loving be,
And the blots of nature's hand
Shall not in their issue stand.
Never mole, harelip, nor scar,
Nor mark prodigious, such as are
Despisèd in nativity;
Shall upon their children be.
With this field dew consecrate
Every fairy take his gait,
And each several chamber bless
Through this palace with sweet peace;
And the owner of it blessed
Ever shall in safety rest.
Trip away; make no stay.
Meet me all by break of day.

January 27 | The Merchant of Venice | Act 3 Scene 1

Anti-Semitism was rife in Shakespeare's day, and Jews had been officially exiled from England since 1290 and would not be allowed to return until the mid-seventeenth century. Those few who remained would worship secretly, though some Jewish scholars (usually converted to Christianity) could be found teaching in the universities. *The Merchant of Venice* is set in Venice, where Jews were allowed to live albeit in harsh circumstances and presents the Jewish moneylender Shylock with ambivalent sympathies. He is indeed a comic, stereotypical, Fagin-like villain who gets his comeuppance. Yet he is also a tragic figure, empathetically drawn at times, who is forcibly dispossessed of his daughter, his money, and his faith. Consequently, Shylock's portrayal, and with it the extent of Shakespeare's anti-Semitism, remain hotly contested today: the role has been both embraced and repudiated by actors and directors. Even where Shylock is at his most cruel, Shakespeare gives him space to respond to some of the hostility he faces on account of his race and religion. This celebrated speech might be regarded today, which is Holocaust Memorial Day, as harrowingly prescient.

SHYLOCK
He hath disgraced me and hindered me half a million, laughed at my losses, mocked at my gains, scorned my nation, thwarted my bargains, cooled my friends, heated mine enemies, and what's his reason? I am a Jew. Hath not a Jew eyes? Hath not a Jew hands, organs, dimensions, senses, affections, passions? Fed with the same food, hurt with the same weapons, subject to the same diseases, healed by the same means, warmed and cooled by the same winter and summer as

a Christian is? If you prick us, do we not bleed? If you tickle us, do we not laugh? If you poison us, do we not die? And if you wrong us, shall we not revenge? If we are like you in the rest, we will resemble you in that. If a Jew wrong a Christian, what is his humility? Revenge. If a Christian wrong a Jew, what should his sufferance be by Christian example? Why, revenge! The villainy you teach me I will execute, and it shall go hard but I will better the instruction.

The Winter's Tale takes its name from the fanciful stories which might be told around a fire during the long, bleak Tudor winters – and Shakespeare's play is nothing if not fanciful. The young prince Mamillius dies after his mother Hermione is accused of adultery, and the Queen herself, dragged to a public trial straight after giving birth to his sister Perdita, soon follows. Although Hermione is miraculously revived sixteen years later at the end of the play, Mamillius is never resurrected. The sad demise of this innocent boy is foreshadowed by his own remark that 'A sad tale's best for winter'.

HERMIONE
Come, sir, now
I am for you again. Pray you, sit by us,
And tell's a tale.

MAMILLIUS
Merry or sad shall't be?

HERMIONE
As merry as you will.

MAMILLIUS
A sad tale's best for winter. I have one
Of sprites and goblins.

HERMIONE
Let's have that, good sir.
Come on, sit down; come on, and do your best
To fright me with your sprites. You're powerful at it.

MAMILLIUS
There was a man –

HERMIONE
Nay, come sit down; then on.

MAMILLIUS
Dwelt by a churchyard – I will tell it softly:
Yond crickets shall not hear it.

HERMIONE
Come on, then,
And give't me in mine ear.

Many plays are set in opposing worlds: *Henry IV* is split
between the tavern and the court; *Antony and Cleopatra*
switches between austere Rome and decadent Egypt; and *As
You Like It* moves from the court to the forest, with each setting
providing consolations to the other. Duke Senior finds life in the
woods to be a welcome contrast to the life of the court he left
behind, or at least tells his fellow exiles that he does. Ironically,
despite these words, he is gratefully restored to the dukedom in
the end.

DUKE SENIOR
Are not these woods
More free from peril than the envious court?
Here feel we but the penalty of Adam,
The seasons' difference, as the icy fang
And churlish chiding of the winter's wind,
Which when it bites and blows upon my body
Even till I shrink with cold, I smile and say
'This is no flattery: these are counsellors
That feelingly persuade me what I am' ?
Sweet are the uses of adversity,
Which, like the toad, ugly and venomous,
Wears yet a precious jewel in his head;
And this our life exempt from public haunt,
Finds tongues in trees, books in the running brooks,
Sermons in stones and good in everything.

January 30 | Hamlet | Act 3 Scene 1

Hamlet is exceptional for many reasons, not least that it has three different early texts – two Quarto texts and the Folio. The variations between the editions are significant: for instance, the most famous soliloquy perhaps in the entire corpus of English literature could have begun rather flatly: the earliest Quarto (Q1) has Hamlet's opening line as, 'To be or not to be; ay, there's the point'. The later, more profound version of this soliloquy is now so well known that the great Shakespearean actor Derek Jacobi said he feared the audience would join in, if ever he misjudged a pause.

HAMLET
To be, or not to be – that is the question;
Whether 'tis nobler in the mind to suffer
The slings and arrows of outrageous fortune
Or to take arms against a sea of troubles
And by opposing end them. To die, to sleep –
No more – and by a sleep to say we end
The heartache and the thousand natural shocks
That flesh is heir to. 'Tis a consummation
Devoutly to be wished. To die, to sleep –
To sleep – perchance to dream. Ay, there's the rub.
For in that sleep of death what dreams may come
When we have shuffled off this mortal coil
Must give us pause. There's the respect
That makes calamity of so long life.
For who would bear the whips and scorns of time,
Th'oppressor's wrong, the proud man's contumely,
The pangs of despised love, the law's delay,
The insolence of office, and the spurns
That patient merit of th'unworthy takes,
When he himself might his quietus make

With a bare bodkin? Who would fardels bear,
To grunt and sweat under a weary life,
But that the dread of something after death,
The undiscovered country, from whose bourn
No traveller returns, puzzles the will,
And makes us rather bear those ills we have
Than fly to others that we know not of?
Thus conscience does make cowards of us all;
And thus the native hue of resolution
Is sicklied o'er with the pale cast of thought,
And enterprises of great pitch and moment
With this regard their currents turn awry,
And lose the name of action. Soft you now,
The fair Ophelia! – Nymph, in thy orisons
Be all my sins remembered.

January 31 | Measure for Measure | Act 3 Scene 1

By contrast to the existentially conflicted *Hamlet,* in *Measure for Measure* the young Claudio, condemned to death for fornication, finds nothing to console him in the 'sleep of death'. Where the Prince of Denmark dithers between life and death, Claudio resolves that no matter how difficult life is, it is always to be opted for over 'what we fear of death'.

CLAUDIO
Ay, but to die, and go we know not where,
To lie in cold obstruction and to rot;
This sensible warm motion to become
A kneaded clod; and the delighted spirit
To bathe in fiery floods, or to reside
In thrilling region of thick-ribbèd ice,
To be imprisoned in the viewless winds
And blown with restless violence round about
The pendent world; or to be worse than worst
Of those that lawless and incertain thought
Imagine howling, 'tis too horrible.
The weariest and most loathèd worldly life
That age, ache, penury, and imprisonment
Can lay on nature is a paradise
To what we fear of death.

February

February 1 | Much Ado About Nothing | Act 5 Scene 4

This is the one and only direct mention of February in all of Shakespeare's works. The pronunciation of 'nothing' and 'noting' was much closer in Shakespeare's time, so *Much Ado About Nothing* might have actually been called *Much Ado About Noting* – noting meaning 'taking note' as well as eavesdropping (a term itself derived from theatre). Towards the play's conclusion, Don Pedro playfully uses the month associated with bitterly cold, stormy weather to comment on Benedick's severe and unwelcoming expression.

DON PEDRO
Good morrow, Benedick. Why, what's the matter,
That you have such a February face,
So full of frost, of storm and cloudiness?

February 2 | Twelfth Night | Act 5 Scene 1

Twins were common devices in comedies of mistaken identity, and feature more than once in Shakespeare, coming up both in *The Comedy of Errors* and *Twelfth Night*. Shakespeare's twin children Hamnet and Judith were baptized on 2 February 1585. On this day in 1602, *Twelfth Night* had its first recorded performance at the Candlemas festivities in Middle Temple. Hamnet had died in 1596, aged just eleven, and it is tempting to see the connection: *Twelfth Night* features a set of twins, who are separated after a shipwreck, and the play opens with Viola thinking her brother has died. After having been mistaken for one another, they are finally reunited – a kind of reunion Shakespeare's own daughter could never have.

SEBASTIAN
Do I stand there? I never had a brother;
Nor can there be that deity in my nature
Of here and everywhere. I had a sister
Whom the blind waves and surges have devoured.
Of charity, what kin are you to me?
What countryman? What name? What parentage?

VIOLA
Of Messaline. Sebastian was my father.
Such a Sebastian was my brother too.
So went he suited to his watery tomb.
If spirits can assume both form and suit
You come to fright us.

SEBASTIAN
A spirit I am indeed,
But am in that dimension grossly clad
Which from the womb I did participate.

Were you a woman, as the rest goes even,
I should my tears let fall upon your cheek,
And say, 'Thrice-welcome, drownèd Viola.'

VIOLA
My father had a mole upon his brow.

SEBASTIAN
And so had mine.

VIOLA
And died that day when Viola from her birth
Had numbered thirteen years.

SEBASTIAN
O, that record is lively in my soul.
He finishèd indeed his mortal act
That day that made my sister thirteen years.

VIOLA
If nothing lets to make us happy both
But this my masculine usurped attire,
Do not embrace me till each circumstance
Of place, time, fortune, do cohere and jump
That I am Viola;

On this day in 1612, Shakespeare's brother Gilbert died, followed by another brother Richard, who died a year and a day later. By the beginning of 1614, only Shakespeare's sister Joan survived of his seven siblings, of whom only four had survived to adulthood. Joan was to outlive her famous brother by thirty years. Little is known about the relationship William might have had with his brothers and sisters, but siblings recur throughout his plays, sometimes as arch rivals and at others as unshakable allies. Relationships between brothers most often become frayed in competition for a throne or over a woman, perhaps nowhere as violently as in *Richard III*. Richard will go on to kill his brothers to gain the throne, but he begins his machinations as their ally as he frames their attempted overthrow of Henry VI as vengeance for their father's death. Seeing an astronomical prodigy on the battlefield – three suns – these sons of York are for the time being united in their cause.

EDWARD
I wonder how our princely father 'scaped,
Or whether he be 'scaped away or no
From Clifford's and Northumberland's pursuit.
Had he been ta'en, we should have heard the news;
Had he been slain, we should have heard the news;
Or had he 'scaped, methinks we should have heard
The happy tidings of his good escape.
How fares my brother? Why is he so sad?

RICHARD
I cannot joy, until I be resolved
Where our right valiant father is become.
I saw him in the battle range about,

And watched him how he singled Clifford forth.
Methought he bore him in the thickest troop
As doth a lion in a herd of neat;
Or as a bear encompassed round with dogs,
Who having pinched a few and made them cry,
The rest stand all aloof and bark at him.
So fared our father with his enemies;
So fled his enemies my warlike father.
Methinks 'tis pride enough to be his son.
See how the morning opes her golden gates,
And takes her farewell of the glorious sun!
How well resembles it the prime of youth,
Trimmed like a younker prancing to his love!

EDWARD
Dazzle mine eyes, or do I see three suns?

RICHARD.
Three glorious suns, each one a perfect sun;
Not separated with the racking clouds,
But severed in a pale clear-shining sky.
See, see! They join, embrace, and seem to kiss,
As if they vowed some league inviolable;
Now are they but one lamp, one light, one sun.
In this the heaven figures some event.

EDWARD.
'T is wondrous strange, the like yet never heard of.
I think it cites us, brother, to the field,
That we, the sons of brave Plantagenet,
Each one already blazing by our meeds,
Should notwithstanding join our lights together
And over-shine the earth, as this the world.
Whate'er it bodes, henceforward will I bear
Upon my target three fair-shining suns.

RICHARD.
Nay, bear three daughters; by your leave I speak it,
You love the breeder better than the male.

[*Enter a Messenger*]

But what art thou, whose heavy looks foretell
Some dreadful story hanging on thy tongue?

MESSENGER
Ah, one that was a woeful looker-on
When as the noble Duke of York was slain,
Your princely father and my loving lord.

EDWARD
O, speak no more, for I have heard too much.

February 4 | Coriolanus | Act 3 Scene 1

On 4 February 1598, Shakespeare was named in Stratford as
a hoarder of malt. Malt hoarding was a significant offence,
as a national shortage of malt meant the markets were
understocked, and beer was watered down. Lear's Fool
identifies it as an ominous sign 'when brewers mar their malt
with water'; in real life, riots ensued in 1607 due to one such
shortage. Around this time, Shakespeare wrote *Coriolanus*,
which features an autocratic general facing a mob uprising
against unfair grain prices. Shakespeare's ancient Rome,
with the rich hoarding grain and the poor starving, holds an
unflattering glass to Elizabethan England: 'Yield us but the
superfluity', say the people, but they are ignored. Instead, the
tyrannical general, Coriolanus, gives voice to the contemptuous
ruling class, saying the starving people have as much grain as
they deserve.

CORIOLANUS
They know the corn
Was not our recompense, resting well assured
That ne'er did service for't. Being pressed to th'war,
Even when the navel of the state was touched,
They would not thread the gates. This kind of service
Did not deserve corn gratis. Being i'th'war,
Their mutinies and revolts, wherein they showed
Most valour, spoke not for them. Th'accusation
Which they have often made against the Senate,
All cause unborn, could never be the native
Of our so frank donation. Well, what then?
How shall this bosom multitude digest
The Senate's courtesy? Let deeds express
What's like to be their words: 'We did request it;
We are the greater poll, and in true fear

They gave us our demands.' Thus we debase
The nature of our seats, and make the rabble
Call our cares fears; which will in time
Break ope the locks o'th'Senate and bring in
The crows to peck the eagles.

Troilus and Cressida is set in the Trojan War, as the Greeks
attempt to storm the city of Troy to rescue Menelaus's ravished
(and ravishing) queen, Helen. Shakespeare's Prologue draws its
audience tantalizingly close into the heart of the action.

PROLOGUE
In Troy there lies the scene. From isles of Greece
The princes orgulous, their high blood chafed,
Have to the port of Athens sent their ships
Fraught with the ministers and instruments
Of cruel war. Sixty and nine that wore
Their crownets regal from th'Athenian bay
Put forth toward Phrygia, and their vow is made
To ransack Troy, within whose strong immures
The ravished Helen, Menelaus' queen,
With wanton Paris sleeps – and that's the quarrel.
To Tenedos they come,
And the deep-drawing barks do there disgorge
Their warlike fraughtage; now on Dardan plains
The fresh and yet unbruisèd Greeks do pitch
Their brave pavilions. Priam's six-gated city,
Dardan and Tymbria, Helias, Chetas, Troien,
And Antenorides, with massy staples
And correspondence and fulfilling bolts,
Stir up the sons of Troy.
Now expectation, tickling skittish spirits
On one and other side, Trojan and Greek,
Sets all on hazard. And hither am I come,
A Prologue armed, but not in confidence
Of author's pen or actor's voice, but suited
In like conditions as our argument,
To tell you, fair beholders, that our play

Leaps o'er the vaunt and firstlings of those broils,
Beginning in the middle; starting thence away
To what may be digested in a play.
Like or find fault; do as your pleasures are;
Now good or bad, 'tis but the chance of war.

By the end of *Troilus and Cressida*, the hitherto sulking
Achilles has been induced to fight Hector after the Trojan has
killed his beloved friend Patroclus. Achilles' swift vengeance
bespeaks a bond with Patroclus that is possibly homosexual
(in the play Thersites calls Patroclus Achilles' 'masculine
whore') and certainly deeper than conventional male
friendship, and this kind of homosocial bonding resurfaces
throughout Shakespeare's stage-writing career. *Twelfth Night*'s
Antonio feels for Sebastian in a similar way: 'I do adore thee
so, - That danger shall seem sport'. Here, Ulysses describes
Achilles' violent expressions of love, paralleled by the similar
vindictiveness of the bereaved Ajax and the betrayed Troilus.

ULYSSES
O, courage, courage, princes! Great Achilles
Is arming, weeping, cursing, vowing vengeance;
Patroclus' wounds have roused his drowsy blood,
Together with his mangled Myrmidons,
That noseless, handless, hacked and chipped, come to him,
Crying on Hector. Ajax hath lost a friend,
And foams at mouth, and he is armed and at it,
Roaring for Troilus, who hath done today
Mad and fantastic execution,
Engaging and redeeming of himself
With such a careless force and forceless care
As if that luck, in very spite of cunning,
Bade him win all.

Robert Devereux, 2nd Earl of Essex, commissioned
Shakespeare's theatre company to perform *Richard II* on
7 February 1601, the night before he attempted an armed
uprising against the ageing Queen Elizabeth's regime. Still
unmarried and childless at the age of sixty-seven, the question
of who would succeed Elizabeth I on the English throne
weighed heavily on people's minds, and Essex offered himself
as the answer. Although characteristically sympathetic to both
monarch and usurper, *Richard II* dramatizes the dethronement
of a weak and tyrannous fourteenth-century king. Interestingly,
Elizabeth requested a play to be performed by Shakespeare's
company on the night of Essex's execution for treason. John of
Gaunt, father of the future Henry IV, reflects on his concern for
England under Richard.

JOHN OF GAUNT
This royal throne of kings, this sceptred isle,
This earth of majesty, this seat of Mars,
This other Eden – demi-paradise –
This fortress built by nature for herself
Against infection and the hand of war,
This happy breed of men, this little world,
This precious stone set in the silver sea,
Which serves it in the office of a wall,
Or as a moat defensive to a house
Against the envy of less happier lands;
This blessèd plot, this earth, this realm, this England,
This nurse, this teeming womb of royal kings,
Feared by their breed, and famous by their birth,
Renownèd for their deeds as far from home
For Christian service and true chivalry
As is the sepulcher in stubborn Jewry

Of the world's ransom, blessèd Mary's son;
This land of such dear souls, this dear dear land,
Dear for her reputation through the world,
Is now leased out – I die pronouncing it –
Like to a tenement or pelting farm.
England, bound in with the triumphant sea,
Whose rocky shore beats back the envious siege
Of watery Neptune, is now bound in with shame,
With inky blots and rotten parchment bonds.
That England that was wont to conquer others
Hath made a shameful conquest of itself.
Ah, would the scandal vanish with my life,
How happy then were my ensuing death!

Mary Queen of Scots was beheaded on 8 February 1586
after becoming complicit in the Babington plot to overthrow
Elizabeth I. It was not the first time Mary had made an attempt
on her cousin's English throne, but Elizabeth prevaricated (for
nineteen years) over having such an influential Catholic figure,
and a queen, executed. One witness observed of Elizabeth, 'I
never knew her fetch a sigh, but when the Queen of Scots was
beheaded.' History plays offered themselves as commentaries
on contemporary events, and King John's hesitation over
having his young cousin Arthur killed might easily be regarded
as resonating with Elizabeth's uncertainties over the execution
of her cousin.

PEMBROKE
This is the man should do the bloody deed;
He showed his warrant to a friend of mine.
The image of a wicked heinous fault
Lives in his eye; that close aspect of his
Does show the mood of a much troubled breast,
And I do fearfully believe 'tis done,
What we so feared he had a charge to do.

SALISBURY
The colour of the King doth come and go
Between his purpose and his conscience,
Like heralds 'twixt two dreadful battles set,
His passion is so ripe it needs must break.

PEMBROKE
And when it breaks, I fear will issue thence
The foul corruption of a sweet child's death.

KING JOHN
We cannot hold mortality's strong hand.
Good lords, although my will to give is living,
The suit which you demand is gone and dead.
He tells us Arthur is deceased tonight.

The writer Ben Jonson remarked that Shakespeare had 'small Latin and less Greek' although to be fair, he did go on to claim that did not diminish his immortal gifts to poetry. Shakespeare was treated with snobbery by some of his peers, such as Robert Greene, who called him an 'upstart crow', because he did not go to university, though the Latin that young Shakespeare would have learned at his grammar school in Stratford would be almost equivalent to degree-level today. The most memorable Latin word that Shakespeare uses – and the longest word to appear anywhere in his canon – is spoken by Costard the clown: bantering with the small pageboy Mote, he enunciates 'honorificabilitudinitatibus' – roughly meaning 'honourableness' – in mockery of the courtier Armado's shaky but pedantic English and the affected tone of his conversation with the schoolmaster Holofernes. As *Love's Labour's Lost* was written after England's triumph over the Spanish Armada, Shakespeare's audience would have enjoyed the ridiculing of the Spaniard Armado.

ARMADO
Chirrah!

HOLOFERNES
Quare 'chirrah', not 'sirrah'?

ARMADO
Men of peace, well encountered.

HOLOFERNES
Most military sir, salutation.

MOTE
[*Aside to* COSTARD] They have been at a great feast
of languages and stolen the scraps.

COSTARD
[*To* MOTE] O, they have lived long on the alms-basket of
  words!
I marvel thy master hath not eaten thee for a word,
for thou art not so long by the head as
honorificabilitudinitatibus. Thou art easier
swallowed than a flap-dragon.

MOTE
Peace! The peal begins.

ARMADO
[*To* HOLOFERNES] Monsieur, are you not lettered?

MOTE
Yes, yes. He teaches boys the horn-book. What is a,
b, spelt backward with the horn on his head?

HOLOFERNES
Ba, *pueritia*, with a horn added.

MOTE
Ba, most silly sheep with a horn. You hear his learning.

HOLOFERNES
Quis, quis, thou consonant?

MOTE
The last of the five vowels, if you repeat them; or
the fifth, if I.

HOLOFERNES
I will repeat them: a, e, i —

MOTE
The sheep. The other two concludes it — o, u.

ARMADO
Now, by the salt wave of the Mediterraneum, a sweet
touch, a quick venue of wit! Snip, snap, quick and
home! It rejoiceth my intellect. True wit!

February 10 | The Merchant of Venice | Act 1 Scene 1

Surviving records show that on 10 February 1605, *The Merchant of Venice* was staged for the court of James I, at the Palace of Whitehall, and James liked it so much that he called for a repeat performance two nights later. This was the first full Christmas season for which Shakespeare's company provided entertainment for James' court, and they offered a rich sampling of their chief scriptwriter's back catalogue, including *Love's Labour's Lost*, *Henry V*, *The Comedy of Errors*, *The Merry Wives of Windsor* and the newer *Othello* and *Measure for Measure*. *The Merchant of Venice*, printed in 1600 and praised by Francis Meres in 1598, was by then already almost a decade old. When Antonio's friend and fellow merchant Salerio refers to 'wealthy Andrew dock'd in sand', he refers to the real life news story of the Spanish ship, the *Andrew*, that was captured by the English in 1596 while run aground in Cádiz harbour. This kind of topical reference is rare for Shakespeare, but it is likely to have gone down well with the play's first audiences.

SALERIO
My wind cooling my broth
Would blow me to an ague when I thought
What harm a wind too great might do at sea.
I should not see the sandy hour-glass run
But I should think of shallows and of flats,
And see my wealthy Andrew docked in sand,
Vailing her high-top lower than her ribs
To kiss her burial. Should I go to church
And see the holy edifice of stone
And not bethink me straight of dangerous rocks,
Which touching but my gentle vessel's side

Would scatter all her spices on the stream,
Enrobe the roaring waters with my silks,
And in a word, but even now worth this,
And now worth nothing? Shall I have the thought
To think on this, and shall I lack the thought
That such a thing bechanced would make me sad?
But tell not me; I know Antonio
Is sad to think upon his merchandise.

Julius Caesar opens during the Roman festival of Lupercalia, which is likely to have been as unfamiliar to Shakespeare's audience as it is to most of us today. Its attendant rituals are certainly bizarre: young men would run naked (apart from a goatskin loincloth) around a race course and strike people they pass with strips of goatskin, which was said to cure infertility. Caesar refers to this when he beseeches his wife, Calpurnia, to stand within striking distance of the athletic Mark Antony and receive the unusual blessing.

Flourish. Enter CAESAR; ANTONY, *for the course;* CALPURNIA, PORTIA, DECIUS BRUTUS, CICERO, BRUTUS, CASSIUS, *and* CASCA; *a great crowd following, among them a Soothsayer*

CAESAR
Calpurnia!

CASCA
Peace, ho! Caesar speaks.

CAESAR
Calpurnia!

CALPURNIA
Here, my lord.

CAESAR
Stand you directly in Antonius' way
When he doth run his course. Antonius.

ANTONY
Caesar, my lord?

CAESAR
Forget not, in your speed, Antonius,
To touch Calpurnia; for our elders say,
The barren, touchèd in this holy chase,
Shake off their sterile curse.

ANTONY
I shall remember:
When Caesar says, 'Do this', it is performed.

CAESAR
Set on, and leave no ceremony out.

In the run-up to Valentine's Day, what do we gain by our labours of love? Shakespeare's *Love's Labour's Lost* plots the blossoming romances of four scholars who are sworn to chastity to focus on their studies until the arrival of four perfectly matched women derails their original intentions. The dynamism of the relationships in this play, the poetry which pulls characters inexorably towards each other, and the sensitivity in which labours of love are ventured and lost, is masterful. Arguing for drastic revisions to their syllabus, Berowne here provides his fellow-students, including King Ferdinand, with a lyrical rationale for abandoning ascetism in favour of romance.

BEROWNE
But love, first learnèd in a lady's eyes,
Lives not alone immurèd in the brain,
But with the motion of all elements
Courses as swift as thought in every power,
And gives to every power a double power,
Above their functions and their offices.
It adds a precious seeing to the eye;
A lover's eyes will gaze an eagle blind.
A lover's ear will hear the lowest sound
When the suspicious head of theft is stopped.
Love's feeling is more soft and sensible
Than are the tender horns of cockled snails.
Love's tongue proves dainty Bacchus gross in taste.
For valour, is not Love a Hercules,
Still climbing trees in the Hesperides?
Subtle as Sphinx; as sweet and musical
As bright Apollo's lute, strung with his hair.
And when Love speaks, the voice of all the gods

Makes heaven drowsy with the harmony.
Never durst poet touch a pen to write
Until his ink were tempered with Love's sighs.
O, then his lines would ravish savage ears
And plant in tyrants mild humility.
From women's eyes this doctrine I derive:
They sparkle still the right Promethean fire;
They are the books, the arts, the academes,
That show, contain, and nourish all the world;
Else none at all in ought proves excellent.
Then fools you were these women to forswear,
Or, keeping what is sworn, you will prove fools.
For wisdom's sake, a word that all men love,
Or for love's sake, a word that loves all men,
Or for men's sake, the authors of these women,
Or women's sake, by whom we men are men –
Let us once lose our oaths to find ourselves,
Or else we lose ourselves to keep our oaths.
It is religion to be thus forsworn,
For charity itself fulfills the law,
And who can sever love from charity?

February 13 | Hamlet | Act 2 Scene 2

Arguably, the most successful marriage in Shakespeare's works
is that of the Macbeths, in so far as they feed off each other's
strengths in securing their mutual ambitions – although this
turns out to be their downfall. The fleeting love affair between
Hamlet and Ophelia is, for different reasons, a poor example
of a successful courtship – she ends up maddened by his
inconstancy. Nevertheless, in the 'salad days' of their courtship,
Hamlet was at least capable of one love poem.

> Doubt thou the stars are fire.
> Doubt that the sun doth move.
> Doubt truth to be a liar.
> But never doubt I love.

Valentine's Day was different in Shakespeare's time: it featured dancing, feasting and pairing games. Shakespeare mentions the day only twice, and one of these comes during Ophelia's mad scene. She sings (to no one in particular): 'Tomorrow is Saint Valentine's day, / All in the morning betime, / And I a maid at your window / To be your Valentine' (4.5.48–51). Today Valentine's Day centres around monogamous declarations of love. This sonnet is maybe not as well known as Sonnet 18 or 130 but it is one of Shakespeare's most affecting and was the favourite love poem of the brooding Romantic poet Samuel Taylor Coleridge. The narrator spends the first twelve lines complaining about his hopeless, friendless, generally quite miserable-sounding life. And then, in the final couplet comes the turning point, or volta; suddenly his beloved comes to mind and he realizes that he's the luckiest man in the world, happier than if he'd even been a king. Well, certainly happier than Richard II, who was murdered on 14 February 1400.

When, in disgrace with Fortune and men's eyes,
I all alone beweep my outcast state,
And trouble deaf heaven with my bootless cries,
And look upon myself and curse my fate,
Wishing me like to one more rich in hope,
Featur'd like him, like him with friends possess'd,
Desiring this man's art and that man's scope,
With what I most enjoy contented least,
Yet in these thoughts myself almost despising,
Haply I think on thee, and then my state,
(Like to the lark at break of day arising),
From sullen earth sings hymns at Heaven's gate,
    For thy sweet love remember'd such wealth brings,
    That then I scorn to change my state with Kings.

Galileo Galilei, the father of modern astronomy, was born in Pisa on this day in 1564, the same year as Shakespeare. Galileo's support for the theory that the earth orbited the sun was met with scepticism – and a possible prison sentence – among religious figures and others, who insisted on the Ptolemaic view that the earth was the centre of the universe. Although Shakespeare's Troilus uses the simile, 'strong as the axeltree on which heaven rides', elsewhere he seems to consider the new theories. Certainly some of his characters, such as Edmund in *King Lear*, reject older astronomical superstitions to the effect that heavenly bodies shape our destiny: Cassius in *Julius Caesar* says 'The fault, dear Brutus, is not in our stars,/ but in ourselves, that we are underlings' (1.2.139–40). That line was recently purloined by the writer John Green for the title of his book and movie, *The Fault in our Stars*. Like Cassius, but for a far more tender reason, Juliet begs Romeo not to swear by the inconstant moon, but by his gracious self.

ROMEO
Lady, by yonder blessèd moon I vow,
That tips with silver all these fruit-tree tops—

JULIET
O, swear not by the moon, th'inconstant moon,
That monthly changes in her circled orb,
Lest that thy love prove likewise variable.

ROMEO
What shall I swear by?

JULIET
Do not swear at all.

Or if thou wilt, swear by thy gracious self,
Which is the god of my idolatry,
And I'll believe thee.

ROMEO
If my heart's dear love—

JULIET
Well, do not swear. Although I joy in thee,
I have no joy of this contract to-night.
It is too rash, too unadvised, too sudden;
Too like the lightning, which doth cease to be
Ere one can say 'It lightens.' Sweet, good night!
This bud of love, by summer's ripening breath,
May prove a beauteous flower when next we meet.
Good night, good night! As sweet repose and rest
Come to thy heart as that within my breast!

February 16 | Richard II | Act 5 Scene 5

We might remember the speaker of Sonnet 29 – who would not change his state for a king's – when we find Richard II in a dungeon, contemplating his fate. The entire play is in verse, and this soliloquy is among Shakespeare's most accomplished moments of artistry as well as one of his longest. It manages to expose Richard's humanity without letting us forget he was king; a delicate balancing act Shakespeare performs with many of his tragic monarchs.

RICHARD
I have been studying how I may compare
This prison where I live unto the world;
And for because the world is populous,
And here is not a creature but myself,
I cannot do it. Yet I'll hammer it out.
My brain I'll prove the female to my soul,
My soul the father, and these two beget
A generation of still-breeding thoughts,
And these same thoughts people this little world,
In humours like the people of this world.
For no thought is contented; the better sort,
As thoughts of things divine, are intermixed
With scruples, and do set the word itself
Against the word; as thus: 'Come, little ones';
And then again,
'It is as hard to come as for a camel
To thread the postern of a small needle's eye.'
Thoughts tending to ambition, they do plot
Unlikely wonders – how these vain weak nails
May tear a passage through the flinty ribs
Of this hard world, my ragged prison walls,
And for they cannot, die in their own pride.

Thoughts tending to content flatter themselves
That they are not the first of Fortune's slaves,
Nor shall not be the last; like silly beggars,
Who, sitting in the stocks, refuge their shame
That many have, and others must sit there.
And in this thought they find a kind of ease,
Bearing their own misfortunes on the back
Of such as have before endured the like.
Thus play I in one person many people,
And none contented. Sometimes am I king.
Then treasons make me wish myself a beggar;
And so I am. Then crushing penury
Persuades me I was better when a king.
Then am I kinged again; and by and by
Think that I am unkinged by Bolingbroke,
And straight am nothing. But whate'er I be,
Nor I, nor any man that but man is,
With nothing shall be pleased till he be eased
With being nothing. [*The music plays*] Music do I hear.
Ha, ha; keep time! How sour sweet music is,
When time is broke, and no proportion kept.
So is it in the music of men's lives;
And here have I the daintiness of ear
To check time broke in a disordered string,
But for the concord of my state and time,
Had not an ear to hear my true time broke.
I wasted time, and now doth time waste me;
For now hath time made me his numbering clock.
My thoughts are minutes, and with sighs they jar
Their watches on unto mine eyes, the outward watch
Whereto my finger, like a dial's point,
Is pointing still in cleansing them from tears.
Now, sir, the sound that tells what hour it is
Are clamorous groans which strike upon my heart,
Which is the bell. So sighs, and tears, and groans
Show minutes, times, and hours. But my time

Runs posting on in Bolingbroke's proud joy,
While I stand fooling here, his jack of the clock.
This music mads me. Let it sound no more;
For though it have holp madmen to their wits,
In me it seems it will make wise men mad.
Yet blessing on his heart that gives it me;
For 'tis a sign of love, and love to Richard
Is a strange brooch in this all-hating world.

As with Richard II, we find a troubled Henry VI alone on
stage in an early example of Shakespeare's exploration of the
humanity of kings. This soliloquy is an intimate portrayal of the
King's now-total sense of powerlessness. He sits on a molehill,
unable to participate in the battle because he is no warrior, but
unable to leave, because he is the King.

KING HENRY VI
This battle fares like to the morning's war,
When dying clouds contend with growing light,
What time the shepherd, blowing of his nails,
Can neither call it perfect day nor night.
Now sways it this way, like a mighty sea
Forced by the tide to combat with the wind;
Now sways it that way, like the selfsame sea
Forced to retire by fury of the wind.
Sometime the flood prevails, and then the wind;
Now one the better, then another best;
Both tugging to be victors, breast to breast,
Yet neither conqueror nor conquerèd;
So is the equal of this fell war.
Here on this molehill will I sit me down.
To whom God will, there be the victory!
For Margaret my Queen, and Clifford too,
Have chid me from the battle, swearing both
They prosper best of all when I am thence.
Would I were dead, if God's good will were so!
For what is in this world but grief and woe?
O God! Methinks it were a happy life
To be no better than a homely swain;
To sit upon a hill, as I do now;
To carve out dials quaintly, point by point

Thereby to see the minutes how they run:
How many make the hour full complete,
How many hours bring about the day,
How many days will finish up the year,
How many years a mortal man may live.
When this is known, then to divide the times:
So many hours must I tend my flock,
So many hours must I take my rest,
So many hours must I contemplate,
So many hours must I sport myself,
So many days my ewes have been with young,
So many weeks ere the poor fools will ean,
So many years ere I shall shear the fleece.
So minutes, hours, days, months, and years,
Passed over to the end they were created,
Would bring white hairs unto a quiet grave.
Ah, what a life were this! How sweet! How lovely!
Gives not the hawthorn bush a sweeter shade
To shepherds looking on their silly sheep
Than doth a rich embroidered canopy
To kings that fear their subjects' treachery?
O, yes, it doth; a thousand-fold it doth.
And to conclude, the shepherd's homely curds,
His cold thin drink out of his leather bottle,
His wonted sleep under a fresh tree's shade,
All which secure and sweetly he enjoys,
Is far beyond a prince's delicates,
His viands sparkling in a golden cup,
His body couchèd in a curious bed,
When care, mistrust, and treason waits on him.

The songs at the end of *Love's Labour's Lost* are sung by two figures, Ver speaks for Spring and Hiems for Winter. Following the promiscuous Cuckoo of Spring, the forlorn Winter Owl concludes the play about frustrated desire with images of hard toil in forbidding conditions. After Winter's song, the usually absurd Spaniard Don Armado aptly reflects in the concluding line of the play, that 'The words of Mercury are harsh after the songs of Apollo'.

HIEMS
When icicles hang by the wall,
And Dick the shepherd blows his nail,
And Tom bears logs into the hall,
And milk comes frozen home in pail,
When blood is nipped, and ways be foul,
Then nightly sings the staring owl: 'Tu-whit
Tu-who!' – a merry note,
While greasy Joan doth keel the pot.
When all aloud the wind doth blow,
And coughing drowns the parson's saw,
And birds sit brooding in the snow,
And Marian's nose looks red and raw,
When roasted crabs hiss in the bowl,
Then nightly sings the staring owl: 'Tu-whit
Tu-who!' – a merry note,
While greasy Joan doth keel the pot.

Shakespeare plundered stories from Ovid, biographies from Plutarch and plots from history; borrowing content from anyone and everyone between Homer and the literary hits of the day. There are, however, some notable exceptions – for instance, the fools including Feste, Falstaff, Touchstone and Autolycus all come from his own pen. Here, Autolycus sings about the dawning spring in a song not dissimilar to those found at the end of *Love's Labour's Lost*. This song, however, appears in the middle of the play, marking where the action shifts from the chilling court tragedies of Sicilia to the bounteous and joyful pastoral landscape of Bohemia.

AUTOLYCUS
[*Singing*]
When daffodils begin to peer,
With heigh, the doxy over the dale,
Why, then comes in the sweet o'the year,
For the red blood reigns in the winter's pale.

The white sheet bleaching on the hedge,
With heigh, the sweet birds O, how they sing!
Doth set my pugging tooth on edge,
For a quart of ale is a dish for a king.

The lark, that tirra-lyra chants,
With heigh, with heigh, the thrush and the jay,
Are summer songs for me and my aunts
While we lie tumbling in the hay.

February 20 | A Midsummer Night's Dream | Act 5 Scene 1

In the last act of *A Midsummer Night's Dream* Shakespeare shows us the newly married Duke Theseus trying to decide which entertainment to have between the ceremony and the wedding night proper. Of course he chooses the workmen's *Pyramus and Thisbe*, whose hapless rehearsals we have been watching throughout the comedy.

THESEUS
Come now, what masques, what dances shall we have
To wear away this long age of three hours
Between our after-supper and bedtime?
Where is our usual manager of mirth?
What revels are in hand? Is there no play
To ease the anguish of a torturing hour?
Call Philostrate.

PHILOSTRATE
Here, mighty Theseus.

THESEUS
Say, what abridgement have you for this evening?
What masque, what music? How shall we beguile
The lazy time, if not with some delight?

PHILOSTRATE
[*Giving a paper*]
There is a brief how many sports are ripe.
Make choice of which your highness will see first.

THESEUS
[*Reads*]
'The Battle with the Centaurs, to be sung
By an Athenian eunuch to the harp.'
We'll none of that. That have I told my love
In glory of my kinsman, Hercules.
[*Reads*]
'The riot of the tipsy Bacchanals,
Tearing the Thracian singer in their rage.'
That is an old device, and it was played
When I from Thebes came last a conqueror.
[*Reads*]
'The thrice three Muses mourning for the death
Of learning, late deceased in beggary.'
That is some satire keen and critical,
Not sorting with a nuptial ceremony.
[*Reads*]
'A tedious brief scene of young Pyramus
And his love Thisbe; very tragical mirth.'
Merry and tragical? Tedious and brief?
That is, hot ice and wondrous strange snow.
How shall we find the concord of this discord?

PHILOSTRATE
A play there is, my lord, some ten words long,
Which is as 'brief' as I have known a play.
But by ten words, my lord, it is too long,
Which makes it 'tedious'. For in all the play
There is not one word apt, one player fitted.
And 'tragical', my noble lord, it is,
For Pyramus therein doth kill himself,
Which when I saw rehearsed, I must confess,
Made mine eyes water: but more 'merry' tears
The passion of loud laughter never shed.

THESEUS
What are they that do play it?

PHILOSTRATE
Hard-handed men that work in Athens here,
Which never laboured in their minds till now,
And now have toiled their unbreathed memories
With this same play against your nuptial.

THESEUS
And we will hear it.

PHILOSTRATE
No, my noble lord,
It is not for you. I have heard it over,
And it is nothing, nothing in the world,
Unless you can find sport in their intents,
Extremely stretched, and conned with cruel pain,
To do you service.

THESEUS
I will hear that play.
For never anything can be amiss
When simpleness and duty tender it.
Go, bring them in; and take your places, ladies.

February 21 | Hamlet | Act 2 Scene 2

On 21 February 1599, Shakespeare – already a successful playwright, with his fortunes rising (and a fortune amassing) – signed a lease with others in his theatre troupe to build the Globe Theatre. Contemporary accounts indicate it had audiences of around 3,000 people, about one per cent of London's population, and it would make Shakespeare, a principal shareholder, a very wealthy man. The theatre is referred to obliquely in his plays – *Hamlet*, in the early scene with the Ghost, talks of 'this distracted globe', then later, perhaps looking up at the stage's painted ceiling (also known as 'the heavens') he delivers the lines about 'this most excellent canopy'.

HAMLET
I have of late – but wherefore I know not – lost all
my mirth, forgone all custom of exercises. And indeed
it goes so heavily with my disposition that this goodly
frame the earth seems to me a sterile promontory.
This most excellent canopy, the air, look you, this brave
o'erhanging firmament, this majestical roof fretted
with golden fire – why, it appeareth nothing to
me but a foul and pestilent congregation of vapours.
What a piece of work is a man, how noble in reason,
how infinite in faculties, in form and moving how
express and admirable, in action how like an angel,
in apprehension how like a god: the beauty of the
world, the paragon of animals! And yet to me
what is this quintessence of dust? Man delights not
me – nor woman neither, though by your smiling
you seem to say so.

Hamlet, seeking to confirm that the late king, his father, had
been murdered by the new king, his uncle, persuades a group of
actors to perform a play 'The Murder of Gonzago' in front of the
court. Carefully watching his uncle's reactions to the plot – which
closely follows the murder of his father according to the Ghost
– Hamlet hopes to 'catch the conscience of the king'. Hamlet
called this legendary 'play within the play', 'The Mousetrap',
and Agatha Christie borrowed the name for her detective drama
which is the longest-running show in London's West End.

HAMLET
O, what a rogue and peasant slave am I!
Is it not monstrous that this player here,
But in a fiction, in a dream of passion,
Could force his soul so to his own conceit
That from her working all his visage wanned,
Tears in his eyes, distraction in his aspect,
A broken voice, and his whole function suiting
With forms to his conceit? And all for nothing.
For Hecuba!
What's Hecuba to him, or he to her,
That he should weep for her? What would he do
Had he the motive and the cue for passion
That I have? He would drown the stage with tears
And cleave the general ear with horrid speech,
Make mad the guilty and appal the free,
Confound the ignorant, and amaze indeed
The very faculties of eyes and ears. Yet I,
A dull and muddy-mettled rascal, peak
Like John-a-dreams, unpregnant of my cause,
And can say nothing, no, not for a king
Upon whose property and most dear life

A damned defeat was made. Am I a coward?
Who calls me villain? Breaks my pate across?
Plucks off my beard and blows it in my face?
Tweaks me by the nose? Gives me the lie i'th'throat
As deep as to the lungs? Who does me this?
Ha, 'swounds, I should take it. For it cannot be
But I am pigeon-livered and lack gall
To make oppression bitter, or ere this
I should ha' fatted all the region kites
With this slave's offal. Bloody, bawdy villain!
Remorseless, treacherous, lecherous, kindless villain!
O, vengeance!
Why, what an ass am I! This is most brave,
That I, the son of a dear father murdered,
Prompted to my revenge by heaven and hell,
Must like a whore unpack my heart with words
And fall a-cursing like a very drab,
A stallion! Fie upon't! foh!
About, my brains. Hum – I have heard
That guilty creatures sitting at a play
Have by the very cunning of the scene
Been struck so to the soul that presently
They have proclaimed their malefactions.
For murder, though it have no tongue, will speak
With most miraculous organ. I'll have these players
Play something like the murder of my father
Before mine uncle. I'll observe his looks.
I'll tent him to the quick. If 'a do blench,
I know my course. The spirit that I have seen
May be the devil, and the devil hath power
T'assume a pleasing shape, yea, and perhaps
Out of my weakness and my melancholy,
As he is very potent with such spirits,
Abuses me to damn me. I'll have grounds
More relative than this. The play's the thing
Wherein I'll catch the conscience of the King.

Over the history of the Academy Awards, Shakespeare's plays
have amassed cabinet-loads of Oscars. The first film to be
adapted from his work was the 1935 *A Midsummer Night's
Dream*, which won two awards and marked the beginning of
Shakespeare's Hollywood career. Kenneth Branagh's *Hamlet*
was even Oscar-nominated for best writer. Robert Wise's
West Side Story, based on *Romeo and Juliet*, swiped an
astonishing ten awards, and *Romeo and Juliet* remains the
play most adapted for the silver screen. Its plot fulfils the age-
old Hollywood trope of forbidden love, and here follows what
is known as the 'balcony' scene, even though, interestingly
enough, Shakespeare makes no mention of a balcony. This
scene is sufficiently iconic to have been much misquoted – it
is worth noting here that 'wherefore' means 'why', not 'where'
– as in 'why are you Romeo Montague, and thus forbidden to
fraternize with me, a Capulet?'

JULIET
O Romeo, Romeo! – wherefore art thou Romeo?
Deny thy father and refuse thy name.
Or, if thou wilt not, be but sworn my love,
And I'll no longer be a Capulet.

ROMEO
[*Aside*] Shall I hear more, or shall I speak at this?

JULIET
'Tis but thy name that is my enemy.
Thou art thyself, though not a Montague.
What's Montague? It is nor hand nor foot
Nor arm nor face nor any other part
Belonging to a man. O, be some other name!

What's in a name? That which we call a rose
By any other name would smell as sweet.
So Romeo would, were he not Romeo called,
Retain that dear perfection which he owes
Without that title.

Shakespeare gives a considerable amount of stage time to
adolescents and their trials and tribulations (although the
term 'teenager' was not coined until 1922). The young love of
passionate Romeo, the bawdiness of rambunctious Prince Hal
and the restlessness of cooped-up Arvirargus and Guiderius are
all recognizably adolescent; and all accord to the description
by the Shepherd in *The Winter's Tale*. Incidentally, this speech
follows the notorious stage direction for the character of
Antigonus (who has brought the baby Perdita to Bohemia):
'Exit, pursued by a bear'.

SHEPHERD
I would there were no age between ten and
three-and-twenty, or that youth would sleep out the
rest: for there is nothing in the between but
getting wenches with child, wronging the ancientry,
stealing, fighting. Hark you now: would any but
these boiled brains of nineteen and two-and-twenty
hunt this weather? They have scared away two of my
best sheep, which I fear the wolf will sooner find
than the master. If anywhere I have them, 'tis by
the seaside, browsing of ivy.

The forty-day period of Lent can begin as early as 10 February and end as late as 25 April, and was a period of major importance for Elizabethans. Theatres would be closed, and Shrovetide, the period immediately preceding Lent, was a time for play before the seriousness of the Lenten period. Many people, then as now, mark Shrove Tuesday with the making and sharing of pancakes: the clown in *All's Well That Ends Well* even mentions 'a pancake for Shrove-Tuesday', Children were encouraged to have a drink – though this was more normal than it sounds. Low-alcohol or 'small' beer was a safer alternative to water, and children would have around four pints a day. The Shrovetide season was a time of much merriment, and, dining with country justices in Gloucestershire, Falstaff's woozy drinking companions embody this infectious spirit.

SILENCE
[*Sings*]
Be merry, be merry, my wife has all,
For women are shrews, both short and tall.
'Tis merry in hall, when beards wag all,
And welcome merry Shrovetide.
Be merry, be merry.

February 26 | The Merry Wives of Windsor | Act 3 Scene 3

Ash Wednesday was welcomed with an ancient custom of dragging a straw man dressed in old clothes through the streets, before burning it or throwing it down a chimney. This figure was called the Jack-a-Lent, and was intended by some to represent Judas Iscariot, although it was often disguised as a more contemporary scapegoat. Jack-a-Lent was synonymous with deception and betrayal, and Mistress Page hurls this insult at the pageboy Robin as Falstaff is approaching.

MISTRESS FORD
How now, my eyas-musket, what news with you?

ROBIN
My master, Sir John, is come in at your back-door, Mistress Ford, and requests your company.

MISTRESS PAGE
You little Jack-a-Lent, have you been true to us?

ROBIN
Ay, I'll be sworn. My master knows not of your being here, and hath threatened to put me into everlasting liberty if I tell you of it; for he swears he'll turn me away.

MISTRESS PAGE
Thou'rt a good boy. This secrecy of thine shall be a tailor to thee and shall make thee a new doublet and hose. I'll go hide me.

MISTRESS FORD
Do so. Go tell thy master I am alone.

Shakespeare's daughter Judith and her husband Thomas
Quiney appeared in court records in Stratford for
marrying during Lent, which was against the law. Another
Lent prohibition forbad the selling of meat: this was to
commemorate the sacrifice of Jesus and at the same time, give
the fisheries a boost in trade. Here, Falstaff tries to get one-up
on his frequent sparring partner Hostess Quickly for serving
meat during Lent.

FALSTAFF
No, I think thou art not; I think thou art quit for
that. Marry, there is another indictment upon thee,
for suffering flesh to be eaten in thy house,
contrary to the law, for the which I think thou wilt howl.

MISTRESS QUICKLY
All victuallers do so. What's a joint of mutton or
two in a whole Lent?

HAL
You, gentlewoman –

DOLL TEARSHEET
What says your grace?

FALSTAFF
His grace says that which his flesh rebels against.

February 28 | The Merchant of Venice | Act 4 Scene 1

The Merchant of Venice is thought to have been partly influenced by the trial of Roderigo Lopez that took place on 28 February 1594. Lopez, a Portuguese doctor of Jewish heritage, was accused of attempting to poison Elizabeth I, and subsequently executed for treason. Echoes of Lopez are detectable in Shakespeare's depiction of Shylock. Portia – the heroine of the play – is disguised here as a male lawyer and attempts to persuade Shylock to spare Antonio the pound of flesh he had foolishly wagered earlier. She does so with an air of markedly Christian righteousness.

PORTIA (as Balthazar):
The quality of mercy is not strained,
It droppeth as the gentle rain from heaven
Upon the place beneath. It is twice blest,
It blesseth him that gives and him that takes.
'Tis mightiest in the mightiest; it becomes
The thronèd monarch better than his crown.
His sceptre shows the force of temporal power,
The attribute to awe and majesty,
Wherein doth sit the dread and fear of kings;
But mercy is above this sceptered sway,
It is enthronèd in the hearts of kings,
It is an attribute to God himself,
And earthly power doth then show likest God's
When mercy seasons justice. Therefore, Jew,
Though justice be thy plea, consider this:
That in the course of justice none of us
Should see salvation. We do pray for mercy,
And that same prayer doth teach us all to render
The deeds of mercy. I have spoke thus much

To mitigate the justice of thy plea,
Which if thou follow, this strict court of Venice
Must needs give sentence 'gainst the merchant
there.

March

March 1 is St David's Day, in honour of the patron saint of
Wales. The best-known Welsh character in Shakespeare's works
is Fluellen, the passionate but comical Celt in *Henry V*. In a play
so concerned with national identity, it is important that Fluellen
draws attention to Henry's Welsh roots; he refers to the King as
'Henry of Monmouth', as Henry was born at Monmouth castle
in Wales. However, Fluellen's patriotism (as well as his diction)
is often a target of humour: the pompous but cowardly soldier
Pistol threatens, 'I'll knock his leek about his pate [*head*] upon
St Davy's day'. Nevertheless, Fluellen has the last laugh when he
forces Pistol to eat the raw leek in retaliation, declaring, 'If you
can mock a leek, you can eat a leek.'

FLUELLEN
Your grandfather of famous memory, an't
please your majesty, and your great-uncle Edward
the Plack Prince of Wales, as I have read in the
chronicles, fought a most prave pattle here in
France.

KING HENRY
They did, Fluellen.

FLUELLEN
Your Majesty says very true. If your majesties
is remembered of it, the Welshmen did good
service in a garden where leeks did grow, wearing
leeks in their Monmouth caps, which your majesty
know to this hour is an honourable badge of the
service; and I do believe your majesty takes no
scorn to wear the leek upon Saint Tavy's day.

KING HENRY
I wear it for a memorable honor;
For I am Welsh, you know, good countryman.

FLUELLEN
All the water in Wye cannot wash your
majesty's Welsh plood out of your pody, I can tell
you that. God pless it and preserve it, as long as it
pleases His grace, and His majesty too!

Seasons in Shakespeare's work feature more as figures of
speech than as strictly delineated time settings. His reticence
to committing his plays to a particular time of year reflects his
flagrant disdain of adhering to Aristotle's unities of Action,
Time and Place – only *The Comedy of Errors* and *The Tempest*
follow the classical rules by confining their action to a single
day. Shakespeare's reasons for flouting the unities were
practical as well as poetic: as Berowne shows, locating the
beginning of spring can be as slippery a business as fixing a
meaning to the season.

BEROWNE
The spring is near when green geese are a-breeding.

DUMAINE
How follows that?

BEROWNE
Fit in his place and time.

DUMAINE
In reason nothing.

BEROWNE
Something then in rhyme.

KING FERDINAND
Berowne is like an envious sneaping frost
That bites the first-born infants of the spring.

The first ever record of a Shakespeare play being staged is for a performance of 'harey the vi' at the Rose Theatre in Southwark on 3 March 1592. This is almost certain to be what we now know as *Henry VI, Part 1*, and joins a limited number of other plays for which we have been able to piece together the first performance dates. In fact, it appears that *Henry VI, Part 1* was composed as what we would today call a 'prequel' to what are now parts 2 and 3 – originally called *The First Part of the Contention of the Two Famous Houses of York and Lancaster* and *The True Tragedy of Richard Duke of York*. *Richard III*, similarly, was a sequel to these *Henry VI* hits. Talbot was a particularly towering figure for Elizabethan schoolboys, representing gallant warrior virtue and patriotic pride. The audience would have been especially moved over these lamentations over his son's death.

TALBOT
Thou antic Death, which laughest us here to scorn,
Anon, from thy insulting tyranny,
Coupled in bonds of perpetuity,
Two Talbots, wingèd through the lither sky,
In thy despite shall 'scape mortality.
O, thou, whose wounds become hard-favoured Death,
Speak to thy father ere thou yield thy breath!
Brave Death by speaking, whether he will or no;
Imagine him a Frenchman, and thy foe.
Poor boy! He smiles, methinks, as who should say
'Had death been French, then Death had died today.'
Come, come, and lay him in his father's arms.
My spirit can no longer bear these harms.
Soldiers, adieu! I have what I would have,
Now my old arms are young John Talbot's grave.
[*Dies*]

Shakespeare's paternal grandfather Richard Shakespeare was a
tenant farmer in Snitterfield, four miles outside Stratford-upon-
Avon, on the land belonging to his maternal grandfather, the
rather more wealthy Robert Arden. Richard's second son John
married the youngest Arden, Mary, and together they moved
into the town of Stratford, but Shakespeare clearly had deep
roots in the Warwickshire countryside. His rural influences are
most apparent in the fifty-odd types of plant which he mentions
in his work, and many of these phrases are in common usage
today: someone may have told you not to 'gild the lily', for
instance, or have defended the title of something by arguing
that 'a rose by any other name would smell as sweet'. The
former is actually misquoted from *King John* – here advised
against having himself crowned for a second time – amidst
a long sequence of metaphors which itself might be seen,
ironically, as labouring the point a little.

SALISBURY
Therefore, to be possessed with double pomp,
To guard a title that was rich before,
To gild refinèd gold, to paint the lily,
To throw a perfume on the violet,
To smooth the ice, or add another hue
Unto the rainbow, or with taper-light
To seek the beauteous eye of heaven to garnish,
Is wasteful and ridiculous excess.

March 5 | Sonnet 99

In Sonnet 99, the speaker upbraids a violet for stealing the sweet-smelling breath of his beloved, only to find other flowers have stolen parts of his lover's beauty too. This poem has fifteen lines, one more than the standard fourteen lines of a sonnet, and the extra one seems most likely to be the first. Do we take it that Shakespeare was experimenting with the sonnet form, or was the first line not intended as part of the sonnet proper? It is one among many mysteries of the sonnet sequence.

The forward violet thus did I chide,
Sweet thief whence didst thou steal thy sweet that smells,
If not from my love's breath? the purple pride,
Which on thy soft cheek for complexion dwells
In my love's veins thou hast too grossly dy'd.
The lily I condemned for thy hand,
And buds of marjoram had stolen thy hair,
The roses fearfully on thorns did stand,
One blushing shame, another white despair:
A third nor red, nor white, had stolen of both,
And to his robb'ry had annex'd thy breath,
But for his theft in pride of all his growth
A vengeful canker eat him up to death.
    More flowers I noted, yet I none could see,
    But sweet, or colour it had stolen from thee.

Laertes makes reference to springtime, but in a far bleaker aspect than the sonneteer who dwells on its beauty. He warns his sister about Hamlet's flip-flopping sentiments, comparing his favour to 'A violet in the youth of primy nature, / Forward, not permanent, sweet, not lasting'. His advice turns to a yet more serious note when he expands on his misgivings about the melancholy prince, comparing her feelings to something as potentially ruinous as a disease to the 'infants of the spring'. It would be easy to see Laertes as overbearing, if he wasn't going to be proved so right.

LAERTES
For nature crescent does not grow alone
In thews and bulk, but as this temple waxes
The inward service of the mind and soul
Grows wide withal. Perhaps he loves you now,
And now no soil nor cautel doth besmirch
The virtue of his will. But you must fear,
His greatness weighed, his will is not his own.
For he himself is subject to his birth.
He may not, as unvalued persons do,
Carve for himself. For on his choice depends
The safety and health of this whole state.
And therefore must his choice be circumscribed
Unto the voice and yielding of that body
Whereof he is the head. Then, if he says he loves you,
It fits your wisdom so far to believe it
As he in his particular act and place
May give his saying deed; which is no further
Than the main voice of Denmark goes withal.
Then weigh what loss your honour may sustain
If with too credent ear you list his songs,
Or lose your heart, or your chaste treasure open

To his unmastered importunity.
Fear it, Ophelia, fear it, my dear sister.
And keep you in the rear of your affection,
Out of the shot and danger of desire.
The chariest maid is prodigal enough
If she unmask her beauty to the moon.
Virtue itself 'scapes not calumnious strokes.
The canker galls the infants of the spring
Too oft before their buttons be disclosed;
And in the morn and liquid dew of youth
Contagious blastments are most imminent.
Be wary then. Best safety lies in fear.
Youth to itself rebels, though none else near.

While the fleeting nature of a violet's bloom is used by Laertes as a warning to his sister to be sceptical of Hamlet's affections, a flower-like threat of fading beauty makes Venus more ardent in her pursuit of Adonis.

'The tender spring upon thy tempting lip
Shows thee unripe; yet mayst thou well be tasted:
Make use of time, let not advantage slip;
Beauty within itself should not be wasted.
Fair flowers that are not gathered in their prime
Rot, and consume themselves in little time.'

Shakespeare wrote more convincing, and more fully developed
female parts than any of his contemporaries. However, female
characters were rarely given an epilogue and even then the
person playing them would be an adolescent man. There are
significant instances of female characters becoming silent
towards the end of certain plays, where outcomes might not
plausibly match their interests: it is unlikely, for instance,
that the prospective nun Isabella would be thrilled at being
snapped up as the Duke's wife in *Measure for Measure*, but
she is given no words to express her wishes either way after
his concluding proposal. On the other hand, there are even
more significant instances of women standing their ground and
speaking truth to powerful men. Paulina's condemnation of
the deplorable Leontes is memorable: 'I'll not call you tyrant; /
But this most cruel usage of your queen,/ Not able to produce
more accusation than/ Your own weak-hinged fancy, something
savours/ Of tyranny and will ignoble make you, / Yea,
scandalous to the world.' Another singular moment is when the
effervescent Rosalind speaks the Epilogue in *As You Like It*.
Her character was possibly intended to mirror the strength and
spirit of Elizabeth I and in any case serves as the perfect herald
to International Women's Day.

ROSALIND
It is not the fashion to see the lady the epilogue,
but it is no more unhandsome than to see the lord
the prologue. If it be true that good wine needs
no bush, 'tis true that a good play needs no
epilogue. Yet to good wine they do use good bushes,
and good plays prove the better by the help of good
epilogues. What a case am I in, then, that am
neither a good epilogue nor cannot insinuate with

you in the behalf of a good play? I am not
furnished like a beggar; therefore to beg will not
become me. My way is to conjure you, and I'll begin
with the women. I charge you, O women, for the love
you bear to men, to like as much of this play as
please you; and I charge you, O men, for the love
you bear to women – as I perceive by your simpering,
none of you hates them – that between you and the
women the play may please. If I were a woman, I
would kiss as many of you as had beards that pleased
me, complexions that liked me, and breaths that I
defied not; and, I am sure, as many as have good
beards, or good faces, or sweet breaths, will, for my
kind offer, when I make curtsy, bid me farewell.

Lucretia's tragic story, as told in *History of Rome* by Roman historian Livy and then again by Ovid, would go on to inspire many more great works of art. Not least among them is Titian's painting *Tarquin and Lucretia*, which is as strikingly sinister as Shakespeare's narrative poem of the same event, *The Rape of Lucrece*. In the poem, Lucrece is assaulted by Tarquin but bravely vows to denounce the terrible crime committed against her. She is furious and defiant as she resolves to overcome her shame and secure justice for her irredeemable suffering.

'For me, I am the mistress of my fate,
And with my trespass never will dispense,
Till life to death acquit my forced offence.

'I will not poison thee with my attaint,
Nor fold my fault in cleanly-coined excuses;
My sable ground of sin I will not paint
To hide the truth of this false night's abuses.
My tongue shall utter all; mine eyes, like sluices,
As from a mountain spring that feeds a dale,
Shall gush pure streams to purge my impure tale.'

March 10 | Henry VI, Part 3 | Act 1 Scene 1

Records show that on 10 March 1613 William Shakespeare was the principal buyer of Blackfriars Gatehouse in London for the considerable sum of £140 (which was even more than the cost of his house New Place in Stratford). There is no evidence that he lived in these lodgings, but in his will he bequeathed the property to his elder daughter, Susanna. Women's interests are protected in his plays too: female characters feature more heavily in his history plays than in their historical sources. Margaret is one such woman, a fierce queen who acts as a counterpart to her weak husband, the King. Shakespeare even writes her into *Richard III* despite the fact that the real Queen Margaret was dead two years before the story starts.

QUEEN MARGARET
Ah, wretched man! Would I had died a maid,
And never seen thee, never borne thee son,
Seeing thou hast proved so unnatural a father!
Hath he deserved to lose his birthright thus?
Hadst thou but loved him half so well as I,
Or felt that pain which I did for him once,
Or nourished him as I did with my blood,
Thou wouldst have left thy dearest heart-blood there,
Rather than have that savage Duke thine heir
And disinherited thine only son.

March 11 | A Midsummer Night's Dream | Act 3 Scene 1

The contractors Shakespeare and his fellow actors commissioned would have been impatient to begin work on the new Globe playhouse, which was delayed by a particularly cold March in 1599. The construction of the Globe, on which Shakespeare would likely have been consulted, was such that the afternoon sun would fall on the audience, warming them as they watched the shaded stage. However, the absence of any elaborate special effects to indicate different settings and times of day, meant that actors had to establish these aspects of the play by other means. The comically literal-minded workmen in *A Midsummer Night's Dream* can be seen hammering out the finer details of their own stagecraft for their upcoming performance of *Pyramus and Thisbe*. They settle, amusingly, on casting members of their group to play the shining moon and a wall. Their consultation of an almanac would have chimed with the first audiences, as almanacs (calendars illustrated with planetary movements) were hugely popular with the Elizabethans – records show that one in three families bought an almanac every year.

SNUG
Doth the moon shine that night we play our play?

BOTTOM
A calendar, a calendar! look in the almanac – find out moonshine, find out moonshine!

QUINCE
Yes, it doth shine that night.

BOTTOM
Why, then, may you leave a casement of the Great
Chamber window – where we play – open, and the moon
may shine in at the casement.

QUINCE
Ay; or else one must come in with a bush of thorns
and a lanthorn, and say he comes to disfigure or to
present the person of Moonshine. Then there is
another thing. We must have a wall in the Great
Chamber; for Pyramus and Thisbe, says the story, did
talk through the chink of a wall.

SNUG
You can never bring in a wall. What say you, Bottom?

BOTTOM
Some man or other must present Wall; and let him
have some plaster, or some loam, or some roughcast
about him to signify Wall; and let him hold his
fingers thus, and through that cranny shall Pyramus
and Thisbe whisper.

QUINCE
If that may be, then all is well. Come, sit down
every mother's son, and rehearse your parts.
Pyramus, you begin. When you have spoken your
speech, enter into that brake; and so every one
according to his cue.

The sun in March was thought to be strong enough to feed nasty
fevers without dispelling them. The fiery rebel soldier Harry
Hotspur uses this well-established association to express his
impatience at the report of King Henry's forces, who are 'as full
of spirit as the month of May'. The bearer of this news is cut
short by Hotspur's counter-simile, which compares this praise
of Henry to the ague-inducing March sun which is incapable of
delivering the soothing heat of war which he so desires.

HOTSPUR
No more, no more! Worse than the sun in March,
This praise doth nourish agues. Let them come!
They come like sacrifices in their trim,
And to the fire-eyed maid of smoky war
All hot and bleeding will we offer them.
The mailèd Mars shall on his altar sit
Up to the ears in blood. I am on fire
To hear this rich reprisal is so nigh,
And yet not ours! Come, let me taste my horse,
Who is to bear me like a thunderbolt
Against the bosom of the Prince of Wales.
Harry to Harry shall, hot horse to horse,
Meet and ne'er part till one drop down a corpse.

Perdita, though she is distributing flowers to her guests at a
sheep-shearing (in late summer), brings the flowers of spring
to life in 3D technicolour and in doing so reveals Shakespeare's
knowledge of the natural world: daffodils do arrive before
the swallows come and all the flowers are true to the season.
Whether they grow in Bohemia, where the story is set, is another
matter. Shakespeare's version of this distant land resembles the
real place in almost nothing but its name. His Bohemia even
has a coast, when the country itself was landlocked. Just as
fancifully, Perdita's account of the flowers and their associations
is strewn with classical references incongruous with her humble
rural upbringing; though, of course, though she does not know
it, she is in fact the daughter of the King and Queen of Sicilia.

PERDITA
I would I had some flowers o'th'spring, that might
Become your time of day – and yours, and yours,
That wear upon your virgin branches yet
Your maidenheads growing. O Proserpina,
For the flowers now that, frighted, thou let'st fall
From Dis's wagon! Daffodils,
That come before the swallow dares, and take
The winds of March with beauty; violets, dim,
But sweeter than the lids of Juno's eyes
Or Cytherea's breath; pale primroses,
That die unmarried ere they can behold
Bright Phoebus in his strength – a malady
Most incident to maids; bold oxlips and
The crown imperial; lilies of all kinds,
The flower-de-luce being one: O, these I lack
To make you garlands of, and my sweet friend
To strew him o'er and o'er!

Brutus' power of persuasion is as compelling to his fellow
conspirators as it is to the audience. However, Shakespeare's
audience would have known the story of Caesar and Brutus
and would have arrived with a view on the most famous
assassination in history, not to mention a knowledge of how
bad its aftermath would be for the conspirators. The story
is politically charged, with Caesar representing monarchy
and Brutus becoming the champion of divided rule – a move
which surprises Caesar, who dies uttering the words 'Et tu
Brute?' (You as well Brutus?) in disbelief. Once he has joined
the conspirators, Brutus argues that his allies do not need to
depend on swearing an oath to spur them to action but need
only to act on their own principles.

BRUTUS
No, not an oath. If not the face of men,
The sufferance of our souls, the time's abuse –
If these be motives weak, break off betimes,
And every man hence to his idle bed;
So let high-sighted tyranny range on
Till each man drop by lottery. But if these,
As I am sure they do, bear fire enough
To kindle cowards and to steel with valour
The melting spirits of women, then, countrymen,
What need we any spur but our own cause
To prick us to redress? What other bond
Than secret Romans that have spoke the word,
And will not palter? and what other oath
Than honesty to honesty engaged
That this shall be, or we will fall for it?
Swear priests and cowards and men cautelous,
Old feeble carrions, and such suffering souls

That welcome wrongs; unto bad causes swear
Such creatures as men doubt; but do not stain
The even virtue of our enterprise,
Nor th'insuppressive mettle of our spirits,
To think that or our cause or our performance
Did need an oath; when every drop of blood
That every Roman bears, and nobly bears,
Is guilty of a several bastardy,
If he do break the smallest particle
Of any promise that hath passed from him.

March 15 | Julius Caesar | Act 1 Scene 2

The Ides of March in the Roman calendar corresponds to 15 March in our modern one. It has become notorious as the date of Julius Caesar's assassination. In the context of the play, the timing of Caesar's death is notable for another reason: it takes place at the beginning of Act 3, making the part relatively minor for a lead role. Julius Caesar has only 141 lines, the least lines of all Shakespeare's title characters; Hamlet has the most.

SOOTHSAYER
Beware the Ides of March.

CAESAR
What man is that?

BRUTUS
A soothsayer bids you beware the Ides of March.

CAESAR
Set him before me; let me see his face.

CASSIUS
Fellow, come from the throng; look upon Caesar.

CAESAR
What sayst thou to me now? Speak once again.

SOOTHSAYER
Beware the Ides of March.

CAESAR
He is a dreamer. Let us leave him. Pass.

Antony and Cleopatra takes place after the events depicted in
Julius Caesar, but its tragic outcome is nevertheless foretold by
a soothsayer. Deviating from the mystic's advice always spells
disaster for Shakespeare's Roman protagonists.

ANTONY
Say to me, whose fortunes shall rise higher,
Caesar's, or mine?

SOOTHSAYER
Caesar's.
Therefore, O Antony, stay not by his side.
Thy daemon – that's thy spirit which keeps thee – is
Noble, courageous high, unmatchable,
Where Caesar's is not. But near him thy angel
Becomes afeared, as being o'erpowered. Therefore
Make space enough between you.

ANTONY
Speak this no more.

SOOTHSAYER
To none but thee; no more but when to thee.
If thou dost play with him at any game,
Thou art sure to lose; and, of that natural luck
He beats thee 'gainst the odds. Thy lustre thickens
When he shines by. I say again, thy spirit
Is all afraid to govern thee near him;
But, he away, 'tis noble.

17 March is St Patrick's Day, after the patron saint of Ireland. Elizabethan England had a rather fraught relationship with Ireland, which, while nominally under Elizabeth's dominion, was predominantly ruled by clan-leaders. They staged a number of rebellions against English rule, and the one Essex was sent to quell was among the closest to being successful. Consequently, on the whole, the Irish do not get an easy time of it in Shakespeare's plays, framed variously as 'shag-haired crafty kern[s]' and 'those rough rug-headed kerns' where they challenge the authority of the King. The Irish are afforded a more compassionate treatment, however, in *Henry V,* which binds English, Irish, Welsh and Scottish soldiers in Henry's 'band of brothers'. Shakespeare had an awareness of St Patrick at least: legend held that the cave of St Patrick on Station Island, County Donegal, was the entrance to Purgatory, and this remained an important site of pilgrimage in the sixteenth century. Hamlet's father's Ghost refers to Purgatory early in Act 1, Sc. 5, 'I am thy father's spirit, / Doom'd for a certain term to walk the night, / And for the day confined to fast in fire / Till the foul crimes done in my days of nature / Are burnt and purged away;' and then later in the scene Hamlet refers to St Patrick:

HORATIO
These are but wild and whirling words, my lord.

HAMLET
I'm sorry they offend you, heartily.
Yes, faith, heartily.

HORATIO
There's no offence, my lord.

HAMLET
Yes, by Saint Patrick, but there is, Horatio,

And much offence too. Touching this vision here,
It is an honest ghost, that let me tell you.
For your desire to know what is between us,
O'ermaster 't as you may. And now, good friends,
As you are friends, scholars, and soldiers,
Give me one poor request.

HORATIO
What is't, my lord? We will.

HAMLET
Never make known what you have seen tonight.

HORATIO and MARCELLUS
My lord, we will not.

HAMLET
Nay, but swear't.

HORATIO
In faith,
My lord, not I.

MARCELLUS
Nor I, my lord – in faith.

HAMLET
Upon my sword.

MARCELLUS
We have sworn, my lord, already.

HAMLET
Indeed, upon my sword, indeed.

GHOST
[*The Ghost cries under the stage*] Swear.

A shrew is a mouse-like animal, which had been wrongly
thought of as venomous in the Middle Ages. As a result the
term has been used to refer to the devil, and as a slur on people
of either sex, but by Shakespeare's day it was predominantly
used against women. Noisy, aggressive and malign, the shrew's
apparent gentleness is quickly exposed as deceptive when any
attempt is made at handling the animal. The sexism of *The
Taming of the Shrew* is as hotly contested as the anti-Semitism
in *The Merchant of Venice*, with critical opinion falling firmly
on either side. The play features Petruchio brashly taming
Katherine, the 'shrew', whom he starves of food and sleep until
she becomes a model of wifely obedience. Many have been
reluctant to view the play as a straightforward endorsement of
such a troubling and inhuman relationship, and rather suppose
it as a moral tale of how not to be. There is some evidence that
it was viewed with discomfort even when it was first performed:
Shakespeare's apprentice John Fletcher wrote a sequel, *The
Woman's Prize*, or, *The Tamer Tamed*, in which Petruchio's
second wife reverses the taming. This passage is one of the
more offensive – or ironically overblown, depending on your
perspective.

PETRUCHIO
They shall go forward, Kate, at thy command.
Obey the bride, you that attend on her.
Go to the feast, revel and domineer,
Carouse full measure to her maidenhead,
Be mad and merry, or go hang yourselves.
But for my bonny Kate, she must with me.
Nay, look not big, nor stamp, nor stare, nor fret,

I will be master of what is mine own.
She is my goods, my chattels, she is my house,
My household stuff, my field, my barn,
My horse, my ox, my ass, my any thing,
And here she stands. Touch her whoever dare!
I'll bring mine action on the proudest he
That stops my way in Padua.

Richard II, deposed by Elizabeth's ancestor Henry Bolingbroke
(later Henry IV), buckles under the full weight of his own
mortality which had been obscured to him by his status as king.
He becomes disorientated: a king is an immortal thing, but
that immortality departs with the hollow crown. Richard's fall
is palpable and devastating, no matter how much he may have
had it coming. This speech, uttered after Richard learns that his
soldiers have deserted his cause, is one of the most remarkable
passages from the play.

KING RICHARD II
No matter where. Of comfort no man speak.
Let's talk of graves, of worms, and epitaphs;
Make dust our paper, and with rainy eyes
Write sorrow on the bosom of the earth.
Let's choose executors and talk of wills –
And yet not so; for what can we bequeath
Save our deposèd bodies to the ground?
Our lands, our lives, and all are Bolingbroke's,
And nothing can we call our own but death
And that small model of the barren earth
Which serves as paste and cover to our bones.
For God's sake let us sit upon the ground
And tell sad stories of the death of kings –
How some have been deposed, some slain in war,
Some haunted by the ghosts they have deposed,
Some poisoned by their wives, some sleeping killed,
All murdered. For within the hollow crown
That rounds the mortal temples of a king
Keeps death his court; and there the antic sits,
Scoffing his state and grinning at his pomp,
Allowing him a breath, a little scene,

To monarchize, be feared and kill with looks,
Infusing him with self and vain conceit,
As if this flesh which walls about our life
Were brass impregnable; and humoured thus,
Comes at the last, and with a little pin
Bores through his castle wall, and – farewell, king!
Cover your heads, and mock not flesh and blood
With solemn reverence. Throw away respect,
Tradition, form, and ceremonious duty;
For you have but mistook me all this while.
I live with bread, like you; feel want,
Taste grief, need friends. Subjected thus,
How can you say to me I am a king?

Henry IV died on this date in 1413. He spends his reign, according to Shakespeare's play, fraught with apparent compunction at having usurped the throne. This and not the pursuit of wealth is cited as the reason for his crusades: pilgrimages to atone for the circumstances surrounding his accession. Richard II had prophesied that Henry IV would die in Jerusalem, and in a way this is fulfilled: but his deathbed lies not in Jerusalem, but in the Jerusalem Chamber of Westminster Abbey, when he awakens to see his son Prince Hal trying on his crown. In this scene, father and son finally reconcile – the old king had been worried about the future of England under his seemingly wayward heir.

KING HENRY IV
Dost thou so hunger for mine empty chair
That thou wilt needs invest thee with my honours
Before thy hour be ripe? O foolish youth!
Thou seekest the greatness that will overwhelm thee.
Stay but a little, for my cloud of dignity
Is held from falling with so weak a wind
That it will quickly drop; my day is dim.
Thou hast stolen that which after some few hours
Were thine without offence, and at my death
Thou hast sealed up my expectation.
Thy life did manifest thou lovedst me not,
And thou wilt have me die assured of it.
Thou hidest a thousand daggers in thy thoughts,
Which thou hast whetted on thy stony heart,
To stab at half an hour of my life.
What, canst thou not forbear me half an hour?
Then get thee gone, and dig my grave thyself,
And bid the merry bells ring to thine ear

That thou art crownèd, not that I am dead.
Let all the tears that should bedew my hearse
Be drops of balm to sanctify thy head;
Only compound me with forgotten dust.
Give that which gave thee life unto the worms.
Pluck down my officers, break my decrees;
For now a time is come to mock at form –
Harry the Fifth is crowned! Up, vanity!
Down, royal state! All you sage counsellors, hence!
And to the English court assemble now,
From every region, apes of idleness!
Now, neighbour confines, purge you of your scum!
Have you a ruffian that will swear, drink, dance,
Revel the night, rob, murder, and commit
The oldest sins the newest kind of ways?
Be happy, he will trouble you no more.
England shall double gild his treble guilt;
England shall give him office, honour, might;
For the fifth Harry from curbed licence plucks
The muzzle of restraint, and the wild dog
Shall flesh his tooth on every innocent.
O my poor kingdom, sick with civil blows!
When that my care could not withhold thy riots,
What wilt thou do when riot is thy care?
O, thou wilt be a wilderness again,
Peopled with wolves, thy old inhabitants!

The spring equinox occurs around this date. The lush pastoral world of *As You Like It* is largely set in the fictitious forest of Arden, which might have been named after Shakespeare's mother whose maiden name was Arden. This song follows a chaotic scene in which convoluted love entanglements have come to a head. Rosalind, disguised as Ganymede, attempts to pacify the desires of Orlando who loves her, but has not recognized her; Phoebe who is in love with 'Ganymede'; and finally Silvius, who loves Phoebe. The song provides welcome relief from the knotty plot, with a page singing of the verdant spring and the kind of idyllic love to be found nowhere else in this chaotic forest. This is one of the few songs in the canon for which we possibly have the music composed for its original appearance on stage: a tune by Henry Morley, who was a close neighbour of Shakespeare's in Southwark in the 1590s.

PAGE
It was a lover and his lass,
With a hey, and a ho, and a hey nonino,
That o'er the green corn field did pass,
In the spring time, the only pretty ring time,
When birds do sing, hey ding a ding, ding,
Sweet lovers love the spring.

Between the acres of the rye,
With a hey, and a ho, and a hey nonino,
These pretty country folks would lie,
In spring time, the only pretty ring time,
When birds do sing, hey ding a ding, ding,
Sweet lovers love the spring.

This carol they began that hour,
With a hey, and a ho, and a hey nonino,
How that a life was but a flower,
In spring time, the only pretty ring time,
When birds do sing, hey ding a ding, ding,
Sweet lovers love the spring.

And therefore take the present time,
With a hey, and a ho, and a hey nonino,
For love is crownèd with the prime,
In spring time, the only pretty ring time,
When birds do sing, hey ding a ding, ding,
Sweet lovers love the spring.

March 22 | A Midsummer Night's Dream | Act 2 Scene 1

Mothering Sunday is held on the fourth Sunday of Lent in the UK, and usually falls in the second half of March or early April. It is a tradition which dates back to the sixteenth century. The old associations with the 'mother church' have been slowly replaced with a general celebration of motherhood. Mothers appear in many and varying roles throughout Shakespeare's dramatic work: Gertrude has conflicting loyalties to the new king (her new husband) and her son; Juliet's mother leaves the nurturing motherhood role to the Nurse; Lady Macbeth is childless; and many of the daughters in the Shakespeare canon – among them Jessica, Desdemona and Miranda – are shown only in relationships with their apparently widowed fathers. That said, some of the most moving moments in the plays feature the reuniting of estranged families, for instance when Marina comes face to face with the mother she believed to have been buried at sea: 'My heart leaps to be gone into my mother's bosom'. One of the more unusual maternal relationships to be found in Shakespeare can be found in *A Midsummer Night's Dream*: Titania, the Fairy Queen has adopted her mortal friend's son after the friend died in childbirth, and now protects this adopted changeling from service to Oberon.

TITANIA
His mother was a votaress of my order,
And in the spicèd Indian air by night
Full often hath she gossiped by my side,
And sat with me on Neptune's yellow sands
Marking th'embarkèd traders on the flood,
When we have laughed to see the sails conceive
And grow big-bellied with the wanton wind;
Which she with pretty and with swimming gait

Following – her womb then rich with my young squire –
Would imitate, and sail upon the land
To fetch me trifles, and return again
As from a voyage, rich with merchandise.
But she, being mortal, of that boy did die,
And for her sake do I rear up her boy;
And for her sake I will not part with him.

March 23 | Sonnet 25

The speaker of Sonnet 25 values the honour he bears in loving the anonymous young man, and the honour he bears in being loved back, as greater and more lasting than any favour that could be won by any other means. The poem features the spring flower, the marigold, which only opens its leaves when the sun shines upon it.

Let those who are in favour with their stars,
Of public honour and proud titles boast,
Whilst I whom fortune of such triumph bars
Unlook'd for joy in that I honour most;
Great Princes' favourites their fair leaves spread,
But as the marigold at the sun's eye,
And in themselves their pride lies buried,
For at a frown they in their glory die.
The painful warrior famoused for worth,
After a thousand victories once foil'd,
Is from the book of honour razed forth,
And all the rest forgot for which he toil'd:
   Then happy I that love and am beloved
   Where I may not remove, nor be removed.

March 24 | The Phoenix and the Turtle

Queen Elizabeth died on 24 March 1603, amidst concerns over who was to succeed her in the absence of a direct heir. Written at the end of her reign, many have attempted to tie Elizabeth to *The Phoenix and the Turtle*, as she had been notably associated with the phoenix, a symbol of chastity. She was painted wearing a pendant of the creature in the so-called 'Phoenix Portrait', attributed to Nicholas Hilliard; and she is referred to as a phoenix in *Henry VIII*, 'when / The bird of wonder dies, the maiden phoenix, / Her ashes new create another heir, / As great in admiration as herself'. This is *The Phoenix and the Turtle* poem in its entirety: it is a peculiar piece that touches on the metaphysical, about the death of an ideal but fruitless love.

Let the bird of loudest lay,
On the sole Arabian tree,
Herald sad and trumpet be,
To whose sound chaste wings obey.

But thou shrieking harbinger,
Foul precurrer of the fiend,
Augur of the fever's end,
To this troop come thou not near!

From this session interdict
Every fowl of tyrant wing,
Save the eagle, feathered king:
Keep the obsequy so strict.

Let the priest in surplice white,
That defunctive music can,
Be the death-divining swan,
Lest the requiem lack his right.

And thou treble-dated crow,
That thy sable gender mak'st
With the breath thou giv'st and tak'st,
'Mongst our mourners shalt thou go.

Here the anthem doth commence:
Love and constancy is dead;
Phoenix and the turtle fled
In a mutual flame from hence.

So they loved, as love in twain
Had the essence but in one;
Two distincts, division none:
Number there in love was slain.

Hearts remote, yet not asunder;
Distance, and no space was seen
'Twixt the turtle and his queen:
But in them it were a wonder.

So between them love did shine,
That the turtle saw his right
Flaming in the phoenix' sight;
Either was the other's mine.

Property was thus appalled,
That the self was not the same;
Single nature's double name
Neither two nor one was called.

Reason, in itself confounded,
Saw division grow together,
To themselves yet either neither,
Simple were so well compounded;

That it cried, How true a twain
Seemeth this concordant one!
Love hath reason, reason none,
If what parts can so remain.

Whereupon it made this threne
To the phoenix and the dove,
Co-supremes and stars of love,
As chorus to their tragic scene.

THRENOS
Beauty, truth, and rarity,
Grace in all simplicity,
Here enclosed, in cinders lie.

Death is now the phoenix' nest;
And the turtle's loyal breast
To eternity doth rest.

Leaving no posterity,
'Twas not their infirmity,
It was married chastity.

Truth may seem, but cannot be;
Beauty brag, but 'tis not she;
Truth and beauty buried be.

To this urn let those repair
That are either true or fair;
For these dead birds sigh a prayer.

March 25 | Sonnet 4

March 25 marked the new calendar year in England until 1752, though Scotland had moved to starting the year on 1 January a century and a half earlier, in 1600; 25 March was also known as 'Lady Day' after the feast of the Annunciation of the Virgin Mary, and was the date when rents had to be paid and business contracts renewed. The UK financial year still begins around this time as a legacy of this old calendar. To welcome in the beginning of the financial year, here is a sonnet on the economics of love: it is bad business to keep beauty to yourself.

Unthrifty loveliness why dost thou spend,
Upon thyself thy beauty's legacy?
Nature's bequest gives nothing but doth lend,
And being frank she lends to those are free:
Then beauteous niggard why dost thou abuse,
The bounteous largess given thee to give?
Profitless usurer why dost thou use
So great a sum of sums yet canst not live?
For having traffic with thyself alone,
Thou of thyself thy sweet self dost deceive,
Then how when nature calls thee to be gone,
What acceptable audit canst thou leave?
　Thy unused beauty must be tomb'd with thee,
　Which used lives th' executor to be.

Scholarly views as to how far Shakespeare, like other playwrights of his time, collaborated with other writers have fluctuated over the years, but it is now generally agreed that some of his earliest plays, such as *Titus Andronicus* and *Henry VI, Part 1,* were co-authored, and so were some of his last. The 1623 Folio of his works, compiled by his colleagues John Heminges and Henry Condell after his death, did not include *Pericles* (printed in 1609, and now thought to have been co-written with George Wilkins) or *The Two Noble Kinsmen* (which was belatedly printed in 1634 as the work of Shakespeare and John Fletcher). However, the Folio did include *Henry VIII*, but this is also now believed to have been co-written with Fletcher. The following song in *Henry VIII*, sung to the grieving Katherine of Aragon, occurs in a scene which is now thought to be by Fletcher, though it is unlikely to disappear from anthologies of Shakespearean songs on this account.

> Orpheus with his lute made trees,
> And the mountain tops that freeze,
> Bow themselves when he did sing.
> To his music plants and flowers
> Ever sprung, as sun and showers
> There had made a lasting spring.
>
> Everything that heard him play,
> Even the billows of the sea,
> Hung their heads, and then lay by.
> In sweet music is such art,
> Killing care and grief of heart
> Fall asleep, or hearing die.

Elizabeth sent her one-time favourite Essex to quell a mounting rebellion in Ireland on 27 March 1599, though he was destined to fail and return in disgrace. The soldiers stationed in Ireland were perpetually underequipped, underpaid and underfed, so desertions were frequent and authority was weak. In an uncommonly direct contemporary reference, the Chorus to *Henry V* refers explicitly to the anticipated homecoming of England's hero, 'the general of our gracious empress' Elizabeth. The Chorus asks the audience to imagine Henry V's homecoming from his victory in France in a similar light.

CHORUS
Vouchsafe to those that have not read the story
That I may prompt them; and of such as have,
I humbly pray them to admit th'excuse
Of time, of numbers, and due course of things,
Which cannot in their huge and proper life
Be here presented. Now we bear the King
Toward Calais. Grant him there: there seen,
Heave him away upon your wingèd thoughts
Athwart the sea. Behold, the English beach
Pales in the flood with men, with wives, and boys,
Whose shouts and claps out-voice the deep-mouthed sea,
Which like a mighty whiffler fore the King
Seems to prepare his way. So let him land,
And solemnly see him set on to London.
So swift a pace hath thought that even now
You may imagine him upon Blackheath,
Where that his lords desire him to have borne
His bruisèd helmet and his bended sword
Before him through the city. He forbids it,
Being free from vainness and self-glorious pride,

Giving full trophy, signal and ostent
Quite from himself to God. But now behold,
In the quick forge and working-house of thought,
How London doth pour out her citizens:
The Mayor and all his brethren in best sort,
Like to the senators of th'antique Rome,
With the plebeians swarming at their heels,
Go forth and fetch their conquering Caesar in:
As, by a lower but loving likelihood,
Were now the General of our gracious Empress,
As in good time he may – from Ireland coming,
Bringing rebellion broachèd on his sword,
How many would the peaceful city quit
To welcome him! Much more, and much more cause,
Did they this Harry. Now in London place him –
As yet the lamentation of the French
Invites the King of England's stay at home.
The Emperor's coming in behalf of France
To order peace between them; and omit
All the occurrences, whatever chanced,
Till Harry's back-return again to France.
There must we bring him; and myself have played
The interim, by remembering you 'tis past.
Then brook abridgment, and your eyes advance,
After your thoughts, straight back again to France.

The poet T.S. Eliot called *Coriolanus* Shakespeare's finest achievement in tragedy, writing in a decade – the 1930s – when the rise of fascism occasioned topical productions of this play about a leader seeking absolute power right across Europe. Coriolanus, like Essex, has great military prowess, but he is fatally impatient with civilian political institutions. Caius Marcius is awarded his title 'Coriolanus' in recognition of his military brilliance at the battle of Corioles, of which Cominius gives this blood-curdling account during the ceremony.

COMINIUS
I shall lack voice. The deeds of Coriolanus
Should not be uttered feebly. It is held
That valour is the chiefest virtue and
Most dignifies the haver. If it be,
The man I speak of cannot in the world
Be singly counterpoised. At sixteen years,
When Tarquin made a head for Rome, he fought
Beyond the mark of others. Our then dictator,
Whom with all praise I point at, saw him fight
When with his Amazonian chin he drove
The bristled lips before him. He bestrid
An o'erpressed Roman and i'th'Consul's view
Slew three opposers. Tarquin's self he met,
And struck him on his knee. In that day's feats,
When he might act the woman in the scene,
He proved best man i'th'field, and for his meed
Was brow-bound with the oak. His pupil age
Man-entered thus, he waxèd like a sea,
And in the brunt of seventeen battles since
He lurched all swords of the garland. For this last,
Before and in Corioles, let me say

I cannot speak him home. He stopped the fliers,
And by his rare example made the coward
Turn terror into sport. As weeds before
A vessel under sail, so men obeyed
And fell below his stem. His sword, death's stamp,
Where it did mark, it took from face to foot.
He was a thing of blood, whose every motion
Was timed with dying cries. Alone he entered
The mortal gate of th'city, which he painted
With shunless destiny; aidless came off,
And with a sudden reinforcement struck
Corioles like a planet. Now all's his,
When by and by the din of war 'gan pierce
His ready sense, then straight his doubled spirit
Requickened what in flesh was fatigate,
And to the battle came he, where he did
Run reeking o'er the lives of men, as if
'Twere a perpetual spoil; and till we called
Both field and city ours he never stood
To ease his breast with panting.

The Battle of Towton was fought on 29 March 1461 in
Yorkshire, and yielded a decisive victory for the Yorkist family
over the Lancastrian Henry VI, installing Edward IV on the
throne. It was the biggest and bloodiest battle in the English
Wars of the Roses – it is thought that 28,000 men lost their
lives on this one day of fighting. In Shakespeare's image of the
conflict, Henry sits alone lamenting his part in the violence,
while on the battlefield there are moving moments of grief.
Among these horrifying scenes of civil war, a son realizes that
the lifeless body of the man he has slain is his own father.

SON
Ill blows the wind that profits nobody.
This man whom hand to hand I slew in fight
May be possessèd with some store of crowns;
And I, that haply take them from him now,
May yet ere night yield both my life and them
To some man else, as this dead man doth me. –
Who's this? O God! It is my father's face,
Whom in this conflict I, unwares, have killed.
O, heavy times, begetting such events!
From London by the king was I pressed forth;
My father, being the Earl of Warwick's man,
Came on the part of York, pressed by his master;
And I, who at his hands received my life,
Have by my hands of life bereavèd him.
Pardon me, God, I knew not what I did!
And pardon, father, for I knew not thee!
My tears shall wipe away these bloody marks;
And no more words till they have flowed their fill.

March 30 | The Two Noble Kinsmen | Act 3 Scene 5

The phrase 'mad as a March hare' has been common in English since long before Lewis Carroll dreamt up the Wonderland tea party. It derived, unsurprisingly, from the antics of male hares in March at the height of the breeding season. In Fletcher and Shakespeare's collaboration *The Two Noble Kinsmen*, the Jailer's Daughter is found drifting around the countryside in a delirium induced by her unrequited love for the nobleman Palamon, whom she has helped break out of jail. Local villagers, about to perform a morris dance, seize the opportunity to exploit her apparent eccentricities as part of their act.

THIRD COUNTRYMAN
There's a dainty madwoman, master,
Comes i'th'nick, as mad as a March hare.
If we can get her dance, we are made again;
I warrant her, she'll do the rarest gambols.

FIRST COUNTRYMAN
A madwoman? We are made, boys!

SCHOOLMASTER
And are you mad, good woman?

DAUGHTER
I would be sorry else. Give me your hand.

SCHOOLMASTER
Why?

DAUGHTER
I can tell your fortune.

141

You are a fool. Tell ten; I have posed him. Buzz!
Friend, you must eat no white bread; if you do,
Your teeth will bleed extremely. Shall we dance, ho?
I know you, you're a tinker; sirrah tinker,
Stop no more holes but what you should.

SCHOOLMASTER
Dii boni,
A tinker, damsel?

DAUGHTER
                    Or a conjurer;
Raise me a devil now, and let him play
Chi passa, o' th'bells and bones.

SCHOOLMASTER
                    Go take her,
And fluently persuade her to a peace.
Et opus exegi, quod nec Iovis ira nec ignis –
Strike up, and lead her in.

SECOND COUNTRYMAN
Come Lass, let's trip it.

DAUGHTER
I'll lead.

THIRD COUNTRYMAN
Do, do.

SCHOOLMASTER
Persuasively and cunningly! Away, boys.

Desdemona's 'Willow song' is among the saddest of the
songs featured in Shakespeare, especially as it precedes the
heartbreaking scene in which Othello strangles the love of his
life in a maddened state of jealousy. It was a common ballad,
and Shakespeare's audience would have known it, but in the
earlier versions the song describes a lovesick man rather than a
lovesick woman.

DESDEMONA
[*Singing*] The poor soul sat sighing by a sycamore tree,
Sing all a green willow;
Her hand on her bosom, her head on her knee,
Sing willow, willow, willow;
The fresh streams ran by her and murmured her moans;
Sing willow, willow, willow;
Her salt tears fell from her and softened the stones –
[*Speaking*] Lay by these.
[*Singing*]
Sing willow, willow, willow –
[*Speaking*] Prithee hie thee; he'll come anon.
[*Singing*]
Sing all a green willow must be my garland.
Let nobody blame him; his scorn I approve –
[. . .]

DESDEMONA
[*Singing*] I called my love false love, but what
said he then?
Sing willow, willow, willow:
If I court moe women, you'll couch with moe men.

April

'The fool doth think he is wise, but the wise man knows himself to be a fool'. These words from Touchstone, the fool in *As You Like It*, are useful to keep in mind on April Fools' Day! Though often a source of comic relief, the Shakespearean fool is a witty and insightful character who is most free to express himself openly. In this passage, Jaques, the melancholy attendant of Duke Senior, envies Touchstone's ability to speak his mind.

JAQUES
A fool, a fool, I met a fool i'th'forest,
A motley fool – a miserable world! –
As I do live by food, I met a fool,
Who laid him down, and basked him in the sun,
And railed on Lady Fortune in good terms,
In good set terms, and yet a motley fool.
'Good morrow, fool,' quoth I. 'No, sir,' quoth he,
'Call me not "fool" till heaven hath sent me
fortune.'
And then he drew a dial from his poke,
And looking on it, with lack-lustre eye,
Says very wisely, 'It is ten o'clock.'
'Thus we may see', quoth he, 'how the world wags:
'Tis but an hour ago since it was nine,
And after one hour more 'twill be eleven,
And so from hour to hour we ripe, and ripe,
And then from hour to hour we rot, and rot,
And thereby hangs a tale.' When I did hear
The motley fool thus moral on the time,
My lungs began to crow like Chanticleer
That fools should be so deep-contemplative;
And I did laugh, sans intermission,
An hour by his dial. O noble fool!
A worthy fool: motley's the only wear!

April 2 | Sonnet 98

Shakespeare sold more printed books of poems than plays in his lifetime. He knew the weights and measures of his words and was a master of verbal acrobatics. April appears more than any other month in his work, being as intimately connected with bounteous spring as it is with the constant threat of rain, capable of delivering up foul and idyllic weather in quick succession. Harnessing these connotations, Antony says of his reluctant wife Octavia, 'The April 's in her eyes: it is love's spring, / And these the showers to bring it on'. Likewise Proteus in *The Two Gentlemen of Verona* observes 'O, how this spring of love resembleth / The uncertain glory of an April day, / Which now shows all the beauty of the sun, / And by and by a cloud takes all away'. Sonnet 98's April-inspired reflections kick off National Poetry Month in America.

From you have I been absent in the spring,
When proud pied April (dress'd in all his trim)
Hath put a spirit of youth in everything:
That heavy Saturn laugh'd and leap'd with him.
Yet nor the lays of birds, nor the sweet smell
Of different flowers in odour and in hue,
Could make me any summer's story tell:
Or from their proud lap pluck them where they grew:
Nor did I wonder at the lilies white,
Nor praise the deep vermilion in the rose,
They were but sweet, but figures of delight:
Drawn after you, you pattern of all those.
    Yet seem'd it Winter still, and, you away,
    As with your shadow I with these did play.

April 3 | Richard II | Act 5 Scene 6

Henry IV was born Henry Bolingbroke on 3 April 1367, and was destined to depose the inadequate King Richard II. As Elizabeth's ancestor, Henry is presented as having done so with a heavy heart, suffering great pangs of conscience all the way: Shakespeare could not be seen to endorse the policies of usurpation and regicide, except when shown in this light. These are the closing lines of *Richard II*, in which Henry vows to launch a crusade to atone for the murder of his predecessor in prison (which he had indirectly requested).

HENRY BOLINGBROKE
They love not poison that do poison need;
Nor do I thee. Though I did wish him dead,
I hate the murderer, love him murderèd.
The guilt of conscience take thou for thy labour,
But neither my good word nor princely favour.
With Cain go wander through shades of night,
And never show thy head by day nor light.
Lords, I protest, my soul is full of woe
That blood should sprinkle me to make me grow.
Come mourn with me for that I do lament,
And put on sullen black incontinent.
I'll make a voyage to the Holy Land
To wash this blood off from my guilty hand.
March sadly after. Grace my mournings here
In weeping after this untimely bier.

Shakespeare uses the structure of poetry to express synchronicity between characters, friends and lovers alike. He even writes an entire fourteen-line sonnet into Romeo and Juliet's first encounter, then they consummate their collaborative poem with a kiss.

ROMEO
If I profane with my unworthiest hand
This holy shrine, the gentle sin is this.
My lips, two blushing pilgrims, ready stand
To smooth that rough touch with a tender kiss.

JULIET
Good pilgrim, you do wrong your hand too much,
Which mannerly devotion shows in this.
For saints have hands that pilgrims' hands do touch,
And palm to palm is holy palmers' kiss.

ROMEO
Have not saints lips, and holy palmers too?

JULIET
Ay, pilgrim, lips that they must use in prayer.

ROMEO
O, then, dear saint, let lips do what hands do!
They pray: grant thou, lest faith turn to despair.

JULIET
Saints do not move, though grant for prayers' sake.

ROMEO
Then move not while my prayer's effect I take.

Poetry and song share the same word in many languages, and are closely associated in our own. For instance, the word 'lyric' originally applied to words intended for singing, to the accompaniment of a lyre; sure enough in recent times, Bob Dylan's lyrics were deemed worthy of the 2016 Nobel Prize for literature. Music interspersed many of Shakespeare's comedies, and sheet music was available for sale by street vendors, including the well-known 'Greensleeves' rumoured to have been composed by Henry VIII. Although almost all the music that featured in Shakespeare's plays is now lost, there is an extant early modern musical setting of this aubade in *Cymbeline*, possibly played by the musicians employed by Cloten to serenade Imogen in the play's first production.

MUSICIAN
[*Sings*]
Hark, hark, the lark at heaven's gate sings,
And Phoebus 'gins arise,
His steeds to water at those springs
On chaliced flowers that lies;
And winking Mary-buds begin to ope their golden eyes;
With every thing that pretty is, my lady sweet arise:
Arise, arise!

April 6 | Sonnet 3

The Sonnets emerged with no consistent or easily identifiable addressee: some seem to address a 'Dark Lady', though the majority are addressed to a young man (or several different young men). On the whole, Shakespeare's sonnets operate to a strict formula, though this does nothing to impede their originality. The volta – the turning point (a term from dancing) – usually occurs in the final couplet, signalled by phrases such as 'and yet' and 'but'. Sonnet 3 is typical of the first seventeen: the young man is urged to promulgate his loveliness through procreation, as if pickling the inheritance of his mother's beauty in his offspring. An engaging poem about the intergenerational relay of virtues.

Look in thy glass and tell the face thou viewest,
Now is the time that face should form another,
Whose fresh repair if now thou not renewest,
Thou dost beguile the world, unbless some mother.
For where is she so fair whose unear'd womb
Disdains the tillage of thy husbandry?
Or who is he so fond will be the tomb,
Of his self-love to stop posterity?
Thou art thy mother's glass, and she in thee
Calls back the lovely April of her prime,
So thou through windows of thine age shalt see,
Despite of wrinkles this thy golden time.
  But if thou live, remember'd not to be,
  Die single, and thine Image dies with thee.

April 7 | The Tempest | Act 4 Scene 1

The masque was principally a courtly entertainment, featuring music, song, dance and allegorical figures, performed by actors and some female members of the court – at a time when women were never seen on the public stage. Henry VIII was partial to this kind of extravagance – the first recorded appearance of the Tudor King's ill-fated second wife, Anne Boleyn, was as a participant in a masque. Shakespeare's long-time friend Ben Jonson would build a lucrative career writing masques under James I; spectacular scenery was produced at great expense for one-off productions. In *The Tempest*, Shakespeare alludes to the court masque when Prospero's spirits perform at his behest: here Iris asks Ceres, the goddess of agriculture, to help conjure a spring wedding scene to celebrate the marriage of Miranda and Ferdinand.

IRIS
Ceres, most bounteous lady, thy rich leas
Of wheat, rye, barley, vetches, oats, and pease;
Thy turfy mountains, where live nibbling sheep,
And flat meads thatched with stover, them to keep;
Thy banks with peonied and twillèd brims,
Which spongy April at thy hest betrims,
To make cold nymphs chaste crowns; and thy broom-
    groves,
Whose shadow the dismissèd bachelor loves,
Being lass-lorn; thy pole-clipped vineyard,
And thy sea-marge, sterile and rocky-hard,
Where thou thyself dost air – the queen o'th'sky,
Whose watery arch and messenger am I,
Bids thee leave these, and with her sovereign grace,
Here on this grass-plot, in this very place
To come and sport. Her peacocks fly amain.
Approach, rich Ceres, her to entertain.

The character of Sir John Falstaff was a runaway success
for Shakespeare, and remains one of his most entertaining
creations – so much so he appeared in a spin-off, *The Merry
Wives of Windsor*, due to popular demand. Though he appears
in the history plays *Henry IV, Parts 1* and *2*, he is not taken
from the historical source material. He embodies the bawdy
and reckless lifestyle which threatens to steer the young prince
Hal from his royal duties. Hal mocks his rotund companion
with something between light-hearted ribaldry and genuine
contempt – a tension which is sustained throughout the *Henry
IV* plays. Here the two play-act an imagined encounter between
Hal and his disapproving father, with Hal as the King and
Falstaff as the young prince.

HAL
Thou art violently carried away from grace.
There is a devil haunts thee in the likeness of an
old fat man, a tun of man is thy companion. Why
dost thou converse with that trunk of humours, that
bolting-hutch of beastliness, that swollen parcel
of dropsies, that huge bombard of sack, that stuffed
cloak-bag of guts, that roasted Manningtree ox with
the pudding in his belly, that reverend Vice, that
grey Iniquity, that Father Ruffian, that Vanity in
years? Wherein is he good, but to taste sack and
drink it? Wherein neat and cleanly, but to carve a
capon and eat it? Wherein cunning, but in craft?
Wherein crafty, but in villainy? Wherein villanous,
but in all things? Wherein worthy, but in nothing?

FALSTAFF
I would your grace would take me with you. Whom
means your grace?

HAL
That villainous abominable misleader of youth,
Falstaff, that old white-bearded Satan.

FALSTAFF
My lord, the man I know.

HAL
I know thou dost.

FALSTAFF
But to say I know more harm in him than in myself
were to say more than I know. That he is old, the
more the pity, his white hairs do witness it, but
that he is, saving your reverence, a whoremaster,
that I utterly deny. If sack and sugar be a fault,
God help the wicked! If to be old and merry be a
sin, then many an old host that I know is damned. If
to be fat be to be hated, then Pharaoh's lean kine
are to be loved. No, my good lord! Banish Peto,
banish Bardolph, banish Poins – but for sweet Jack
Falstaff, kind Jack Falstaff, true Jack Falstaff,
valiant Jack Falstaff – and therefore more valiant,
being as he is old Jack Falstaff – banish not him
thy Harry's company, banish not him thy Harry's
company. Banish plump Jack, and banish all the world.

The charismatic Falstaff was probably originally played
by Will Kemp, the Chamberlain's Men's star comic actor,
famed for his funny dances and clowning skill. In the
Epilogue of *Henry IV, Part 2* more misadventures involving
Falstaff are promised – but in the sequel *Henry V* Falstaff
never appears and Shakespeare has him dying offstage.
It isn't known if Kemp left the company because he was
upset that his character had been cut, or whether 'gentle
Shakespeare' had forced the actor from his company for
drawing attention away from the genius of his writing.
Kemp would, like his character, die penniless in obscurity.
Hal, now crowned Henry V, here rejects Falstaff, striking
a visceral blow to his one-time friend and mentor. This
moment would spell the end of Falstaff's – and Kemp's –
part in *Henry V*.

KING HENRY V
I know thee not, old man. Fall to thy prayers.
How ill white hairs become a fool and jester.
I have long dreamt of such a kind of man,
So surfeit-swelled, so old, and so profane,
But being awaked I do despise my dream.
Make less thy body hence, and more thy grace;
Leave gormandizing; know the grave doth gape
For thee thrice wider than for other men.
Reply not to me with a fool-born jest.
Presume not that I am the thing I was,
For God doth know, so shall the world perceive,
That I have turned away my former self;
So will I those that kept me company.
When thou dost hear I am as I have been,
Approach me, and thou shalt be as thou wast,

The tutor and the feeder of my riots;
Till then I banish thee, on pain of death,
As I have done the rest of my misleaders,
Not to come near our person by ten mile.

April 10 | King John | Act 1 Scene 1

Rituals of the Easter weekend were widely observed by the Elizabethans: Elizabeth herself sustained the tradition of washing the feet of the poor every Maundy Thursday, however reticent she tended to be around overtly religious affiliations. Good Friday was traditionally a fast day, in reverence of Christ's death. Phillip Faulconbridge, the 'Bastard', reaches for the image of this abstinence as he tells his mother, fresh from being knighted by his biological uncle King John, that his father could not have been Robert, as she has always claimed, but King Richard I. This illegitimate son of Richard the Lionheart is one of the largest parts in the canon, fourth only to Hamlet, Richard III and Iago.

BASTARD
Madam, I was not old Sir Robert's son.
Sir Robert might have eat his part in me
Upon Good Friday and ne'er broke his fast,
Sir Robert could do well – marry, to confess –
Could he get me! Sir Robert could not do it!
We know his handiwork. Therefore, good mother,
To whom am I beholding for these limbs?
Sir Robert never holp to make this leg.

LADY FAULCONBRIDGE
Hast thou conspirèd with thy brother too,
That for thine own gain shouldst defend mine honour?
What means this scorn, thou most untoward knave?

BASTARD
Knight, knight, good mother, Basilisco-like!
What! I am dubbed, I have it on my shoulder,
But, mother, I am not Sir Robert's son.

I have disclaimed Sir Robert and my land;
Legitimation, name, and all is gone.
Then, good my mother, let me know my father;
Some proper man, I hope. Who was it, mother?

LADY FAULCONBRIDGE
Hast thou denied thyself a Faulconbridge?

BASTARD
As faithfully as I deny the devil.

LADY FAULCONBRIDGE
King Richard Coeur-de-lion was thy father.
By long and vehement suit I was seduced
To make room for him in my husband's bed.
Heaven lay not my transgression to my charge!
Thou art the issue of my dear offence,
Which was so strongly urged past my defence.

Shakespeare paints Lucrece in her bed like a portrait, showing us contrasting colours and contrasting states, such as light and dark, sleep and death, wantonness and modesty. We see a perfect picture of calm before the storm; a quiet moment before the terrible act of violence is committed.

Without the bed her other fair hand was,
On the green coverlet, whose perfect white
Showed like an April daisy on the grass,
With pearly sweat resembling dew of night.
Her eyes like marigolds had sheathed their light,
And canopied in darkness sweetly lay
Till they might open to adorn the day.

Her hair like golden threads played with her breath:
O modest wantons, wanton modesty!
Showing life's triumph in the map of death,
And death's dim look in life's mortality:
Each in her sleep themselves so beautify
As if between them twain there were no strife,
But that life lived in death and death in life.

Timon of Athens is the riches to rags story of a wealthy Athenian who fritters his wealth away on parasitic artists and writers and ends up in a cave in the wilderness, digging for roots to eat. A bitter Timon is here berating gold itself for the misdeeds it is responsible for: in particular, he laments the way it enables a 'wappened widow' – a woman riddled with venereal disease – to marry again through the purchase of disguises like balms and spices. Not surprisingly, this was one of Karl Marx's favourite passages in Shakespeare.

TIMON
Who seeks for better of thee, sauce his palate
With thy most operant poison. What is here?
Gold? Yellow, glittering, precious gold?
No, gods, I am no idle votarist.
Roots, you clear heavens! Thus much of this will make
Black white, foul fair, wrong right,
Base noble, old young, coward valiant.
Ha, you gods! Why this? What, this, you gods? Why, this
Will lug your priests and servants from your sides,
Pluck stout men's pillows from below their heads.
This yellow slave
Will knit and break religions, bless th'accursed,
Make the hoar leprosy adored, place thieves,
And give them title, knee, and approbation,
With senators on the bench. This is it
That makes the wappened widow wed again –
She, whom the spital-house and ulcerous sores
Would cast the gorge at, this embalms and spices
To th'April day again. Come, damned earth,
Thou common whore of mankind, that puts odds
Among the rout of nations, I will make thee
Do thy right nature.

The loyal Roman soldier Titus Andronicus here pleads with the earth that, if he could saturate the ground with his continuous weeping, the dirt will refuse to take the blood of his sons, who are about to be executed for a murder they didn't commit.

TITUS ANDRONICUS
Hear me, grave fathers; noble tribunes, stay!
For pity of mine age, whose youth was spent
In dangerous wars whilst you securely slept,
For all my blood in Rome's great quarrel shed,
For all the frosty nights that I have watched,
And for these bitter tears which now you see
Filling the agèd wrinkles in my cheeks,
Be pitiful to my condemnèd sons,
Whose souls are not corrupted as 'tis thought.
For two-and-twenty sons I never wept
Because they died in honour's lofty bed;

[*Andronicus lieth down, and the judges and others pass by him*]

For these two, tribunes, in the dust I write
My heart's deep languor and my soul's sad tears.
Let my tears stanch the earth's dry appetite;
My sons' sweet blood will make it shame and blush.
O earth, I will befriend thee more with rain
That shall distil from these two ancient ruins
Than youthful April shall with all his showers.
In summer's drought I'll drop upon thee still;
In winter with warm tears I'll melt the snow
And keep eternal springtime on thy face,
So thou refuse to drink my dear sons' blood.

At the conclusion of *Love's Labour's Lost*, a play all about frustrated desire, Ver speaking for Spring contributes a mocking ode playing on the similarity between cuckoo and cuckold. A cuckold is a term for a man whose wife commits adultery; a cuckoo is a bird of spring, known for its trick of deceptively laying its eggs in another bird's nest.

VER
When daisies pied and violets blue
And lady-smocks all silver-white
And cuckoo-buds of yellow hue
Do paint the meadows with delight,
The cuckoo then, on every tree,
Mocks married men; for thus sings he:
'Cuckoo! Cuckoo, cuckoo!'
O, word of fear,
Unpleasing to a married ear!
When shepherds pipe on oaten straws,
And merry larks are ploughmen's clocks,
When turtles tread, and rooks, and daws,
And maidens bleach their summer smocks,
The cuckoo then, on every tree,
Mocks married men; for thus sings he:
'Cuckoo! Cuckoo, cuckoo!'
O, word of fear,
Unpleasing to a married ear!

The Globe was demolished on 15 April 1644, during the decade
of Oliver Cromwell's Puritan rule in England after the English
Civil War. All plays were banned. Prospero, the banished duke-
magician, whose masque-like entertainment for his newly engaged
daughter has been interrupted by his recollection of an impending
attempt on his life, reflects on the transience of theatre, with one of
a few allusions to the Globe to be found in the plays.

PROSPERO
Our revels now are ended. These our actors,
As I foretold you, were all spirits, and
Are melted into air, into thin air;
And, like the baseless fabric of this vision,
The cloud-capped towers, the gorgeous palaces,
The solemn temples, the great globe itself,
Yea, all which it inherit, shall dissolve,
And like this insubstantial pageant faded,
Leave not a rack behind. We are such stuff
As dreams are made on, and our little life
Is rounded with a sleep. Sir, I am vexed.
Bear with my weakness; my old brain is troubled.
Be not disturbed with my infirmity.
If you be pleased, retire into my cell,
And there repose. A turn or two I'll walk
To still my beating mind.

April 16 | As You Like It | Act 4 Scene 1

Rosalind makes friends with Orlando, whom she loves, while disguised as a shepherd called Ganymede. She tests his feelings for her, undetected, after Orlando vows to have Rosalind 'forever and a day'. She chides Orlando, rather cynically comparing the manner of men in courtship to their behaviour after they are married, as spring-like April is to wintry December. Rosalind speaks in prose, as part of her disguise; though here, confusingly, 'Ganymede' is pretending to be Rosalind.

ROSALIND
Say 'a day' without the 'ever.' No, no, Orlando,
men are April when they woo, December when
they wed; maids are May when they are maids,
but the sky changes when they are wives. I will
be more jealous of thee than a Barbary cock-pigeon
over his hen, more clamorous than a parrot against
rain, more new-fangled than an ape, more giddy in
my desires than a monkey; I will weep for nothing,
like Diana in the fountain, and I will do that when
you are disposed to be merry; I will laugh like a hyena,
and that when thou are inclined to sleep.

In *The Winter's Tale*, Prince Florizel of Bohemia dons a peasant's outfit as Doricles, in order to woo Perdita (who has been brought up by a shepherd, but is in fact a princess). At their engagement party, Perdita is lavished with pastoral compliments by her husband-to-be: 'These your unusual weeds to each part of you / Do give a life: no shepherdess, but Flora / Peering in April's front.' However, Shakespeare's pastoral settings were not always idyllic. We might readily imagine what *As You Like It*'s Rosalind would think of such effusive praise, as she is always ready to challenge pastoral idealism. Here she mocks the shepherd Silvius who has been acting just like Florizel, but wooing a less responsive shepherdess, the disdainful Phoebe.

ROSALIND
You foolish shepherd, wherefore do you follow her,
Like foggy south, puffing with wind and rain?
You are a thousand times a properer man
Than she a woman. 'Tis such fools as you
That makes the world full of ill-favoured children.
'Tis not her glass but you that flatters her,
And out of you she sees herself more proper
Than any of her lineaments can show her.
But, mistress, know yourself; down on your knees
And thank heaven, fasting, for a good man's love!
For I must tell you friendly in your ear,
Sell when you can, you are not for all markets.
Cry the man mercy, love him, take his offer.
Foul is most foul, being foul to be a scoffer.
So take her to thee, shepherd. Fare you well.

Shakespeare's first published work was licensed for printing on 18 April 1593, during an outbreak of plague which had closed down the theatres. The narrative poem *Venus and Adonis* was printed by Richard Field, a neighbour of William Shakespeare from Stratford-upon-Avon, and is dedicated to Shakespeare's patron, Henry Wriothesley, 3rd Earl of Southampton – whom many believe to be the young man to whom the first sonnets are addressed. Although we know more copies of this were sold than of any of his other works in his lifetime, there is now only one extant copy of the first edition, in Oxford's Bodleian Library. This might have been because the texts were so well thumbed – Venus's poetic passion made for a popular read. These are the opening stanzas of the poem, which began the most remarkable literary career in the English-speaking world.

Even as the sun with purple-coloured face
Had ta'en his last leave of the weeping morn,
Rose-cheeked Adonis hied him to the chase;
Hunting he loved, but love he laughed to scorn.
Sick-thoughted Venus makes amain unto him,
And like a bold-faced suitor 'gins to woo him.

'Thrice-fairer than myself,' thus she began,
'The field's chief flower, sweet above compare,
Stain to all nymphs, more lovely than a man,
More white and red than doves or roses are;
Nature that made thee with herself at strife
Saith that the world hath ending with thy life.

'Vouchsafe, thou wonder, to alight thy steed,
And rein his proud head to the saddle-bow;
If thou wilt deign this favour, for thy meed
A thousand honey secrets shalt thou know.
Here come and sit, where never serpent hisses,
And being set, I'll smother thee with kisses;

'And yet not cloy thy lips with loathed satiety,
But rather famish them amid their plenty,
Making them red and pale with fresh variety;
Ten kisses short as one, one long as twenty.
A summer's day will seem an hour but short,
Being wasted in such time-beguiling sport.'

With this she seizeth on his sweating palm,
The precedent of pith and livelihood,
And, trembling in her passion, calls it balm,
Earth's sovereign salve to do a goddess good.
Being so enraged, desire doth lend her force
Courageously to pluck him from his horse.

Over one arm the lusty courser's rein,
Under her other was the tender boy,
Who blushed and pouted in a dull disdain,
With leaden appetite, unapt to toy;
She red and hot as coals of glowing fire,
He red for shame, but frosty in desire.

April 19 | The Merchant of Venice | Act 2 Scene 9

A messenger forewarns the rich heiress Portia of the arrival of
Bassanio, who is destined to choose the lead casket and win
Portia's hand in marriage by the terms of her late father's will.
The suggestion is that Bassanio will prevail in love as surely as
summer follows April.

MESSENGER
Madam, there is alighted at your gate
A young Venetian, one that comes before
To signify th'approaching of his lord,
From whom he bringeth sensible regreets,
To wit, besides commends and courteous breath,
Gifts of rich value. Yet I have not seen
So likely an ambassador of love.
A day in April never came so sweet,
To show how costly summer was at hand,
As this fore-spurrer comes before his lord.

April 20 | Macbeth | Act 1 Scene 5

Theatregoer Simon Foreman wrote in his diary that he attended a public performance of *Macbeth* on 20 April 1610. He noted, 'Macbeth contrived to kill Duncan and through the persuasion of his wife did that night murder the King in his own castle, being his guest; and there were many prodigies seen that night and the day before.' It is the first recorded performance of the play, but it may have been presented at the court of James I as early as 1606, when the dangers of regicide were still vivid from the Gunpowder Plot of 1605. Here is one of the classic speeches by Lady Macbeth, which begins with the ominous prodigy of the raven croaking the arrival of Duncan.

LADY MACBETH
The raven himself is hoarse
That croaks the fatal entrance of Duncan
Under my battlements. Come, you spirits
That tend on mortal thoughts, unsex me here
And fill me from the crown to the toe top-full
Of direst cruelty. Make thick my blood;
Stop up the access and passage to remorse,
That no compunctious visitings of nature
Shake my fell purpose, nor keep peace between
The effect and it. Come to my woman's breasts,
And take my milk for gall, you murdering ministers,
Wherever, in your sightless substances,
You wait on nature's mischief. Come, thick night,
And pall thee in the dunnest smoke of hell,
That my keen knife see not the wound it makes,
Nor heaven peep through the blanket of the dark
To cry, 'Hold, hold!'

In *Julius Caesar*, Mark Antony, left alone with the murdered body of Caesar, predicts that the consequences of his friend's assassination will include a savage civil war. This issue would have hit close to home in Elizabethan England, with mounting anxieties over the succession of the ageing and heirless queen.

ANTONY
O, pardon me, thou bleeding piece of earth,
That I am meek and gentle with these butchers.
Thou art the ruins of the noblest man
That ever livèd in the tide of times.
Woe to the hand that shed this costly blood!
Over thy wounds now do I prophesy –
Which like dumb mouths do ope their ruby lips,
To beg the voice and utterance of my tongue –
A curse shall light upon the limbs of men;
Domestic fury and fierce civil strife
Shall cumber all the parts of Italy;
Blood and destruction shall be so in use,
And dreadful objects so familiar,
That mothers shall but smile when they behold
Their infants quartered with the hands of war,
All pity choked with custom of fell deeds;
And Caesar's spirit, ranging for revenge,
With Ate by his side, come hot from hell,
Shall in these confines with a monarch's voice
Cry havoc and let slip the dogs of war,
That this foul deed shall smell above the earth
With carrion men, groaning for burial.

In the immediate aftermath of Caesar's assassination on the
fateful Ides of March, Rome is uncertain as to whether to revile
him as a tyrant or mourn him as a great leader. Antony's funeral
speech is a rhetorical tour de force – although at first it pretends
otherwise, it is carefully calculated to destabilize the people's
trust in Brutus. Amusingly, Cicero – who is one of history's
celebrated rhetoricians – is only given four lines in this play
and is made out to be a bit of a self-fancier: Brutus says of him
that 'he will never follow anything that other men begin', and
Casca ridicules the renowned orator for speaking Greek for no
useful purpose; 'it was Greek to me' he famously remarks. It is
Antony who is endowed with textbook oratory finesse: among
other rhetorical devices, this remarkable politician uses laudatio
(praise, of Brutus), miseratio (condemnation, of Caesar) and
cohortatio (incitement, to riot). The content of Antony's speech
is Shakespeare's invention; Plutarch's *Life of Brutus*, the main
source for the play, mentions that Antony spoke at this point,
but does not record in detail what he said. Shakespeare captures
the moment, and fills the silence.

ANTONY
Friends, Romans, countrymen, lend me your ears;
I come to bury Caesar, not to praise him.
The evil that men do lives after them,
The good is oft interrèd with their bones;
So let it be with Caesar. The noble Brutus
Hath told you Caesar was ambitious.
If it were so, it was a grievous fault,
And grievously hath Caesar answered it.
Here, under leave of Brutus and the rest –
For Brutus is an honourable man;
So are they all, all honourable men –

Come I to speak in Caesar's funeral.
He was my friend, faithful and just to me;
But Brutus says he was ambitious,
And Brutus is an honourable man.
He hath brought many captives home to Rome,
Whose ransoms did the general coffers fill:
Did this in Caesar seem ambitious?
When that the poor have cried, Caesar hath wept;
Ambition should be made of sterner stuff:
Yet Brutus says he was ambitious,
And Brutus is an honourable man.
You all did see that on the Lupercal
I thrice presented him a kingly crown,
Which he did thrice refuse. Was this ambition?
Yet Brutus says he was ambitious,
And sure he is an honourable man.
I speak not to disprove what Brutus spoke,
But here I am to speak what I do know.
You all did love him once, not without cause;
What cause withholds you then, to mourn for him?
O judgment! thou art fled to brutish beasts,
And men have lost their reason. Bear with me;
My heart is in the coffin there with Caesar,
And I must pause till it come back to me.

Characteristically for the master of antithesis, Shakespeare's birthday, 23 April 1564, is the same as the day he died in 1616 (although we can only estimate these dates from his baptism and burial records). He was fifty-two, and considering he survived childhood and was not slain in a war, this was not that impressive an age to reach. The 'Ages of Man' speech of Jaques (even though Shakespeare never went through phases of soldiering or serving as a justice of the peace) could be read as the perfect epilogue for a man who spent his life in the theatre.

JAQUES
All the world's a stage,
And all the men and women merely players;
They have their exits and their entrances,
And one man in his time plays many parts,
His acts being seven ages. At first the infant,
Mewling and puking in the nurse's arms;
Then, the whining school-boy, with his satchel
And shining morning face, creeping like snail
Unwillingly to school; and then the lover,
Sighing like furnace, with a woeful ballad
Made to his mistress' eyebrow; then, a soldier,
Full of strange oaths, and bearded like the pard,
Jealous in honour, sudden and quick in quarrel,
Seeking the bubble reputation
Even in the cannon's mouth; and then, the justice,
In fair round belly, with good capon lined,
With eyes severe, and beard of formal cut,
Full of wise saws and modern instances,
And so he plays his part; the sixth age shifts
Into the lean and slippered pantaloon,
With spectacles on nose and pouch on side,

His youthful hose, well saved, a world too wide
For his shrunk shank, and his big manly voice,
Turning again toward childish treble, pipes
And whistles in his sound; last Scene of all,
That ends this strange eventful history,
Is second childishness, and mere oblivion,
Sans teeth, sans eyes, sans taste, sans everything.

Shakespeare returned to Stratford towards the end of his life.
For the backdrop to this homecoming, these are Lucrece's
reflections on the nature of time, which returns things to their
original state, which turns children to men and back again
(just as in Jaques's monologue), and sees gold tarnished and
monuments decayed. Shakespeare wrote these verses as a
young man.

'Time's glory is to calm contending kings,
To unmask falsehood and bring truth to light,
To stamp the seal of time in agèd things,
To wake the morn and sentinel the night,
To wrong the wronger till he render right,
To ruinate proud buildings with thy hours,
And smear with dust their glittering golden towers;

'To fill with worm-holes stately monuments,
To feed oblivion with decay of things,
To blot old books and alter their contents,
To pluck the quills from ancient ravens' wings,
To dry the old oak's sap and cherish springs,
To spoil antiquities of hammered steel,
And turn the giddy round of Fortune's wheel;

'To show the beldame daughters of her daughter,
To make the child a man, the man a child,
To slay the tiger that doth live by slaughter,
To tame the unicorn and lion wild,
To mock the subtle in themselves beguiled,
To cheer the ploughman with increaseful crops,
And waste huge stones with little water-drops'.

April 25 | Sonnet 55

On 25 April 1616, Shakespeare was buried at Holy Trinity Church, Stratford-upon-Avon. The epitaph on his tombstone warns: 'Good friend, for Jesus' sake forbear, To dig the dust enclosed here. Blest be the man that spares these stones, And curst be he that moves my bones.' Sonnet 55 considers the legacy of a writer's work. Here Shakespeare writes how the speaker's beloved will live on in his words long after they have died and buildings and statues have collapsed. Given that we are still reading this poem over 400 years later, it's safe to say that he was right.

Not marble, nor the gilded monuments
Of Princes shall outlive this powerful rhyme,
But you shall shine more bright in these contents
Than unswept stone, besmeared with sluttish time.
When wasteful war shall statues overturn,
And broils root out the work of masonry,
Nor Mars his sword, nor war's quick fire shall burn
The living record of your memory.
'Gainst death and all oblivious enmity
Shall you pace forth, your praise shall still find room,
Even in the eyes of all posterity
That wear this world out to the ending doom.
  So till the judgment that yourself arise,
   You live in this, and dwell in lovers' eyes.

April 26 | Much Ado About Nothing | Act 2 Scene 1

Shakespeare's baptism on 26 April 1564 was recorded in
the Parish Register in Stratford-upon-Avon, Warwickshire.
The entry reads '*Guilielmus filius Johannes Shakspere*', or,
in English, 'William, son of John Shakespeare'. There are
several variants on the spelling of his name in records from
his life, noting it as variously as *Shakesspere, Shakysper,
Shaxpeer, Schakespeire, Shackper, Shexpere, Shaxkspere*, and
Shakspeyre. For making sense of births and death, there was a
strong inclination towards Astrology and the movements of the
stars around these moments are often mentioned in his plays
as benchmarks by which certain fates were foreclosed. Beatrice
excuses herself with as much in her refusal of Don Pedro's
(somewhat random) offer of marriage.

DON PEDRO
Will you have me, lady?

BEATRICE
No, my lord, unless I might have another for
working-days: your grace is too costly to wear
every day. But, I beseech your grace, pardon me; I
was born to speak all mirth and no matter.

DON PEDRO
Your silence most offends me, and to be merry best
becomes you; for, out of question, you were born in
a merry hour.

BEATRICE
No, sure, my lord, my mother cried; but then there
was a star danced, and under that was I born.

Juliet's father, Capulet, prods Paris to woo Juliet, even though we know from the play's title and its spoiler-ridden prologue that Paris is not going to be *the one.*

CAPULET
Earth hath swallowed all my hopes but she;
She's the hopeful lady of my earth.
But woo her, gentle Paris, get her heart,
My will to her consent is but a part,
And, she agreed, within her scope of choice
Lies my consent and fair according voice.
This night I hold an old accustomed feast,
Whereto I have invited many a guest,
Such as I love; and you among the store,
One more, most welcome, makes my number more.
At my poor house look to behold this night
Earth-treading stars that make dark heaven light.
Such comfort as do lusty young men feel
When well-apparelled April on the heel
Of limping winter treads, even such delight
Among fresh female buds shall you this night
Inherit at my house. Hear all; all see;
And like her most whose merit most shall be;
Which, on more view, of many, mine, being one,
May stand in number, though in reckoning none.
Come, go with me. [*To Servant*] Go, sirrah, trudge about
Through fair Verona; find those persons out
Whose names are written there, and to them say,
My house and welcome on their pleasure stay.

The tinker Autolycus here touts a ballad about a fish, which he claims is based in truth: though the events depicted are about as likely as the date, the 'fourscore [i.e. 80th] of April'. This is pretty standard for ballads of the time, which often described such portentous freaks of nature, and is amusing for the enormity of the exaggerations and the credulity of the peasants. Unfortunately we never get to hear this particular ballad as he doesn't get round to singing it.

AUTOLYCUS
Here's another ballad, of a fish, that appeared upon
the coast on Wednesday the fourscore of April,
forty thousand fathom above water, and sung this
ballad against the hard hearts of maids. It was
thought she was a woman, and was turned into a cold
fish for she would not exchange flesh with one that
loved her. The ballad is very pitiful, and as true.

April 29 | Sonnet 145

Although there is no proof that Shakespeare wrote directly
to or about his wife, Anne Hathaway, there has been some
speculation that the sonnet published as one of the last in the
sequence was in fact one of the first he ever wrote. Some believe
Shakespeare was a young man, perhaps as young as eighteen,
when he penned Sonnet 145. In Elizabethan pronunciation, the
phrase 'hate away' would have sounded very similar to Anne's
maiden name, while 'And sav'd my life', it has been argued, is
not far off 'Anne saved my life'. While we can only conjecture,
it is touching to think of a young Shakespeare taking his first
furtive steps in love and in poetry.

Those lips that Love's own hand did make,
Breath'd forth the sound that said I hate,
To me that languish'd for her sake:
But when she saw my woeful state,
Straight in her heart did mercy come,
Chiding that tongue that ever sweet,
Was us'd in giving gentle doom:
And taught it thus anew to greet:
I hate she alter'd with an end,
That follow'd it as gentle day,
Doth follow night who like a fiend
From heaven to hell is flown away.
  I hate from hate away she threw,
  And sav'd my life saying, not you.

Food and drink appear abundantly throughout Shakespeare's plays, and often derogatively. 'Small beer', which was low in flavour and alcohol content, is associated with lower social orders; Old King Hamlet's 'funeral-baked meats' are allegedly recycled for his wife's swift remarriage, and Katherine in *The Taming of the Shrew* is reduced by Petruchio to the status of his 'household cates': nonspecific items of food.

In contrast to the starving peasants of *Coriolanus*, Falstaff is fat. Really fat. In fact, he is so fat that it is almost the first thing we learn about him, and adjectives conveying the fact are appended to his name whenever he is referred to or even addressed directly. Shakespeare rarely specifies the physique of his characters: Falstaff's belly, Richard III's hunchback and Andrew Aguecheek's ungainly height are anomalies, perhaps because he was conscious that different-size actors would play his parts. Here, Hal (Prince Henry) jibes at his fat friend's gluttony, which Falstaff receives with characteristic jocularity and faux dignity.

HAL
Thou art so fat-witted with drinking of old sack,
and unbuttoning thee after supper, and sleeping upon
benches after noon, that thou hast forgotten to
demand that truly which thou wouldst truly know.
What a devil hast thou to do with the time of the
day? Unless hours were cups of sack, and minutes
capons, and clocks the tongues of bawds, and dials the
signs of leaping-houses, and the blessed sun himself
a fair hot wench in flame-coloured taffeta, I see no
reason why thou shouldst be so superfluous to demand
the time of the day.

FALSTAFF
Indeed, you come near me now Hal, for we that take
purses go by the moon and the seven stars, and not
'by Phoebus, he, that wandering knight so fair'. And
I prithee sweet wag, when thou art King, as God
save thy grace – majesty I should say, for grace
thou wilt have none –

HAL
What, none?

FALSTAFF
No by my troth, not so much as will serve to
prologue to an egg and butter.

May

May Day has been observed since Roman times and was a major Elizabethan festival marking the first day of summer. A festive spirit of subversion coursed through the celebrations, which included dances, plays, music and storytelling. Illustrations of upright fish catching men with rods, and carts pulling oxen, circulated among noisy crowds who observed this day as lying outside the usually binding rules and laws. Lysander in *A Midsummer Night's Dream* likens the woods beyond Athens to the permissive atmosphere of a May Day, vowing to marry Hermia outside the city walls against her father's wishes.

LYSANDER
I have a widow aunt, a dowager,
Of great revenue; and she hath no child.
From Athens is her house remote seven leagues;
And she respects me as her only son.
There, gentle Hermia, may I marry thee;
And to that place the sharp Athenian law
Cannot pursue us. If thou lovest me, then
Steal forth thy father's house tomorrow night,
And in the wood, a league without the town –
Where I did meet thee once with Helena
To do observance to a morn of May –
There will I stay for thee.

May Day festivities were characterized by the weird and the wonderful. Songs such as 'London Bridge is Falling Down' originated amidst these rituals, and the day had developed over the centuries to encompass mumming, minstrels, and recitations of legendary stories such as George and the Dragon and the adventures of Robin Hood. A Robin Hood and a Maid Marion would be appointed for the duration of the festivities, as well as a Lord and Lady of May to lead the revels in a dance around the maypole. The festival's pagan pedigree and subversive character saw it banished by the Puritans in 1644; but the May Day tradition of morris dancing lives on in some towns and villages to this day. Dancing the morris crops up in several of Shakespeare's plays, but only among the rustic characters. The dance is explained most amusingly by Gerrold the Schoolmaster, a verbose and pedantic character in *The Two Noble Kinsmen* similar to Holofernes in *Love's Labour's Lost*, who speaks a prologue before he and his rustic colleagues perform for Duke Theseus.

SCHOOLMASTER
We are a few of those collected here
That ruder tongues distinguish villager;
And to say verity, and not to fable,
We are a merry rout, or else a rabble,
Or company, or, by a figure, *chorus,*
That 'fore thy dignity will dance a morris.
And I that am the rectifier of all,
By title *pedagogus,* that let fall
The birch upon the breeches of the small ones,
And humble with a ferula the tall ones,
Do here present this machine, or this frame;
And, dainty Duke, whose doughty dismal fame

From Dis to Daedalus, from post to pillar,
Is blown abroad, help me, thy poor well-willier,
And with thy twinkling eyes look right and straight
Upon this mighty 'Morr', of mickle weight;
'Is' now comes in, which being glued together
Makes 'Morris', and the cause that we came hither,
The body of our sport, of no small study.
I first appear, though rude, and raw, and muddy,
To speak before thy noble grace this tenor,
At whose great feet I offer up my penner;
The next, the Lord of May and Lady bright;
The chambermaid and servingman, by night
That seek out silent hanging; then mine host
And his fat spouse, that welcomes to their cost
The gallèd traveller, and with a beckoning
Informs the tapster to inflame the reckoning;
Then the beast-eating clown, and next the fool,
The bavian, with long tail and eke long tool,
Cum multis aliis that make a dance;
Say 'ay', and all shall presently advance.

May 3 | Sonnet 18

The Romantic poet Samuel Taylor Coleridge described Shakespeare as 'myriad-minded' for his ability to hold several ideas in play at once. His fellow poet John Keats later described a similar ability of the dramatist to surrender any opinions of his own to his vision of the world as it is, even to the point of uncertainty and confusion, which he called 'negative capability'. Both of these virtues are present in spades throughout Sonnet 18, in which the speaker declares that the charm of a beautiful day in summer pales in comparison to the almost unimaginable magnificence of his beloved. It has become one of the most well-known love poems in the English language.

Shall I compare thee to a Summer's day?
Thou art more lovely and more temperate:
Rough winds do shake the darling buds of May,
And Summer's lease hath all too short a date:
Sometime too hot the eye of heaven shines,
And often is his gold complexion dimm'd,
And every fair from fair sometime declines,
By chance, or nature's changing course untrimm'd:
But thy eternal Summer shall not fade,
Nor lose possession of that fair thou ow'st,
Nor shall Death brag thou wander'st in his shade,
When in eternal lines to time thou grow'st:
    So long as men can breathe or eyes can see,
    So long lives this, and this gives life to thee.

Shakespeare bought New Place, an unimaginatively named
but enormous house in Stratford-upon-Avon, on 4 May 1597.
The house was passed down to his daughter and finally his
granddaughter, who died without an heir, and the building
was subsequently knocked down. We can but speculate on his
sentiments towards his home and his marriage, and there may
well have been something of Valentine, one of the two gentlemen
of Verona, in him. These lines on the subject of home open
the play.

VALENTINE
Cease to persuade, my loving Proteus;
Home-keeping youth have ever homely wits.
Were't not affection chains thy tender days
To the sweet glances of thy honoured love,
I rather would entreat thy company
To see the wonders of the world abroad
Than, living dully sluggardized at home,
Wear out thy youth with shapeless idleness.
But, since thou lovest, love still, and thrive therein,
Even as I would when I to love begin.

PROTEUS
Wilt thou be gone? Sweet Valentine, adieu.
Think on thy Proteus, when thou haply seest
Some rare noteworthy object in thy travel.
Wish me partaker in thy happiness,
When thou dost meet good hap; and in thy danger –
If ever danger do environ thee –
Commend thy grievance to my holy prayers,
For I will be thy beadsman, Valentine.

Christopher Columbus landed in Jamaica on 5 May 1494. He quickly set about enslaving and killing off the peaceful Arawak inhabitants of the island as part of his search for gold. Writing from Jamaica in 1504, Columbus proclaims that 'Gold is a wonderful thing! Whoever possesses it is lord of whatever he wants. By means of gold, one can even get souls into paradise.' Karl Marx would later build his economic theories around the corrupting allure of money and gold, to which Columbus's world-shaping voyages bear devastating witness. For Marx, Columbus and Shakespeare's Antipholus of Syracuse, 'gold' is the answer to everything. In this extract from *The Comedy of Errors* – in which each one of a separated pair of identical twins employs another separated twin as their servant – the servant Dromio of Ephesus is baffled by an exchange with Antipholus of Syracuse, having mistaken him for his master Antipholus of Ephesus, who in turn mistakes him for his own servant to whom he had given 1000 marks.

DROMIO OF EPHESUS
But sure he is stark mad.
When I desired him to come home to dinner
He ask'd me for a thousand marks in gold.
'Tis dinner-time,' quoth I. 'My gold,' quoth he.
'Your meat doth burn,' quoth I. 'My gold,' quoth he.
'Will you come?' quoth I. 'My gold,' quoth he.
'Where is the thousand marks I gave thee, villain?'
'The pig,' quoth I, 'is burned.' 'My gold,' quoth he.
'My mistress, sir –' quoth I – 'Hang up thy mistress!
I know not thy mistress. Out on thy mistress!'

Francis Drake became the first Englishman to circumnavigate the world in 1580, when Shakespeare was sixteen – a feat unimaginable to the previous generation of seafarers. The voyage took nearly three years, and made an absolute fortune for the sponsors of the trip including Elizabeth I, whose income was doubled. For the English imagination, the world was turned overnight from an expanse of unfathomable dimensions to a finite, navigable unit, and the shift makes an impression in some of Shakespeare's plays. A comparable but faster feat of circumnavigation is credited to the fairies in *A Midsummer Night's Dream,* where Oberon conjectures that 'We the globe can compass soon, / Swifter than the wandering moon.' Puck makes an even more extravagant claim, one which even now we haven't managed without his fantastical powers: he says 'I'll put a girdle round about the earth / In forty minutes.' (The sole British satellite to be launched by a British rocket, in 1971, after the funding for the British space programme had already been cancelled, was originally called Puck for this reason, but, fearing that the name might be misheard in Parliament, the ministry involved called it Prospero instead.) Dromio's description of a fat kitchen maid is outrageous for its xenophobia but its sheer creative audacity can still get laughs today.

DROMIO OF SYRACUSE
No longer from head to foot than from hip to hip.
She is spherical, like a globe. I could find out countries in her.

ANTIPHOLUS OF SYRACUSE
In what part of her body stands Ireland?

DROMIO OF SYRACUSE
Marry, sir, in her buttocks. I found it out by the bogs.

ANTIPHOLUS OF SYRACUSE
Where Scotland?

DROMIO OF SYRACUSE
I found it by the barrenness, hard in the palm of the hand.

ANTIPHOLUS OF SYRACUSE
Where France?

DROMIO OF SYRACUSE
In her forehead, armed and reverted, making war
against her heir.

ANTIPHOLUS OF SYRACUSE
Where England?

DROMIO OF SYRACUSE
I looked for the chalky cliffs, but I could find no
whiteness in them. But I guess it stood in her chin,
by the salt rheum that ran between France and it.

ANTIPHOLUS OF SYRACUSE
Where Spain?

DROMIO OF SYRACUSE
Faith, I saw it not, but I felt it hot in her breath.

ANTIPHOLUS OF SYRACUSE
Where America, the Indies?

DROMIO OF SYRACUSE
O, sir, upon her nose all o'er embellished with

rubies, carbuncles, sapphires, declining their rich
aspect to the hot breath of Spain, who sent whole
armadoes of carracks to be ballast at her nose.

ANTIPHOLUS OF SYRACUSE
Where stood Belgia, the Netherlands?

DROMIO OF SYRACUSE
O, sir, I did not look so low.

May 7 | Henry VIII | Act 5 Scene 4

Walter Raleigh was the one-time favourite of Elizabeth I
who embarked on several profitable adventures during her
reign. Raleigh is memorable to English schoolchildren, since
history textbooks traditionally credited him with bringing
the potato and tobacco (a commodity, surprisingly, never
mentioned by Shakespeare) to English shores. On a bleaker
note, indigenous people were also taken from their lands to be
exhibited as foreign curiosities: Epenow, a Nauset inhabitant
of Massachusetts, was a local celebrity among the frequenters
of London's taverns and coffeehouses, and was taught to cry
'Welcome! Welcome!' to the thirsty patrons. In the closing
scene of *Henry VIII,* one such 'strange Indian' is referred to by
the disgruntled Porter, who is bemoaning his task of controlling
the enthusiastic crowds at the christening of the future Queen
Elizabeth.

PORTER
What should you do, but knock 'em down by th'dozens?
Is this Moorfields to muster in? or have we
some strange Indian with the great tool come to
court, the women so besiege us? Bless me, what a
fry of fornication is at door! On my Christian
conscience, this one christening will beget a
thousand: here will be father, godfather, and all together.

Epenow went on to become a pioneering figure of colonial
resistance. While in England he convinced his captor Captain
Edward Harlow that there was a wealth of gold in his native
Massachusetts, and that he was willing to act as the guide.
Once back in his homeland, Epenow quietly conspired with his
family. Although he had been decked out in baggy clothes so
he could be easily grabbed by the English crew, Epenow was
able to escape; and Harlow returned to England empty-handed.
Epenow's anguish, and his resolution to resist, is echoed by
Shakespeare's Cleopatra, as she movingly laments the prospect
of being exhibited as a foreign marvel if she were taken to
Rome. There would have been a note of irony in this speech for
the original viewers: Cleopatra would have been played by the
very sort of 'squeaking . . . boy' she shudders to think of here.

CLEOPATRA
Now, Iras, what think'st thou?
Thou, an Egyptian puppet, shall be shown
In Rome as well as I. Mechanic slaves
With greasy aprons, rules, and hammers shall
Uplift us to the view. In their thick breaths,
Rank of gross diet, shall be enclouded,
And forced to drink their vapour.

IRAS
The gods forbid!

CLEOPATRA
Nay, 'tis most certain, Iras. Saucy lictors
Will catch at us like strumpets, and scald rhymers
Ballad us out o' tune. The quick comedians
Extemporally will stage us, and present

Our Alexandrian revels. Antony
Shall be brought drunken forth, and I shall see
Some squeaking Cleopatra boy my greatness
I'th'posture of a whore.

The Rape of Lucrece was first registered on 9 May 1594, and was dedicated to Henry Wriothesley, Earl of Southampton – the alleged addressee of the Sonnets. The dedication is evidence of the intimacy between the poet and the patron, and is one of Shakespeare's few surviving texts writing as himself. He signs it off with these words:

> What I have done is yours; what I have to do is yours; being part
> in all I have, devoted yours. Were my worth greater, my duty would
> show greater; meantime, as it is, it is bound to your lordship, to
> whom I wish long life, still lengthened with all happiness.
> Your lordship's in all duty,
> William Shakespeare.

The Rape of Lucrece did not reach the heights of popularity of *Venus and Adonis*, but nevertheless ran through six editions within forty years of its first publication. Again, the story is taken from Ovid and is characteristically grim. The opening lines of the poem are packed with foreboding as Tarquin, inflamed with dreadful lust at Collatine's vivid descriptions of his wife Lucrece, makes his way to her house to satisfy his lurid desire.

From the besiegèd Ardea all in post,
Borne by the trustless wings of false desire,
Lust-breathèd Tarquin leaves the Roman host
And to Collatium bears the lightless fire
Which, in pale embers hid, lurks to aspire
And girdle with embracing flames the waist
Of Collatine's fair love, Lucrece the chaste.

Haply that name of 'chaste' unhapp'ly set
This bateless edge on his keen appetite,
When Collatine unwisely did not let
To praise the clear unmatchèd red and white
Which triumphed in that sky of his delight,
Where mortal stars as bright as heaven's beauties
With pure aspects did him peculiar duties.

For he the night before in Tarquin's tent
Unlocked the treasure of his happy state;
What priceless wealth the heavens had him lent
In the possession of his beauteous mate;
Reckoning his fortune at such high-proud rate
That kings might be espousèd to more fame,
But king nor peer to such a peerless dame.

O happiness enjoyed but of a few,
And, if possessed, as soon decayed and done
As is the morning silver melting dew
Against the golden splendor of the sun!
An expired date cancelled ere well begun!
Honour and beauty in the owner's arms
Are weakly fortressed from a world of harms.

May 10 | Sir Thomas More | Scene 6

On 10 May 1849, a massive riot which left up to thirty people dead at New York's Astor Opera House started from a dispute over who was the greatest Shakespearean actor. The British William Macready and the American Edwin Forrest had amassed enormous followings over their careers, and the loyalties of their respective fans were enmeshed with the intensifying Anglo-American tensions before the American Civil War. British actors touring the country became the focus of hostility from the American working class, and the Astor riots were a boiling point of the stewing aggression. In a lesser known collaborative work, *Sir Thomas More* – preserved in the British Library and which is thought to be the only example of a manuscript featuring Shakespeare's handwriting – More speaks these lines to quell a rioting crowd swelling with anti-immigration sentiment.

SIR THOMAS MORE
Grant them removed, and grant that this your noise
Hath chid down all the majesty of England.
Imagine that you see the wretched strangers,
Their babies at their backs, with their poor luggage,
Plodding to th' ports and coasts for transportation,
And that you sit as kings in your desires,
Authority quite silenced by your brawl,
And you in ruff of your opinions clothed.
What had you got? I'll tell you: you had taught
How insolence and strong hand should prevail,
How order should be quelled. And by this pattern
Not one of you should live an agèd man;
For other ruffians, as their fancies wrought,
With selfsame hand, self reasons, and self right,
Would shark on you, and men, like ravenous fishes
Would feed on one another.

May 11 | Much Ado About Nothing | Act 1 Scene 1

The month of May, like April, is frequently used as a metaphor for youth and beauty, in contrast with old age and withered looks associated with December. When Claudio waxes lyrical over Hero, Benedick says her cousin Beatrice is much more beautiful, who is to Hero as May is to December – at least she would be, if she weren't so bad-tempered.

CLAUDIO
In mine eye she is the sweetest lady that ever I looked on.

BENEDICK
I can see yet without spectacles, and I see no such matter; there's her cousin, an she were not possessed with a fury, exceeds her as much in beauty as the first of May doth the last of December. But I hope you have no intent to turn husband, have you?

CLAUDIO
I would scarce trust myself, though I had sworn the contrary, if Hero would be my wife.

BENEDICK
Is't come to this? In faith, hath not the world one man but he will wear his cap with suspicion? Shall I never see a bachelor of threescore again? Go to, i'faith; an thou wilt needs thrust thy neck into a yoke, wear the print of it, and sigh away Sundays.

May 12 | Much Ado About Nothing | Act 5 Scene 1

Later on in *Much Ado About Nothing*, when everything seems
to have gone sour, Leonato berates the misinformed Claudio for
making false accusations about his daughter Hero's fidelity. As
a result she has apparently died of a broken heart. Don't worry,
this is just a ruse on Hero's part intended to extract remorse
from her accusers, and confessions from those who misled
them. Here it is Claudio who is associated with the youthfulness
of May when Leonato threatens to overcome the former's
advantage in age with the strength of his conviction.

LEONATO
Know, Claudio, to thy head,
Thou hast so wronged mine innocent child and me
That I am forced to lay my reverence by,
And with grey hairs and bruise of many days,
Do challenge thee to trial of a man.
I say thou hast belied mine innocent child.
Thy slander hath gone through and through her heart,
And she lies buried with her ancestors –
O, in a tomb where never scandal slept,
Save this of hers, framed by thy villainy!

CLAUDIO
My villainy?

LEONATO
Thine, Claudio; thine, I say.

DON PEDRO
You say not right, old man.

LEONATO
My lord, my lord,
I'll prove it on his body if he dare,
Despite his nice fence and his active practise,
His May of youth and bloom of lustihood.

CLAUDIO
Away! I will not have to do with you.

The association of May with the happy vivacity of love was so established for Shakespeare that it could function as a comical cliché. Dumaine, one of the lords attending the King of Navarre, becomes lovesick over Lady Catherine, despite his vow of abstinence. He recites a rhyme in honour of his love, oblivious to the fact that his friends are within earshot, mocking him with the audience from their hiding place.

DUMAINE
[*Reads*]
On a day – alack the day! –
Love, whose month is ever May,
Spied a blossom passing fair
Playing in the wanton air.
Through the velvet leaves the wind,
All unseen, can passage find;
That the lover, sick to death,
Wish himself the heaven's breath.
Air, quoth he, thy cheeks may blow;
Air, would I might triumph so!
But, alack, my hand is sworn
Ne'er to pluck thee from thy thorn.
Vow, alack, for youth unmeet,
Youth so apt to pluck a sweet!
Do not call it sin in me,
That I am forsworn for thee;
Thou for whom Jove would swear
Juno but an Ethiop were,
And deny himself for Jove,
Turning mortal for thy love.

May is a month for loving in Shakespeare's universe, providing
the perfect setting in *As You Like It* for Rosalind to tentatively
pursue her union with the exiled young nobleman, Orlando.
Disguised as a young man of lowly status, Rosalind speaks in
prose to obscure her noble birth rather than the verse form
more fitting to her station as the daughter of a duke. The
simplicity of her words does nothing to dull the tender irony of
her description of how her cousin Celia and Orlando's brother
Oliver met and fell in love.

ROSALIND
[. . .] no sooner met but they looked; no sooner
looked but they loved;
no sooner loved but they sighed, no sooner
sighed but they asked one another the reason; no
sooner knew the reason but they sought the remedy:
and in these degrees have they made a pair of stairs
to marriage which they will climb incontinent or
else be incontinent before marriage. They are in
the very wrath of love and they will together; clubs
cannot part them.

The astrologer Simon Forman records that he saw *The Winter's Tale* on 15 May 1611, the same year in which he died. After his death, Forman's name became tarnished with an involvement in an assassination plot, and he was subsequently depicted by writers such as Ben Jonson as either a foolish sort or an evil magician. *The Winter's Tale* has an ambiguous relationship to magic, considered by many at the time to be satanic. In the final scene, a statue of Hermione, the long dead wife of Leontes, King of Sicilia, steps off her plinth having been resurrected by her friend and defender Paulina: or rather, the statue turns out to be Hermione herself, who has not died but has remained in hiding for sixteen years. Even in the face of the miracle, the King acknowledges the potential profaneness of the event.

PAULINA
Music, awake her, strike!
[*Music*]
'Tis time: descend; be stone no more; approach;
Strike all that look upon with marvel. Come,
I'll fill your grave up. Stir, nay, come away.
Bequeath to death your numbness, for from him
Dear life redeems you. You perceive she stirs.

[HERMIONE *descends*]

Start not: her actions shall be holy as
You hear my spell is lawful. [*To Leontes*] Do not shun her
Until you see her die again, for then
You kill her double. Nay, present your hand.
When she was young you wooed her; now, in age,
Is she become the suitor?

LEONTES
O, she's warm!
If this be magic, let it be an art
Lawful as eating.

Here is part of Ophelia's harrowing mad scene. Her
flabbergasted brother laments the premature mental decline
of his sister, apparently driven insane by Hamlet's fickleness –
though this is open to debate. Ophelia, a 'rose of May',
distributes flowers and herbs to her dumbstruck onlookers.

LAERTES
How now! What noise is that?
[*Enter* OPHELIA]

O heat, dry up my brains! Tears seven times salt
Burn out the sense and virtue of mine eye!
By heaven, thy madness shall be paid with weight,
Till our scale turn the beam. O rose of May,
Dear maid, kind sister, sweet Ophelia!
O heavens, is't possible a young maid's wits
Should be as mortal as an old man's life?
Nature is fine in love, and where 'tis fine,
It sends some precious instance of itself
After the thing it loves.

OPHELIA
[*Sings*]
They bore him barefaced on the bier,
Hey non nony, nony, hey nony,
And in his grave rained many a tear –
Fare you well, my dove!

LAERTES
Hadst thou thy wits, and didst persuade revenge,
It could not move thus.

OPHELIA
[*Sings*]
You must sing 'A-down a-down,
and you call him a-down-a.'
O, how the wheel becomes it! It is the false
steward, that stole his master's daughter.

LAERTES
This nothing's more than matter.

OPHELIA
There's rosemary, that's for remembrance. Pray you,
love, remember. And there is pansies, that's for thoughts.

LAERTES
A document in madness: thoughts and remembrance
fitted.

OPHELIA
There's fennel for you, and columbines. There's rue
for you; and here's some for me. We may call it
herb of grace o'Sundays. O, you must wear your rue with
a difference. There's a daisy. I would give you
some violets, but they withered all when my father
died. They say 'a made a good end.
[*Sings*]
For bonny sweet Robin is all my joy.

May 17 | Macbeth | Act 1 Scene 3

On 17 May 1603, a month after becoming king, James I commanded that Shakespeare's theatre company, the Chamberlain's Men be renamed the King's Men and fall under his own patronage. As part of this name change, the company had to agree to be available for James' 'solace and pleasure when we shall thinke good to see them'. It is likely that Shakespeare adapted his writing to appeal to James, who claimed ancestry from Banquo, a fellow nobleman of the medieval king Macbeth. Despite being Macbeth's co-conspirator in the historical source material, Holinshed's *Chronicles,* Shakespeare's Banquo is a noble and likeable character who isn't taken in by the witches' prophecies, nor driven by greed or ambition.

MACBETH
Do you not hope your children shall be kings,
When those that gave the Thane of Cawdor to me
Promised no less to them?

BANQUO
That trusted home
Might yet enkindle you unto the crown
Besides the Thane of Cawdor. But 'tis strange;
And oftentimes, to win us to our harm,
The instruments of darkness tell us truths;
Win us with honest trifles, to betray's
In deepest consequence.
Cousins, a word, I pray you.

MACBETH
[*Aside*] Two truths are told,
As happy prologues to the swelling act

Of the imperial theme. – I thank you, gentlemen.
[*Aside*] This supernatural soliciting
Cannot be ill, cannot be good. If ill,
Why hath it given me earnest of success,
Commencing in a truth? I am Thane of Cawdor.
If good, why do I yield to that suggestion
Whose horrid image doth unfix my hair,
And make my seated heart knock at my ribs
Against the use of nature? Present fears
Are less than horrible imaginings.
My thought, whose murder yet is but fantastical,
Shakes so my single state of man
That function is smothered in surmise,
and nothing is but what is not.

BANQUO
Look, how our partner's rapt.

MACBETH
[*Aside*] If chance will have me king, why, chance may
    crown me,
Without my stir.

BANQUO
New horrors come upon him
Like our strange garments, cleave not to their mould
But with the aid of use.

MACBETH
[*Aside*] Come what come may,
Time and the hour runs through the roughest day.

When Troilus first becomes smitten with Cressida, he entreats her uncle, Pandarus, to put in a good word for him. Trying to present Troilus as a witty sort of chap, Pandarus relays to Cressida a funny comment that Troilus was supposed to have made in banter with his brother Paris, in front of Paris's wife, Helen. One gets the sense that this is a you-had-to-be-there joke.

CRESSIDA
At what was all this laughing?

PANDARUS
Marry, at the white hair that Helen spied on Troilus' chin.

CRESSIDA
An't had been a green hair I should have laughed too.

PANDARUS
They laughed not so much at the hair as at his pretty answer.

CRESSIDA
What was his answer?

PANDARUS
Quoth she: 'Here's but two and fifty hairs on your chin, and one of them is white.'

CRESSIDA
This is her question.

PANDARUS
That's true; make no question of that. 'Two and
fifty hairs,' quoth he, 'and one white: that white
hair is my father, and all the rest are his sons.'
'Jupiter,' quoth she, 'which of these hairs is Paris,
my husband?' 'The forked one,' quoth he; 'pluck't
out, and give it him.' But there was such laughing,
and Helen so blushed, and Paris so chafed, and all the
rest so laughed, that it passed.

CRESSIDA
So let it now; for it has been while going by.

PANDARUS
Well, cousin, I told you a thing yesterday; think on't.

CRESSIDA
So I do.

PANDARUS
I'll be sworn 'tis true; he will weep you an 'twere
a man born in April.

CRESSIDA
And I'll spring up in his tears, an 'twere a nettle
against May.

When William Camden wrote that 'a wondrous excess of Apparel had spread itself all over England' in the late sixteenth century, he was referring to the diminished influence of the Sumptuary Laws which affected people's clothing. These laws, which set out which cloth and colours were appropriate for each social class to wear, were not strictly enforced; nevertheless, there would have been an acute awareness of someone's apparel transgressing the social order. In *Twelfth Night,* for example, Malvolio's excruciating cross-gartering was associated with nobility (albeit an unfashionable kind), which follows his assumption that Countess Olivia regards him as an equal. When Shakespeare's acting troupe became the King's Men, as a mark of their promoted status the king gave them permission to wear the red cloth that was usually reserved for members of the royal household. In this context, clothes could communicate as well as obscure, and the multiple disguises employed in *The Taming of the Shrew* lead to scenes of delightful confusion. Here, Tranio is dressed as his master, Lucentio, to distract Baptista, so Lucentio can woo Baptista's daughter behind his back. Disastrously, Lucentio's father Vincentio sees through Tranio's disguise, and the hapless pedant whom Tranio had enlisted in his plot, makes matters worse by declaring himself to be the real Vincentio.

TRANIO
Sir, what are you that offer to beat my servant?

VINCENTIO
What am I, sir? Nay, what are you, sir? O immortal gods! O fine villain! A silken doublet! a velvet hose, a scarlet cloak, and a copatain hat! O, I am undone, I am undone! While I play the good

husband at home, my son and my servant spend all at the university.

TRANIO
How now, what's the matter?

BAPTISTA
What, is the man lunatic?

TRANIO
Sir, you seem a sober ancient gentleman by your habit, but your words show you a madman. Why, sir, what 'cerns it you if I wear pearl and gold? I thank my good father, I am able to maintain it.

VINCENTIO
Thy father? O villain, he is a sailmaker in Bergamo.

BAPTISTA
You mistake, sir, you mistake, sir. Pray, what do you think is his name?

VINCENTIO
His name? As if I knew not his name! I have brought him up ever since he was three years old, and his name is Tranio.

PEDANT
Away, away, mad ass! His name is Lucentio, and he is mine only son, and heir to the lands of me, Signor Vincentio.

May 20 | King John | Act 2 Scene 1

The Treaty of Le Goulet, one among many ill-fated treaties between England and France, was signed in May 1200 by King John and Philip II only to be broken two years later. Four hundred years on, relations between England and continental Europe were still politically sensitive – if you can imagine such a thing – so Shakespeare did not dare refer to them but through the prism of history. Here are the kings, forging a deal.

KING JOHN
Peace be to France – if France in peace permit
Our just and lineal entrance to our own.
If not, bleed France, and peace ascend to heaven,
Whiles we, God's wrathful agent, do correct
Their proud contempt that beats His peace to heaven.

KING PHILIP
Peace be to England – if that war return
From France to England, there to live in peace.
England we love, and for that England's sake
With burden of our armour here we sweat.
This toil of ours should be a work of thine;

May 21 | King John | Act 4 Scene 2

Ascension Day falls forty days after Easter, and it is the day on which a prophet warns King John that he should give up his crown. Prophecies are not usually good news in Shakespeare, and the Bastard relates the 'harsh sounding rhymes' to the King: indeed, the lines ending 'noon' and 'crown' do make for a jarring half-rhyme.

KING JOHN
Bear with me, cousin, for I was amazed
Under the tide; but now I breathe again
Aloft the flood, and can give audience
To any tongue, speak it of what it will.

BASTARD
How I have sped among the clergymen
The sums I have collected shall express.
But as I travelled hither through the land,
I find the people strangely fantasied,
Possessed with rumours, full of idle dreams,
Not knowing what they fear, but full of fear.
And here's a prophet that I brought with me
From forth the streets of Pomfret, whom I found
With many hundreds treading on his heels;
To whom he sung, in rude harsh-sounding rhymes,
That, ere the next Ascension Day at noon,
Your highness should deliver up your crown.

May 22 | Henry VI, Part 2 | Act 5 Scene 3

The first Battle of St Albans was also the first of the Wars of the Roses, which would eventually see the House of York triumph over Queen Elizabeth's ancestors from the House of Lancaster. Shakespeare depicts mounting tensions through the first two parts of *Henry VI* and features this culminating battle at the end of the second play.

YORK
Of Salisbury, who can report of him,
That winter lion, who in rage forgets
Agèd contusions and all brush of time;
And, like a gallant in the brow of youth,
Repairs him with occasion? This happy day
Is not itself, nor have we won one foot,
If Salisbury be lost.

RICHARD
My noble father,
Three times today I holp him to his horse,
Three times bestrid him; thrice I led him off,
Persuaded him from any further act;
But still where danger was, still there I met him,
And like rich hangings in a homely house,
So was his will in his old feeble body.
But, noble as he is, look where he comes.
[*Enter* SALISBURY]

SALISBURY
Now, by my sword, well hast thou fought today;
By th'mass, so did we all. I thank you, Richard:
God knows how long it is I have to live,
And it hath pleased Him that three times today

You have defended me from imminent death.
Well, lords, we have not got that which we have;
'Tis not enough our foes are this time fled,
Being opposites of such repairing nature.

YORK
I know our safety is to follow them;
For, as I hear, the King is fled to London,
To call a present court of parliament.
Let us pursue him ere the writs go forth.
What says Lord Warwick? Shall we after them?

WARWICK
After them! Nay, before them, if we can.
Now by my hand, lords, 'twas a glorious day.
Saint Albans battle, won by famous York,
Shall be eternized in all age to come.
Sound drums and trumpets, and to London all,
And more such days as these to us befall!

May 23 | Henry VIII | Act 2 Scene 4

Katherine of Aragon, Henry VIII's first wife, is a significant figure in European history, and a captivating character in Shakespeare and Fletcher's play about the notorious Tudor monarch. Henry declared his union with Katherine invalid on 23 May 1533 after twenty years of marriage. She reacts with considerable dismay in Shakespeare's version. It was a bold move to draw the Catholic Katherine as a virtuous and sympathetic character considering Henry VIII was the father of Elizabeth I and the first head of the Church of England, but the play is known to have been written and performed after the accession of James I.

QUEEN KATHERINE
Sir, I desire you do me right and justice,
And to bestow your pity on me; for
I am a most poor woman, and a stranger,
Born out of your dominions, having here
No judge indifferent, nor no more assurance
Of equal friendship and proceeding. Alas, sir,
In what have I offended you? What cause
Hath my behavior given to your displeasure
That thus you should proceed to put me off
And take your good grace from me? Heaven witness,
I have been to you a true and humble wife,
At all times to your will conformable,
Ever in fear to kindle your dislike,
Yea, subject to your countenance, glad or sorry
As I saw it inclined. When was the hour
I ever contradicted your desire,
Or made it not mine too? Or which of your friends
Have I not strove to love, although I knew
He were mine enemy? What friend of mine

That had to him derived your anger did I
Continue in my liking, nay, gave notice
He was from thence discharged? Sir, call to mind
That I have been your wife in this obedience
Upward of twenty years, and have been blessed
With many children by you. If, in the course
And process of this time, you can report,
And prove it too, against mine honour aught,
My bond to wedlock, or my love and duty
Against your sacred person, in God's name
Turn me away, and let the foul'st contempt
Shut door upon me, and so give me up
To the sharp'st kind of justice. Please you, sir,
The King your father was reputed for
A prince most prudent, of an excellent
And unmatched wit and judgment. Ferdinand,
My father, King of Spain, was reckoned one
The wisest prince that there had reigned, by many
A year before. It is not to be questioned
That they had gathered a wise council to them
Of every realm, that did debate this business,
Who deemed our marriage lawful. Wherefore I humbly
Beseech you, sir, to spare me, till I may
Be by my friends in Spain advised, whose counsel
I will implore. If not, i'th'name of God,
Your pleasure be fulfilled.

218

In May 1596, the Dutch explorer Willem Barentz set out on his third attempt to navigate the North-East Passage across the Arctic Circle. After having failed a third time, the renowned Dutchman died on the return journey along with many of his crew. In a rare topical allusion, Fabian warns the drunkard Sir Andrew that 'you are now sailed into the north of my lady's opinion, where you will hang like an icicle on a Dutchman's beard.' Elsewhere, Maria apparently refers to a more positive legacy of Barentz's voyages when talking about the creases on Malvolio's bewildered face: a new map, drawn by Edward Wright in 1600.

MARIA
If you desire the spleen, and will laugh yourself
into stitches, follow me. Yond gull Malvolio is
turned heathen, a very renegado; for there is no
Christian, that means to be saved by believing
rightly, can ever believe such impossible passages
of grossness. He's in yellow stockings!

SIR TOBY BELCH
And cross-gartered?

MARIA
Most villanously; like a pedant that keeps a school
i'the church. I have dogged him like his
murderer. He does obey every point of the letter
that I dropped to betray him. He does smile his
face into more lines than is in the new map with the
augmentation of the Indies. You have not seen such
a thing as 'tis.

Harry Hotspur's challenge for the English throne was heavily defeated when Henry IV was able to rally the prince and the allies of the crown against the rebellion. Shakespeare depicts fearsome armies with no small measure of beauty. Here, Vernon is warning the impetuous rebel leader of the King and the Prince's approach, and the spectacle presented is masterfully sumptuous.

HOTSPUR
He shall be welcome too. Where is his son,
The nimble-footed madcap Prince of Wales,
And his comrades that daffed the world aside
And bid it pass?

VERNON
All furnished, all in arms,
All plumed like estridges that with the wind
Bated, like eagles having lately bathed,
Glittering in golden coats like images,
As full of spirit as the month of May,
And gorgeous as the sun at midsummer,
Wanton as youthful goats, wild as young bulls.

May 26 | The Tempest | Act 1 Scene 2

Shakespeare's first child, Susanna, was baptized on 26 May 1583 in the local church at Stratford-upon-Avon. Shakespeare writes many father and daughter relationships into his plays and the dynamic between them ranges from the coolest contempt to the warmest affection. In this late play, Prospero tenderly reassures his daughter that she was a help to him when he was banished, set adrift in an open boat and forced to endure the rough seas with her as a toddler.

MIRANDA
Alack, what trouble
Was I then to you!

PROSPERO
O, a cherubin
Thou wast that did preserve me. Thou didst smile,
Infusèd with a fortitude from heaven,
When I have decked the sea with drops full salt,
Under my burthen groaned, which raised in me
An undergoing stomach to bear up
Against what should ensue.

May 27 | King John | Act 3 Scene 1

King John's controversial coronation fell on 27 May 1199 against a backdrop of civil strife in England, and trouble in his territories in France. John would eventually come to rue the complacency with which he regarded the authority and loyalty commanded by kingship. Pope Innocent III shared John's sense of an inalienable right to govern all his subjects, and John's refusal to recognize the Pope as his feudal overlord led to the former's swift excommunication. (The complete schism with Rome came eventually under Henry VIII.)

KING JOHN
What earthy name to interrogatories
Can task the free breath of a sacred king?
Thou canst not, Cardinal, devise a name
So slight, unworthy, and ridiculous,
To charge me to an answer, as the Pope.
Tell him this tale, and from the mouth of England
Add thus much more: that no Italian priest
Shall tithe or toll in our dominions;
But as we, under heaven, are supreme head,
So, under Him, that great supremacy
Where we do reign, we will alone uphold,
Without th'assistance of a mortal hand.
So tell the Pope, all reverence set apart
To him and his usurped authority.

In stark contrast to King John's arrogant view of his nobility,
the far more successful Henry V pragmatically emphasizes
his common manhood over and above his royalty. While
disguised as one of his own soldiers, the King dons simple
prose as he tries to settle the pre-battle qualms of his brothers
in arms.

KING HENRY V
For though I speak it to you, I think the King is but a man,
as I am: the violet smells to him as it doth to me; the
element shows to him as it doth to me; all his
senses have but human conditions. His ceremonies
laid by, in his nakedness he appears but a man; and
though his affections are higher mounted than ours,
yet, when they stoop, they stoop with the like
wing. Therefore, when he sees reason of fears, as we
do, his fears, out of doubt, be of the same relish
as ours are: yet, in reason, no man should possess
him with any appearance of fear, lest he, by showing
it, should dishearten his army.

BATES
He may show what outward courage he will, but I
believe, as cold a night as 'tis, he could wish
himself in Thames up to the neck; and so I would he
were, and I by him, at all adventures, so we were quit here.

KING HENRY V
By my troth, I will speak my conscience of the King:
I think he would not wish himself anywhere but
where he is.

BATES
Then I would he were here alone; so should he be
sure to be ransomed, and a many poor men's lives saved.

KING HENRY V
I dare say you love him not so ill to wish him here
alone, howsoever you speak this to feel other men's
minds. Methinks I could not die anywhere so
contented as in the King's company, his cause being
just and his quarrel honourable.

May 29 | A Lover's Complaint

A Lover's Complaint is a narrative poem written largely from the female point of view, whose content is not wildly different from that of some modern pop music; a woman tells of how she was courted, seduced and abandoned by her lover, and how she would fall for him again in a heartbeat. The complaint poem form was as familiar then just as its perennial theme is now: the pain of unrequited love. The rhyme scheme, identical to that of *The Rape of Lucrece*, is called 'Rhyme royal' and was pioneered by Chaucer. Each stanza has seven lines and the metric pattern is iambic pentameter, a metre which pulses throughout Shakespeare's verse. You could say iambic pentameter is like the rhythm of a human heartbeat – de dum de dum de dum de dum de dum.

His qualities were beauteous as his form,
For maiden-tongu'd he was, and thereof free;
Yet, if men mov'd him, was he such a storm
As oft 'twixt May and April is to see,
When winds breathe sweet, unruly though they be.
His rudeness so with his authoriz'd youth
Did livery falseness in a pride of truth.

May 30 | Sonnet 86

One of the more far-fetched conspiracy theories regarding Shakespeare's relationship to Christopher Marlowe, his great predecessor and friend, is that Marlowe faked his death to avoid spy charges, escaped to France, and continued to write plays under the name of William Shakespeare. This story, however appealing, has been widely debunked; Marlowe, the writer of celebrated works including the plays *Dr Faustus, The Jew of Malta* and *Edward II* and the poem, 'The Passionate Shepherd to his Love', is known to have been killed in a house in Deptford on 30 May 1593, an event hinted at by Shakespeare in *As You Like It*. According to some, Shakespeare's Sonnet 86 alludes to Marlowe, in homage to his death and ghost.

Was it the proud full sail of his great verse,
Bound for the prize of (all too precious) you,
That did my ripe thoughts in my brain inhearse,
Making their tomb the womb wherein they grew?
Was it his spirit, by spirits taught to write,
Above a mortal pitch, that struck me dead?
No, neither he, nor his compeers by night
Giving him aid, my verse astonished.
He, nor that affable familiar ghost
Which nightly gulls him with intelligence,
As victors of my silence cannot boast,
I was not sick of any fear from thence.
   But when your countenance fill'd up his line,
   Then lack'd I matter; that enfeebled mine.

With summer fast approaching, *All's Well That Ends Well*
moves towards its final scenes. Helena is about to win Count
Bertram, the man she has followed across Europe, a man
unwillingly allocated to her as bridegroom as her reward
for curing the King's illness, whom she has tricked into
impregnating her after faking her own death and arranging to
be exchanged in the dark with the Italian girl Bertram really
fancied. It's a puzzling play with an unusual plot, not least
because it is the woman, and not the man, who is inspired to
perform great gestures by love.

HELENA
Yet, I pray you.
But with the word the time will bring on summer,
When briers shall have leaves as well as thorns
And be as sweet as sharp. We must away;
Our wagon is prepared, and time revives us.
All's well that ends well; still the fine's the crown.
Whate'er the course, the end is the renown.

June

Whitsun day – or 'Wheeson', as the publican Mistress Quickly calls it in *Henry IV, Part 2* – falls on the seventh Sunday after Easter and is still marked in parts of England with games and sports, especially morris dancing. In contrast to the abstinence of Lent, Whitsun celebrations were characterized by excess; drunken carousing in the churchyard was commonplace in Elizabethan revels on this day. Whitsun is now more commonly recognized as Pentecost.

DAUPHIN
My most redoubted father,
It is most meet we arm us 'gainst the foe;
For peace itself should not so dull a kingdom,
Though war nor no known quarrel were in question,
But that defences, musters, preparations,
Should be maintain'd, assembled and collected,
As were a war in expectation.
Therefore, I say, 'tis meet we all go forth
To view the sick and feeble parts of France:
And let us do it with no show of fear –
No, with no more than if we heard that England
Were busied with a Whitsun morris-dance;
For, my good liege, she is so idly kinged,
Her sceptre so fantastically borne
By a vain, giddy, shallow, humorous youth,
That fear attends her not.

Shortly after becoming king, James I granted a royal charter
to the Virginia Company of London to begin sending ships
and settlers to North America. In recognition of this charter,
the first English settlement was called Jamestown, and the
river it sat on became known, logically enough, as the James.
On 2 June 1609, three years after James I started sending the
settlers, the ship *Sea Venture* ran aground during a storm
in Bermuda. After spending the winter there, its crew were
able to build two ships from the wreckage and make it home
safely, and the incident caused enough of a stir in England that
Shakespeare's *The Tempest* would have made a timely debut on
the Jacobean stage. Shakespeare's play takes some details from
an account of the incident, which he had apparently seen in
manuscript before its publication, possibly thanks to his patron
Southampton's involvement in the Virginia Company. Ariel
describes the tempest he had conjured to attack the King's ship
at Prospero's behest.

ARIEL
I boarded the King's ship; now on the beak,
Now in the waist, the deck, in every cabin,
I flamed amazement. Sometime I'd divide
And burn in many places; on the topmast,
The yards and bowsprit, would I flame distinctly,
Then meet and join. Jove's lightning, the precursors
O'th'dreadful thunderclaps, more momentary
And sight out-running were not. The fire and cracks
Of sulphurous roaring the most mighty Neptune
Seem to besiege, and make his bold waves tremble,
Yea, his dread trident shake.

June 3 | The Tempest | Act 1 Scene 2

North America was not uninhabited when Europeans first started to disembark on its shores, which makes the term 'settler' a little misleading. Although some European leaders occasionally sought alliances with indigenous chiefs, the advance through the continent mostly saw the local population exploited or decimated. However, relations could be complex: Pocahontas was initially taken hostage by the English as leverage over her father, a powerful Native American chief. When given the opportunity to return to her people, she chose to remain with the English and married an Englishman, John Rolfe. Her arrival in England in 1616 attracted great public interest: she and her husband were James I's guests of honour at Ben Jonson's masque *The Vision of Delight* at Twelfth Night, 1617. Aged only twenty-one, she died of an illness before the ship taking her and her family back to Virginia had passed the mouth of the Thames. Although Pocahontas' visit to England took place just after Shakespeare's death, his late play *The Tempest* resonates with the casualties of colonialism. Meeting Caliban, the child of the now-dead Sycorax (an Algerian witch banished to the island before the arrival of any Europeans), the shipwrecked clown Trinculo immediately plans to take him to England and exploit him as a fairground attraction, since when the English 'will not give a doit to relieve a lame beggar, they will lay out ten to see a dead Indian.' Caliban himself has been enslaved by Prospero, the exiled Duke of Milan, who during his twelve years on the island has taken on the role of a powerful 'settler'. Shakespeare allows Caliban to protest eloquently against his treatment.

CALIBAN
This island's mine, by Sycorax my mother,
Which thou tak'st from me. When thou cam'st first

Thou strok'st me, and made much of me; wouldst give me
Water with berries in't, and teach me how
To name the bigger light, and how the less,
That burn by day and night. And then I loved thee,
And showed thee all the qualities o'th'isle,
The fresh springs, brine-pits, barren place and fertile –
Cursed be I that did so! All the charms
Of Sycorax – toads, beetles, bats – light on you!
For I am all the subjects that you have,
Which first was mine own king; and here you sty me
In this hard rock, whiles you do keep from me
The rest o'th'island.

June 4 | Twelfth Night | Act 1 Scene 2

Viola and her twin brother Sebastian are shipwrecked and are washed up, separately, on the shores of Illyria (present-day Croatia, where this play is especially popular), and their status as strangers gives rise to the mistaken identities which drive the plot forwards.

VIOLA
What country, friends, is this?

CAPTAIN
This is Illyria, lady.

VIOLA
And what should I do in Illyria?
My brother, he is in Elysium.
Perchance he is not drowned. What think you, sailors?

CAPTAIN
It is perchance that you yourself were saved.

VIOLA
O, my poor brother! and so perchance may he be.

CAPTAIN
True, madam, and to comfort you with chance,
Assure yourself, after our ship did split,
When you and those poor number saved with you
Hung on our driving boat, I saw your brother,
Most provident in peril, bind himself –
Courage and hope both teaching him the practice –
To a strong mast that lived upon the sea;
Where, like Arion on the dolphin's back,

I saw him hold acquaintance with the waves
So long as I could see.

VIOLA
For saying so, there's gold.
Mine own escape unfoldeth to my hope,
Whereto thy speech serves for authority,
The like of him.

June 5 | Sonnet 27

To the credit of how far her father had risen, on 5 June 1607, Susanna Shakespeare married John Hall, a respected Cambridge-educated physician. They had one child who survived infancy, Elizabeth. When Elizabeth Hall died childless, Shakespeare's direct bloodline ended; however, his son-in-law's profession is immortalized in many of his plays. Unlike his colleague Ben Jonson, Shakespeare never represents doctors as cynical quacks. Medicine is often central to a plot: Helena offers to remedy the king's fistula to get closer to marrying Bertram in *All's Well That Ends Well*, and Romeo and Juliet naively usher in their tragic fate first with the help of Friar Lawrence's sleeping drug, then with the apothecary's poison. Elsewhere, infection is often a metaphor, quite alarmingly in those plague-ridden days, for love-related maladies. The resonant Sonnet 27 treads the line between sickness of the mind and of the body.

Weary with toil, I haste me to my bed,
The dear repose for limbs with travel tired,
But then begins a journey in my head
To work my mind, when body's work's expired.
For then my thoughts (from far where I abide)
Intend a zealous pilgrimage to thee,
And keep my drooping eyelids open wide,
Looking on darkness which the blind do see.
Save that my soul's imaginary sight
Presents thy shadow to my sightless view,
Which like a jewel (hung in ghastly night)
Makes black night beauteous, and her old face new.
　Lo thus by day my limbs, by night my mind,
　For thee, and for myself, no quiet find.

June 6 | Richard III | Act 4 Scene 1

Although the fact is contested in some history books, Shakespeare's play unambiguously shows Richard ordering the killing of the young princes in the Tower of London, despite serving as their Lord Protector. In June 1493, a month after their murder, he was crowned King Richard III. The boys' mother, Queen Elizabeth, has been forbidden to visit her sons on Richard's orders; she appeals to the walls of the tower to protect her sons.

QUEEN ELIZABETH
Stay, yet look back with me unto the Tower.
Pity, you ancient stones, those tender babes
Whom envy hath immured within your walls –
Rough cradle for such little pretty ones!
Rude ragged nurse, old sullen playfellow
For tender princes – use my babies well!
So foolish sorrow bids your stones farewell.

June 7 | The Two Gentlemen of Verona |
Act 4 Scene 4

Elizabethan revels around Trinity Sunday and Pentecost
involved dressing up, parades and pageants. Festivities could
become debauched and one bacchanal involved disrupting
pairs of lovers – this was the end of the period of Lent when
marriage was banned. Here, a boy describes to Silvia how he
was mistaken for Julia during a Pentecost game. Little does
Silvia know, but 'the boy' is actually Julia herself in disguise,
desperate as her beloved Proteus has fallen for Silvia.

SILVIA
How tall was she?

JULIA
About my stature; for, at Pentecost,
When all our pageants of delight were played,
Our youth got me to play the woman's part,
And I was trimmed in Madam Julia's gown,
Which servèd me as fit, by all men's judgments,
As if the garment had been made for me;
Therefore I know she is about my height.
And at that time I made her weep agood,
For I did play a lamentable part.
Madam, 'twas Ariadne passioning
For Theseus' perjury and unjust flight;
Which I so lively acted with my tears
That my poor mistress, movèd therewithal,
Wept bitterly; and would I might be dead
If I in thought felt not her very sorrow.

Henry IV scolds Prince Hal for the depraved company he keeps, a window in to a royal version of a concerned father berating his rambunctious son. During this supreme telling-off, Henry refers to his predecessor Richard II whom he usurped for being an inadequate king who surrounded himself with preening jesters. He threatens Hal with a similar fate.

KING HENRY IV
God pardon thee! Yet let me wonder, Harry,
At thy affections, which do hold a wing
Quite from the flight of all thy ancestors.
Thy place in Council thou hast rudely lost,
Which by thy younger brother is supplied,
And art almost an alien to the hearts
Of all the court and princes of my blood.
The hope and expectation of thy time
Is ruined, and the soul of every man
Prophetically doth forethink thy fall.
Had I so lavish of my presence been,
So common-hackneyed in the eyes of men,
So stale and cheap to vulgar company,
Opinion, that did help me to the crown,
Had still kept loyal to possession,
And left me in reputeless banishment,
A fellow of no mark nor likelihood.
By being seldom seen, I could not stir
But like a comet I was wondered at,
That men would tell their children, 'This is he!'
Others would say 'Where, which is Bolingbroke?'
And then I stole all courtesy from heaven,
And dressed myself in such humility
That I did pluck allegiance from men's hearts,

Loud shouts and salutations from their mouths,
Even in the presence of the crownèd King.
Thus did I keep my person fresh and new,
My presence, like a robe pontifical,
Ne'er seen but wondered at, and so my state,
Seldom, but sumptuous, showed like a feast,
And won by rareness such solemnity.
The skipping King, he ambled up and down,
With shallow jesters and rash bavin wits,
Soon kindled and soon burnt, carded his state,
Mingled his royalty with capering fools,
Had his great name profanèd with their scorns,
And gave his countenance against his name
To laugh at gibing boys, and stand the push
Of every beardless vain comparative,
Grew a companion to the common streets,
Enfeoffed himself to popularity,
That, being daily swallowed by men's eyes,
They surfeited with honey, and began
To loathe the taste of sweetness, whereof a little
More than a little is by much too much.
So, when he had occasion to be seen,
He was but as the cuckoo is in June,
Heard, not regarded; seen, but with such eyes
As, sick and blunted with community,
Afford no extraordinary gaze,
Such as is bent on sun-like majesty
When it shines seldom in admiring eyes,

June 9 | Timon of Athens | Act 4 Scene 3

Words from Shakespeare's works have been adopted as titles by writers, moviemakers and musicians. H. E. Bates's *The Darling Buds of May*, Aldous Huxley's *Brave New World*, Noel Coward's *Present Laughter*, Alistair MacLean's *Where Eagles Dare* and Pink Floyd's *The Dogs of War* are just some who owe their titles to Shakespeare. Vladimir Nabokov's *Pale Fire* is one of the great works of fiction from the twentieth century, famed for its originality and depth. The first half of the book consists of the eponymous poem written by a fictional poet, who takes the title from *Timon of Athens* – an ironic move, since the quotation concerns the poaching of others' greatness.

TIMON
The sun's a thief, and with his great attraction
Robs the vast sea. The moon's an arrant thief,
And her pale fire she snatches from the sun.
The sea's a thief, whose liquid surge resolves
The moon into salt tears. The earth's a thief,
That feeds and breeds by a composture stolen
From general excrement. Each thing's a thief.
The laws, your curb and whip, in their rough power
Has unchecked theft.

June 10 | A Midsummer Night's Dream |
Act 2 Scene 2

A Midsummer Night's Dream occupies an enchanted setting,
thrumming with fairies who serve Oberon and Titania, the fairy
king and queen. Their lullaby appeals to all of the nocturnal
creatures not to stir the sleeping Titania.

FIRST FAIRY
You spotted snakes with double tongue,
Thorny hedgehogs, be not seen.
Newts and blindworms, do no wrong,
Come not near our Fairy Queen.

CHORUS
Philomel with melody
Sing in our sweet lullaby,
Lulla, lulla, lullaby; lulla, lulla, lullaby.
Never harm
Nor spell nor charm
Come our lovely lady nigh.
So good night, with lullaby.

FIRST FAIRY
Weaving spiders, come not here;
Hence, you longlegged spinners, hence!
Beetles black, approach not near,
Worm nor snail, do no offence.

CHORUS
Philomel with melody
Sing in our sweet lullaby,
Lulla, lulla, lullaby; lulla, lulla, lullaby.
Never harm

Nor spell nor charm
Come our lovely lady nigh.
So good night, with lullaby.

SECOND FAIRY
Hence, away! Now all is well:
One aloof stand sentinel.

June 11 | Sonnet 65

The speaker of Sonnet 65 is afflicted with the concern that all things are subject to decay, which is the law of nature – even his love and his lover's beauty. He hopes that putting his subject into poetry will secure it against decay, and we can happily say that his wish has been granted.

Since brass, nor stone, nor earth, nor boundless sea,
But sad mortality o'ersways their power,
How with this rage shall beauty hold a plea,
Whose action is no stronger than a flower?
O how shall summer's honey breath hold out,
Against the wrackful siege of batt'ring days,
When rocks impregnable are not so stout,
Nor gates of steel so strong but Time decays?
O fearful meditation, where alack,
Shall Time's best jewel from Time's chest lie hid?
Or what strong hand can hold his swift foot back?
Or who his spoil of beauty can forbid?
  O none, unless this miracle have might,
  That in black ink my love may still shine bright.

June 12 | Henry V | Prologue

A conjectural replica of the Globe Theatre opened in London
on 12 June 1997 with a production of *Henry V*; the first play to
have been performed at the original Globe exactly 398 years
earlier – according to one tradition, though impossible to prove.
As a co-owner, the Globe Theatre's success made Shakespeare
a wealthy man. The monarch of the second Elizabethan era,
Elizabeth II, arrived at the opening night to 'behold the swelling
scene', from a barge that sailed her down the River Thames to
Southwark.

CHORUS
O for a Muse of fire, that would ascend
The brightest heaven of invention,
A kingdom for a stage, princes to act,
And monarchs to behold the swelling scene!
Then should the warlike Harry, like himself,
Assume the port of Mars, and at his heels,
Leashed in like hounds, should famine, sword, and fire
Crouch for employment. But pardon, gentles all,
The flat unraisèd spirits that hath dared
On this unworthy scaffold to bring forth
So great an object. Can this cockpit hold
The vasty fields of France? Or may we cram
Within this wooden O the very casques
That did affright the air at Agincourt?
O, pardon! since a crooked figure may
Attest in little place a million;
And let us, ciphers to this great accompt,
On your imaginary forces work.
Suppose within the girdle of these walls
Are now confined two mighty monarchies,
Whose high upreared and abutting fronts

The perilous narrow ocean parts asunder:
Piece out our imperfections with your thoughts;
Into a thousand parts divide on man,
And make imaginary puissance;
Think when we talk of horses, that you see them
Printing their proud hoofs i' the receiving earth;
For 'tis your thoughts that now must deck our kings,
Carry them here and there; jumping o'er times,
Turning the accomplishment of many years
Into an hour-glass: for the which supply,
Admit me Chorus to this history;
Who prologue-like your humble patience pray,
Gently to hear, kindly to judge, our play.

This iconic depiction of Cleopatra's barge on the Nile is far more decadent than a barge down London's River Thames. Here, Antony's friend Enobarbus describes the attractions of Egypt to Caesar's officers: his vision of Cleopatra paints her as a goddess. It captures the dichotomy which lies at the heart of *Antony and Cleopatra*, between Shakespeare's feminine and exotic portrayal of Egypt, and the self-restrained, masculine virtue of Rome.

ENOBARBUS
The barge she sat in, like a burnished throne,
Burned on the water. The poop was beaten gold;
Purple the sails, and so perfumèd that
The winds were lovesick with them. The oars were silver,
Which to the tune of flutes kept stroke and made
The water which they beat to follow faster,
As amorous of their strokes. For her own person,
It beggared all description. She did lie
In her pavilion, cloth-of-gold of tissue,
O'erpicturing that Venus where we see
The fancy outwork nature. On each side her
Stood pretty dimpled boys, like smiling cupids,
With divers-coloured fans, whose wind did seem
To glow the delicate cheeks which they did cool,
And what they undid did.
[. . .]
Her gentlewomen, like the Nereides,
So many mermaids, tended her i'th'eyes,
And made their bends adornings. At the helm
A seeming mermaid steers. The silken tackle
Swell with the touches of those flower-soft hands,
That yarely frame the office. From the barge

A strange invisible perfume hits the sense
Of the adjacent wharfs. The city cast
Her people out upon her; and Antony,
Enthroned i'th' market-place, did sit alone,
Whistling to th'air; which, but for vacancy,
Had gone to gaze on Cleopatra too,
And made a gap in nature.

Antony was once such a great warrior, with such a large army, that he could have taken on all of Rome and won. However, as a result of his infatuation with the Egyptian Queen Cleopatra, when her naval forces withdraw from the Battle of Actium, he follows her, dispensing with all strategy – much to the chagrin of his other allies. The men close to Antony regard Cleopatra – with considerable sexism – as a seducer who has corrupted their great friend and leader, and they hurl great Shakespearean insults at her feet.

ENOBARBUS
Naught, naught, all naught! I can behold no longer.
Th'*Antoniad*, the Egyptian admiral,
With all their sixty, fly and turn the rudder.
To see't mine eyes are blasted.
[*Enter* SCARUS]

SCARUS
Gods and goddesses,
All the whole synod of them!

ENOBARBUS
What's thy passion?

SCARUS
The greater cantle of the world is lost
With very ignorance. We have kissed away
Kingdoms and provinces.

ENOBARBUS
How appears the fight?

SCARUS
On our side like the tokened pestilence,
Where death is sure. Yon ribaudred nag of Egypt –
Whom leprosy o'ertake! – i'th'midst o'th'fight,
When vantage like a pair of twins appeared,
Both as the same, or rather ours the elder,
The breese upon her, like a cow in June,
Hoists sails and flies.

ENOBARBUS
That I beheld.
Mine eyes did sicken at the sight, and could not
Endure a further view.

SCARUS
She once being loofed,
The noble ruin of her magic, Antony,
Claps on his sea wing and, like a doting mallard,
Leaving the fight in height, flies after her.
I never saw an action of such shame.
Experience, manhood, honour, ne'er before
Did violate so itself.

ENOBARBUS
Alack, alack!

June 15 | King John | Act 4 Scene 2

The Magna Carta was drawn up on 15 June 1215 and has since become the foundation of modern democracy. It was brokered between King John, a very unpopular king, and rebellious barons who were tired of his habit of taking their resources without warning and spending them on pointless wars, among other things. Crucially, it established that no one, not even the king, was above the law, and that everybody had the right to a fair trial – principles which went on to inspire the US Constitution and the Universal Declaration of Human Rights hundreds of years later. Shakespeare makes no mention of this momentous document in his play – perhaps he was being careful not to trump up such a triumph of subjects over the monarchy – but he nonetheless puts his finger on the dynamic between king and barons. Here the nobles convince John to release Arthur, who has a rival claim to the throne, from jail, and they criticize his counter-productive stunt of having himself crowned for a second time.

PEMBROKE
When workmen strive to do better than well,
They do confound their skill in covetousness;
And oftentimes excusing of a fault
Doth make the fault the worse by th'excuse,
As patches set upon a little breach
Discredit more in hiding of the fault
Than did the fault before it was so patched.

SALISBURY
To this effect, before you were new crowned,
We breathed our counsel. But it pleased your highness
To overbear it, and we are all well pleased,

Since all and every part of what we would
Doth make a stand at what your highness will.

KING JOHN
Some reasons of this double coronation
I have possessed you with and think them strong;
And more, more strong, then lesser is my fear,
I shall indue you with. Meantime but ask
What you would have reformed that is not well,
And well shall you perceive how willingly
I will both hear and grant you your requests.

June 16 | A Midsummer Night's Dream | Act 5 Scene 1

Elizabethans would observe Corpus Christi every year, sixty days after Easter Sunday. Before the Reformation, Corpus Christi would feature religious plays, but the festival was secularized by the mid 1500s: luckily for Shakespeare, Corpus Christi performances of 'mystery' plays dramatizing the entire story of the Bible continued at Coventry, only a day's walk from Stratford, until 1579, and allusions in his plays suggest he must have seen them. Although the forest in *A Midsummer Night's Dream* appears to be set in midsummer, Athens, where the action begins and ends, seems to be set around May Day. This means that when Theseus extends a two-week holiday after the nuptials at the end of the play, it could stretch to the Corpus Christi celebrations on a lucky year, meaning yet another week of revels.

THESEUS
The iron tongue of midnight hath told twelve.
Lovers, to bed; 'tis almost fairy time.
I fear we shall outsleep the coming morn
As much as we this night have overwatched.
This palpable-gross play hath well beguiled
The heavy gait of night. Sweet friends, to bed.
A fortnight hold we this solemnity
In nightly revels and new jollity.

June 17 | Sonnet 104

The speaker of the sonnet reflects on the three years since he first laid eyes on his fair friend. It is a poem that considers how the seasons and months turn and the years pass, but his love and his lover's beauty do not wither.

To me fair friend you never can be old,
For as you were when first your eye I eyed,
Such seems your beauty still: three Winters cold,
Have from the forests shook three Summers' pride,
Three beauteous springs to yellow Autumn turn'd,
In process of the seasons have I seen,
Three April perfumes in three hot Junes burn'd,
Since first I saw you fresh which yet are green.
Ah yet doth beauty like a dial hand,
Steal from his figure, and no pace perceiv'd,
So your sweet hue, which methinks still doth stand,
Hath motion, and mine eye may be deceiv'd.
  For fear of which, hear this thou age unbred,
  Ere you were born was beauty's summer dead.

Katherine in *The Taming of the Shrew*, once married off to
Petruchio, then starved and bullied by him, is finally 'tamed'
into an exemplar wife, and urges her audience to follow her
obedient example. Most modern audiences find the treatment
of Kate and her final speech troubling. George Bernard Shaw
called the play 'altogether disgusting to modern sensibility,'
and said, 'No man with any decency of feeling can sit it out in
the company of a woman without feeling extremely ashamed.'
Some modern productions, including the updated Hollywood
teen rom-com version *10 Things I Hate About You*, choose to
change the ending.

KATHERINE
Thy husband is thy lord, thy life, thy keeper,
Thy head, thy sovereign; one that cares for thee,
And for thy maintenance; commits his body
To painful labour both by sea and land,
To watch the night in storms, the day in cold,
Whilst thou liest warm at home, secure and safe;
And craves no other tribute at thy hands
But love, fair looks, and true obedience –
Too little payment for so great a debt.
Such duty as the subject owes the prince,
Even such a woman oweth to her husband.
And when she is froward, peevish, sullen, sour,
And not obedient to his honest will,
What is she but a foul contending rebel
And graceless traitor to her loving lord?
I am ashamed that women are so simple
To offer war where they should kneel for peace,
Or seek for rule, supremacy, and sway,
When they are bound to serve, love, and obey.

Why are our bodies soft, and weak, and smooth,
Unapt to toil and trouble in the world,
But that our soft conditions and our hearts
Should well agree with our external parts?

In stark contrast to Katherine in *The Taming of the Shrew*, Emilia in *Othello* inveighs heavily against the compulsory subservience of women to men. She scandalizes her mistress, the unflinchingly virtuous Desdemona, with her candid support for women's autonomy and her criticism of men's double standards.

EMILIA
But I do think it is their husbands' faults
If wives do fall. Say that they slack their duties,
And pour our treasures into foreign laps;
Or else break out in peevish jealousies,
Throwing restraint upon us; or say they strike us,
Or scant our former having in despite –
Why, we have galls, and though we have some grace,
Yet have we some revenge. Let husbands know
Their wives have sense like them: they see and smell,
And have their palates both for sweet and sour
As husbands have. What is it that they do,
When they change us for others? Is it sport?
I think it is. And doth affection breed it?
I think it doth. Is't frailty that thus errs?
It is so too. And have not we affections,
Desires for sport, and frailty, as men have?
Then let them use us well: else let them know
The ills we do, their ills instruct us so.

June 20 | Sir Thomas More | Scene 6

June 20 is now World Refugee Day, instituted by the United Nations in 2000 – although the plight of refugees is not a new one. Shakespeare's small contribution to *The Book of Sir Thomas More* contains some powerful rhetoric for the legendary politician, urging empathy in the treatment of refugees from foreign lands. The play had originally been composed by a team of other playwrights, but was refused performance on the grounds that it was too sympathetic towards the Catholic More. Shakespeare's additional material, in which More quells a race riot, does not seem to have changed the censor's mind.

SIR THOMAS MORE
You'll put down strangers,
Kill them, cut their throats, possess their houses,
And lead the majesty of law in lyam
To slip him like a hound. Alas, alas! Say now the King
As he is clement if th'offender mourn,
Should so much come too short of your great trespass
As but to banish you: whither would you go?
What country, by the nature of your error,
Should give you harbour? Go you to France or Flanders,
To any German province, Spain or Portugal,
Nay, anywhere that not adheres to England:
Why, you must needs be strangers.

Father's Day falls on the third Sunday in June. It is a twentieth-century invention (unlike Mothering Sunday that dates back to the Elizabethan era). In the first act of the play, Polixenes, King of Bohemia, away from home on a diplomatic visit to his friend Leontes, King of Sicilia, tenderly asserts his love for his son. In the second half of the play, their relationship undergoes something of a crisis when Prince Florizel, now grown up, tries to marry a shepherdess without his royal father's knowledge or blessing, but they are reconciled when she turns out to be Leontes' long-lost daughter.

POLIXENES
He's all my exercise, my mirth, my matter;
Now my sworn friend, and then mine enemy;
My parasite, my soldier, statesman, all.
He makes a July's day short as December,
And with his varying childness cures in me
Thoughts that would thick my blood.

June 22 | A Midsummer Night's Dream | Act 2 Scene 1

Elizabethans used 'wood' as a term for 'mad', which Shakespeare pounced upon as ripe for punning. In *A Midsummer Night's Dream* – largely set in a wood – an exasperated Demetrius spurns Helena's love with 'here am I, and wood [i.e. mad] within this wood [i.e. forest], / Because I cannot meet my Hermia'. Midsummer had connotations with madness and is mentioned in conjunction with it across many of Shakespeare's plays. Oberon the fairy king uses a flower with magic aphrodisiac powers to create even more Midsummer madness and mischief.

OBERON
That very time I saw – but thou couldst not –
Flying between the cold moon and the earth
Cupid all arm'd. A certain aim he took
At a fair vestal thronèd by the west,
And loosed his loveshaft smartly from his bow
As it should pierce a hundred thousand hearts;
But I might see young Cupid's fiery shaft
Quenched in the chaste beams of the watery moon,
And the imperial votaress passed on
In maiden meditation, fancy-free.
Yet marked I where the bolt of Cupid fell:
It fell upon a little western flower,
Before, milk-white; now purple with love's wound:
And maidens call it 'love-in-idleness'.
Fetch me that flower – the herb I showed thee once.
The juice of it on sleeping eye-lids laid
Will make or man or woman madly dote
Upon the next live creature that it sees.
Fetch me this herb, and be thou here again
Ere the leviathan can swim a league.

June 23 | A Midsummer Night's Dream |
Act 2 Scene 2

Hermia, having fallen asleep in the woods, awakes in fear of
her dream, calling for her lover Lysander with whom she has
eloped. Lysander, however, has tottered off after Helena, as
Puck has mistakenly dosed him with Oberon's love potion. Poor
Hermia has this realization yet to come.

HERMIA
[*Awaking*] Help me, Lysander, help me! Do thy best
To pluck this crawling serpent from my breast!
Ay me, for pity! – What a dream was here!
Lysander, look how I do quake with fear!
Methought a serpent ate my heart away,
And you sat smiling at his cruel pray.
Lysander – what, removed? Lysander, lord!
What, out of hearing? Gone? No sound, no word?
Alack, where are you? Speak an if you hear.
Speak, of all loves! I swoon almost with fear.
No? Then I well perceive you all not nigh.
Either death or you I'll find immediately.

June 24 | A Midsummer Night's Dream |
Act 3 Scene 2

Helena, who began the play with nobody loving her, ends up, as a result of Puck's liberal sprinkling of the magic potion, as the object of desire for both Lysander who has eloped with her best friend and Demetrius over whom she has pined unrequitedly for some time. She is naturally convinced it is some kind of nasty joke.

HELENA
O spite! O hell! I see you all are bent
To set against me for your merriment.
If you were civil and knew courtesy
You would not do me thus much injury.
Can you not hate me – as I know you do –
But you must join in souls to mock me too?
If you were men – as men you are in show –
You would not use a gentle lady so,
To vow, and swear, and superpraise my parts,
When, I am sure, you hate me with your hearts.
You both are rivals, and love Hermia;
And now both rivals to mock Helena.
A trim exploit, a manly enterprise –
To conjure tears up in a poor maid's eyes
With your derision. None of noble sort
Would so offend a virgin, and extort
A poor soul's patience, all to make you sport.

June 25 | A Midsummer Night's Dream | Act 2 Scene 1

Oberon gives a rundown of several flowers you might find at this time of year: musk roses are *Rosa arvensis*, and eglantine is *R. rubiginosa*. Woodbine is an old name for honeysuckle, and oxlips are similar to cowslips, but larger. He is giving Puck instructions: first to humiliate his wife by making her fall in love with an ass; and second, to help Demetrius fall in love with Helena who has chased him into the woods. These high jinks are typical of Midsummer's Day, which is replete with crazy rituals. In reference to these, for instance, *Twelfth Night*'s Olivia calls Malvolio's strange conduct 'a very midsummer madness'.

OBERON
I know a bank where the wild thyme blows,
Where oxlips and the nodding violet grows,
Quite over-canopied with luscious woodbine,
With sweet muskroses and with eglantine.
There sleeps Titania sometime of the night,
Lulled in these flowers with dances and delight.
And there the snake throws her enamelled skin,
Weed wide enough to wrap a fairy in.
And with the juice of this I'll streak her eyes;
And make her full of hateful fantasies.
Take thou some of it, and seek through this grove.
A sweet Athenian lady is in love
With a disdainful youth – anoint his eyes;
But do it when the next thing he espies
May be the lady. Thou shalt know the man
By the Athenian garments he hath on.
Effect it with some care, that he may prove
More fond on her than she upon her love.
And look thou meet me ere the first cock crow.

June 26 | Richard III | Act 3 Scene 4

On 26 June 1483, Richard III was named king; he was crowned the following month. At this point in Shakespeare's play about his reign, Hastings, arrested on trumped-up charges of witchcraft and treason, realizes how deeply mistaken he was to help the murderous tyrant Richard to become Protector. The deposed Queen Margaret's curse is coming home to roost as Hastings senses he is in danger. Her words seem to ring loudly in his ear: 'God, I pray him, / That none of you may live his natural age, / But by some unlooked accident cut off!'

HASTINGS
Woe, woe for England, not a whit for me!
For I, too fond, might have prevented this.
Stanley did dream the boar did raze our helms,
And I did scorn it and disdain to fly.
Three times today my footcloth horse did stumble,
And startled when he looked upon the Tower,
As loath to bear me to the slaughterhouse.
O, now I want the priest that spake to me!
I now repent I told the pursuivant,
As too triumphing, how mine enemies
Today at Pomfret bloodily were butchered,
And I myself secure, in grace and favour.
O Margaret, Margaret, now thy heavy curse
Is lighted on poor Hastings' wretched head!

There was an Ottoman invasion of Cyprus on 27 June 1570 and Shakespeare seems to set *Othello* around this time. Othello is reunited with Desdemona after a perilous journey to Cyprus, where he has been sent by the Venetian authorities to fight against a threatened Turkish invasion which in the play is thwarted by bad weather. The seemingly indestructible bond between them, and their tender love, is heart-wrenching in the context of the tragedy that is to follow.

OTHELLO
O, my fair warrior!

DESDEMONA
My dear Othello!

OTHELLO
It gives me wonder great as my content
To see you here before me. O, my soul's joy!
If after every tempest come such calms,
May the winds blow till they have wakened death,
And let the labouring bark climb hills of seas,
Olympus-high, and duck again as low
As hell's from heaven. If it were now to die,
'Twere now to be most happy; for, I fear
My soul hath her content so absolute
That not another comfort like to this
Succeeds in unknown fate.

DESDEMONA
The heavens forbid
But that our loves and comforts should increase,
Even as our days do grow.

OTHELLO
Amen to that, sweet Powers!
I cannot speak enough of this content;
It stops me here; it is too much of joy.
[*They kiss*]
And this, and this the greatest discords be
That e'er our hearts shall make.

Although 'the fool' is a stock character, Shakespeare carefully characterizes each of his fools – Touchstone in *As You Like It*, the Fool in *Lear* – with unique manners and personalities, and places them very carefully in relation to the protagonists of each play. Lear's fool is one of the most ingeniously drawn, as his sympathies change and adapt with the King's misfortunes. Far from being mere light relief to the waning monarch, the Fool represents a conscience where the King loses his own, and quiet compassion when all the world has risen against him. His prophecy is bitterly satirical: all the supposed portents he lists add up to a description of the everyday corruption of the world.

FOOL
I'll speak a prophecy ere I go:
When priests are more in word than matter,
When brewers mar their malt with water,
When nobles are their tailors' tutors,
No heretics burned, but wenches' suitors –
Then shall the realm of Albion
Come to great confusion.

When every case in law is right,
No squire in debt, nor no poor knight,
When slanders do not live in tongues,
Nor cutpurses come not to throngs,
When usurers tell their gold i'the field,
And bawds and whores do churches build –
Then comes the time, who lives to see't,
That going shall be used with feet.
This prophecy Merlin shall make; for I live before his time.

June 29 | Henry VIII | Prologue

On 29 June 1613, the theatrical cannon used during a
performance of *Henry VIII* misfired and burned the Globe
Theatre to the ground. One account explains that nobody
was hurt although 'one man had his breeches set on fire, that
would perhaps have broyled him, if he had not by the benefit
of a provident wit, put it out with a bottle of ale.' The replica
Globe Theatre is the only building in central London allowed to
have a thatched roof since the Great Fire of 1666, and despite
its gestures towards Tudor authenticity it is carefully fitted
with a sprinkler system. Here is the Prologue the unsuspecting
playgoers would have heard at the opening of that fateful 1613
performance.

> I come no more to make you laugh. Things now
> That bear a weighty and a serious brow,
> Sad, high, and working, full of state and woe,
> Such noble scenes as draw the eye to flow,
> We now present. Those that can pity here
> May, if they think it well, let fall a tear;
> The subject will deserve it. Such as give
> Their money out of hope they may believe
> May here find truth too. Those that come to see
> Only a show or two, and so agree
> The play may pass, if they be still, and willing,
> I'll undertake may see away their shilling
> Richly in two short hours. Only they
> That come to hear a merry, bawdy play,
> A noise of targets, or to see a fellow
> In a long motley coat guarded with yellow,
> Will be deceived; for, gentle hearers, know
> To rank our chosen truth with such a show
> As fool and fight is, beside forfeiting

Our own brains, and the opinion that we bring
To make that only true we now intend,
Will leave us never an understanding friend.
Therefore, for goodness' sake, and as you are known
The first and happiest hearers of the town,
Be sad, as we would make ye. Think ye see
The very persons of our noble story
As they were living; think you see them great,
And followed with the general throng and sweat
Of thousand friends: then, in a moment, see
How soon this mightiness meets misery.
And if you can be merry then, I'll say
A man may weep upon his wedding day.

June 30 | Sonnet 94

The eminent critic and poet William Empson, whose first
degree was in mathematics, calculated that Sonnet 94 contains
'4096 possible movements of thought, with other possibilities'.
It is a difficult poem which reads with deceptive ease: perhaps,
like the mysterious young man to whom the poem is addressed,
more treacherous intentions lurk beneath the surface. The
seeming disjunction between the first eight and last six lines
gives rise to that dizzying array of possibilities. What is the
poet's tone, and to whom is he speaking? Are his meanings
clear even to himself? These and countless other questions
swill around the closing image, of a beautiful summer flower,
stinking and infected with disease.

They that have power to hurt, and will do none,
That do not do the thing they most do show,
Who moving others, are themselves as stone,
Unmoved, cold, and to temptation slow:
They rightly do inherit heaven's graces,
And husband nature's riches from expense,
They are the Lords and owners of their faces,
Others, but stewards of their excellence:
The summer's flower is to the summer sweet,
Though to itself, it only live and die,
But if that flower with base infection meet,
The basest weed outbraves his dignity:
   For sweetest things turn sourest by their deeds,
   Lilies that fester, smell far worse than weeds.

July

July 1 | Love's Labour's Lost | Act 1 Scene 1

Shakespeare mentions July just three times throughout his work: Don Pedro mentions the month in *Much Ado*; to his father Polixenes in *The Winter's Tale*, the young Florizel makes 'July's day short as December' and *Henry VIII*'s Lord Buckingham describes 'proofs as clear as founts [springs] in July', referring to the light and clarity which characterizes this summer month. *Love's Labour's Lost* appears to be set amongst the long clear days of summer, and begins with Ferdinand of Navarre and his three lords, including Berowne, swearing off women for three years so that they can devote themselves to study. Berowne's reluctant embrace of the virtues of study is cast off the moment he meets one of the visiting Princess of France's companions, the irresistible Rosaline.

BEROWNE
Study is like the heaven's glorious sun,
That will not be deep-searched with saucy looks.
Small have continual plodders ever won,
Save base authority from others' books.
These earthly godfathers of heaven's lights,
That give a name to every fixèd star,
Have no more profit of their shining nights
Than those that walk and wot not what they are.
Too much to know is to know naught but fame,
And every godfather can give a name.

Queen Cleopatra of Egypt's infatuation with the Roman general Antony reaches a comical pitch in his absence. She is constantly testing Antony's affections, and conducts her affair with him as if it were a campaign of psychological warfare. At one point she extravagantly demands, 'Get me ink and paper: / He shall have every day a several greeting, / Or I'll unpeople Egypt.' In another fit of affection, she declares that Antony is to be told, whatever his mood may be, that hers is the opposite: this is because she knows, like Shakespeare, that using antitheses holds her audience in her thrall.

CLEOPATRA
See where he is, who's with him, what he does.
I did not send you. If you find him sad,
Say I am dancing; if in mirth, report
That I am sudden sick. Quick, and return.

CHARMIAN
Madam, methinks, if you did love him dearly,
You do not hold the method to enforce
The like from him.

CLEOPATRA
What should I do I do not?

CHARMIAN
In each thing give him way. Cross him nothing.

CLEOPATRA
Thou teachest like a fool: the way to lose him.

There is an ancient superstition that Sirius, the Dog-star, was responsible for causing madness in dogs. The time of year when the star is visible, between 3 July and 17 August, was known by the Romans as the 'dog days'. Shakespeare alludes to it here, in this comical description of crowds thronging to a royal occasion (the christening of Henry VIII's daughter, the future Elizabeth I).

PORTER'S MAN
The spoons will be the bigger, sir. There is a
fellow somewhat near the door, he should be a
brazier by his face, for, o'my conscience, twenty
of the dog-days now reign in's nose; all that stand
about him are under the line, they need no other
penance. That fire-drake did I hit three times on
the head, and three times was his nose discharged
against me; he stands there like a mortar-piece, to
blow us. There was a haberdasher's wife of small
wit near him, that railed upon me till her pinked
porringer fell off her head, for kindling such a
combustion in the state. I missed the meteor once,
and hit that woman, who cried out 'Clubs!', when I
might see from far some forty truncheoners draw to
her succor, which were the hope o'th'Strand, where
she was quartered. They fell on; I made good my
place. At length they came to th'broomstaff to
me; I defied 'em still; when suddenly a file of
boys behind 'em, loose shot, delivered such a shower
of pebbles that I was fain to draw mine honour in,
and let 'em win the work. The devil was amongst
'em, I think, surely.

The month of July takes its name from the legendary Roman emperor Julius Caesar, who was born on the fourth of the month. Now, of course, that day is best known as American Independence Day, which put America on the path to becoming one of the world's most powerful nations. In Shakespeare's play, Julius Caesar, defying warnings against appearing in public on the Ides of March, speaks lines which resonated with Nelson Mandela during his political imprisonment. The future president of South Africa had a copy of Shakespeare's complete works in prison, its jacket disguised by a fellow prisoner as a Hindu text to avoid confiscation. This volume was referred to as the 'Robben Island Bible', and the following passage was highlighted by Mandela in ballpoint pen.

CAESAR
Cowards die many times before their deaths;
The valiant never taste of death but once.
Of all the wonders that I yet have heard,
It seems to me most strange that men should fear,
Seeing that death, a necessary end,
Will come when it will come.

July 5 | A Midsummer Night's Dream | Act 5 Scene 1

This is the wonderfully mispunctuated prologue to the mechanicals' play *Pyramus and Thisbe*, spoken towards the end of *A Midsummer Night's Dream* by Peter Quince, the leader of the amateur troupe. The nobles mock Quince and compare his delivery to a child playing the recorder, but audiences then and now enjoy his amateur performance and the elaborately stilted dialogue of the 'very tragical mirth' which it presents. There is evidence that both the noblemen and the mechanicals would have had counterparts in the audience. Recent excavations on the site of London's Elizabethan Rose Theatre found remains of oysters (then a poor person's snack) alongside Italian forks (a new and expensive affectation of the wealthy). There were also remnants of ceramic money-collecting boxes, which is the likely origin of the term 'box office'. There is very possibly a little pun in Quince's prologue: 'our good will' may refer to the playwright himself.

QUINCE
If we offend, it is with our good will.
That you should think, we come not to offend
But with good will. To show our simple skill,
That is the true beginning of our end.
Consider then we come but in despite.
We do not come as minding to contest you,
Our true intent is. All for your delight
We are not here. That you should here repent you,
The actors are at hand, and by their show
You shall know all that you are like to know.
[. . .]

Gentles, perchance you wonder at this show;
But wonder on, till truth make all things plain.
This man is Pyramus, if you would know;
This beauteous lady Thisbe is, certain.
This man with lime and rough-cast doth present
Wall – that vile wall which did these lovers sunder;
And through Wall's chink, poor souls, they are content
To whisper. At the which let no man wonder.
This man with lantern, dog, and bush of thorn
Presenteth Moonshine. For, if you will know,
By moonshine did these lovers think no scorn
To meet at Ninus' tomb, there, there to woo.
This grisly beast – which Lion hight by name –
The trusty Thisbe coming first by night
Did scare away, or rather did affright.
And as she fled, her mantle she did fall,
Which Lion vile with bloody mouth did stain.
Anon comes Pyramus – sweet youth and tall –
And finds his trusty Thisbe's mantle slain.
Whereat with blade – with bloody, blameful blade –
He bravely broached his boiling bloody breast.
And Thisbe, tarrying in mulberry shade,
His dagger drew, and died. For all the rest,
Let Lion, Moonshine, Wall, and lovers twain
At large discourse while here they do remain.

Don Pedro and Claudio mock their friend Benedick by pretending to write an absurdly formal letter from him to Leonato about the mundane business of dinner: "'To the tuition of God: From my house'" begins Claudio; "'The sixth of July: Your loving friend, Benedick'" continues Don Pedro. The sixth of July is a quarter day on which rents were due, and business letters likely to be written. Not everybody has such a command of basic sequences: elsewhere, the diligent but obtuse village policeman Dogberry fudges his report of a crime to Don Pedro with his total misuse of 'sixth and lastly' to denote the fourth item in a list five items long. Don Pedro imitates him mockingly.

DON PEDRO
Officers, what offence have these men done?

DOGBERRY
Marry, sir, they have committed false report;
moreover they have spoken untruths; secondarily,
they are slanders; sixth and lastly, they have
belied a lady; thirdly, they have verified unjust
things; and, to conclude, they are lying knaves.

DON PEDRO
First, I ask thee what they have done; thirdly, I
ask thee what's their offence; sixth and lastly, why
they are committed; and, to conclude, what you lay
to their charge.

CLAUDIO
Rightly reasoned, and in his own division; and, by
my troth, there's one meaning well suited.

DON PEDRO
Who have you offended, masters, that you are thus
bound to your answer? This learned Constable is
too cunning to be understood.

King Duncan expects to enjoy the Macbeths' hospitality whilst his hosts advance their dastardly scheme to take the crown. The darkness of the Macbeths' ambition contrasts with the delicate summer air which Duncan remarks upon as he is welcomed into their castle.

DUNCAN
This castle hath a pleasant seat; the air
Nimbly and sweetly recommends itself
Unto our gentle senses.

BANQUO
This guest of summer,
The temple-haunting martlet, does approve
By his loved mansionry that the heaven's breath
Smells wooingly here; no jutty, frieze,
Buttress, nor coign of vantage, but this bird
Hath made his pendent bed and procreant cradle;
Where they most breed and haunt I have observed
The air is delicate.

Romeo and Juliet is set 'a fortnight and odd days' before Lammas Eve, which is Juliet's fourteenth birthday. It is probably no coincidence that Shakespeare gives a character called Juliet a birthday in July, though this puts her in a small minority of characters whose age is explicitly revealed: in Hamlet's case, for instance, he is consistently referred to as 'young', even though the gravedigger implies he is thirty years old. Juliet is the same age as both her nurse's now-dead daughter, and Shakespeare's own, Susanna, in 1595 when the play was probably written. Alexander Pope would later criticize Shakespeare's interest in the lower classes, though they are often ingenious and important elements of the dramas. These characters were not excluded from the plays, as they were not excluded from its audience, and Shakespeare develops them convincingly and sympathetically. Like the Nurse to her Capulet employers, Shakespeare is bound to his audience by an intricate mixture of financial need and genuine sympathy.

NURSE
Come Lammas Eve at night shall she be fourteen.
Susan and she – God rest all Christian souls! –
Were of an age. Well, Susan is with God.
She was too good for me. But, as I said,
On Lammas Eve at night shall she be fourteen.
That shall she, marry! I remember it well.
'Tis since the earthquake now eleven years;
And she was weaned – I never shall forget it –
Of all the days of the year, upon that day.
For I had then laid wormwood to my dug,
Sitting in the sun under the dovehouse wall.
My lord and you were then at Mantua.
Nay, I do bear a brain. But, as I said,

When it did taste the wormwood on the nipple
Of my dug and felt it bitter, pretty fool,
To see it tetchy and fall out wi' th' dug!
Shake, quoth the dovehouse! 'Twas no need, I trow,
To bid me trudge.
And since that time it is eleven years.
For then she could stand high-lone. Nay, by th' rood,
She could have run and waddled all about.
For even the day before, she broke her brow.
And then my husband – God be with his soul!
'A was a merry man – took up the child.
'Yea,' quoth he, 'dost thou fall upon thy face?
Thou wilt fall backward when thou hast more wit.
Wilt thou not, Jule?' and, by my holidam,
The pretty wretch left crying and said 'Ay'.
To see, now, how a jest shall come about!
I warrant, an I should live a thousand years,
I never should forget it. 'Wilt thou not, Jule?' quoth he,
And, pretty fool, it stinted and said 'Ay'.

Aristotle observed that tragedies usually play out the consequences of a protagonist's tragic flaw, and critics who subscribe to this formula point to Macbeth's ambition and Othello's jealousy. It has been hotly contested whether Romeo and Juliet qualify under this rule, being too young, and too fatally 'star-crossed' to be entirely responsible for their destiny. The course of their love affair speeds along at such a pace, at once exhilarating and terrifying, that the lovers find themselves happily and dangerously disorientated. At the end of their clandestine wedding night, Juliet claims she hears a nocturnal nightingale, as she tries to assure Romeo that the night is still young. But Romeo knows the bird was a lark, announcing the midsummer dawn, and reluctantly she too has to concede that it is time for him to make his escape towards Mantua.

JULIET
Wilt thou be gone? It is not yet near day.
It was the nightingale, and not the lark,
That pierced the fearful hollow of thine ear.
Nightly she sings on yond pomegranate tree.
Believe me, love, it was the nightingale.

ROMEO
It was the lark, the herald of the morn;
No nightingale. Look, love, what envious streaks
Do lace the severing clouds in yonder East.
Night's candles are burnt out, and jocund day
Stands tiptoe on the misty mountain tops.
I must be gone and live, or stay and die.

JULIET
Yon light is not daylight; I know it, I.

It is some meteor that the sun exhales
To be to thee this night a torchbearer
And light thee on thy way to Mantua.
Therefore stay yet. Thou needest not to be gone.

ROMEO
Let me be ta'en, let me be put to death.
I am content, so thou wilt have it so.
I'll say yon grey is not the morning's eye;
'Tis but the pale reflex of Cynthia's brow.
Nor that is not the lark, whose notes do beat
The vaulty heaven so high above our heads.
I have more care to stay than will to go.
Come, death, and welcome! Juliet wills it so.
How is't, my soul? Let's talk. It is not day.

JULIET
It is, it is! Hie hence, be gone, away!
It is the lark that sings so out of tune,
Straining harsh discords and unpleasing sharps.
Some say the lark makes sweet division.
This doth not so, for she divideth us.
Some say the lark and loathèd toad change eyes.
O, now I would they had changed voices too,
Since arm from arm that voice doth us affray,
Hunting thee hence with hunt's-up to the day.
O, now be gone! More light and light it grows.

ROMEO
More light and light: more dark and dark our woes.

This speech is truly legendary. It is given by the electric
Mercutio, who sets about dispelling Romeo's ominous dream
to the effect that if they crash the Capulets' party there will be
tragic consequences. Having told Romeo 'that dreamers often
lie', he goes on to explain how Queen Mab, the fairies' midwife,
gives out dreams corresponding to the dreamer's desires: hence,
for example, a parson dreams of obtaining a lucrative parish,
and a lover of love. His description of Queen Mab as a tiny
creature helped to establish the fairy image we recognize today.

MERCUTIO
O, then I see Queen Mab hath been with you.
She is the fairies' midwife, and she comes
In shape no bigger than an agate stone
On the forefinger of an alderman,
Drawn with a team of little atomies
Over men's noses as they lie asleep.
Her chariot is an empty hazelnut,
Made by the joiner squirrel or old grub,
Time out o' mind the fairies' coachmakers.
Her wagon spokes made of long spinners' legs;
The cover, of the wings of grasshoppers;
Her traces, of the smallest spider web;
Her collars, of the moonshine's watery beams;
Her whip, of cricket's bone: the lash, of film;
Her wagoner, a small grey-coated gnat,
Not half so big as a round little worm
Pricked from the lazy finger of a maid.
And in this state she gallops night by night
Through lovers' brains, and then they dream of love;
O'er courtiers' knees, that dream on curtsies straight;
O'er lawyers' fingers, who straight dream on fees;

O'er ladies' lips, who straight on kisses dream,
Which oft the angry Mab with blisters plagues,
Because their breaths with sweetmeats tainted are.
Sometime she gallops o'er a courtier's nose,
And then dreams he of smelling out a suit.
And sometime comes she with a tithe-pig's tail
Tickling a parson's nose as 'a lies asleep;
Then he dreams of another benefice.
Sometime she driveth o'er a soldier's neck;
And then dreams he of cutting foreign throats,
Of breaches, ambuscados, Spanish blades,
Of healths five fathom deep; and then anon
Drums in his ear, at which he starts and wakes,
And being thus frighted, swears a prayer or two
And sleeps again. This is that very Mab
That plaits the manes of horses in the night
And bakes the elf-locks in foul sluttish hairs,
Which once untangled, much misfortune bodes.
This is the hag, when maids lie on their backs,
That presses them and learns them first to bear,
Making them women of good carriage.

If you are so inclined, you may visit the Casa di Giulietta in Verona, which has a bronze statue of Juliet, a balcony, and a wall covered with love notes. Visitors rub the statue or leave a note to ask Juliet for advice of the heart, which is all a little perplexing considering how her own brief affair ended. She fakes her death with the aid of a narcotic medicine so convincingly that Romeo sees her apparently dead and then kills himself. She wakes up twenty-seven lines of dialogue too late and follows suit.

JULIET
O comfortable Friar! Where is my lord?
I do remember well where I should be,
And there I am. Where is my Romeo?
[. . .]

What's here? A cup, closed in my true love's hand?
Poison, I see, hath been his timeless end.
O churl! drunk all, and left no friendly drop
To help me after? I will kiss thy lips.
Haply some poison yet doth hang on them
To make me die with a restorative.
[*Kisses him*]
Thy lips are warm!
[. . .]

Yea, noise? Then I'll be brief. O happy dagger!
[*She snatches* ROMEO's dagger]
This is thy sheath;
[*She stabs herself*]
there rust, and let me die.
[*Falls on* ROMEO's *body and dies*]

Rushbearing was a communal practice undertaken around
this time in July, whereby village communities would gather
dry rushes and strew them about the mud floors of churches
and houses as a form of insulation, and as a sign of hospitality.
Hence 'Is supper ready, the house / trimm'd, rushes strew'd,
cobwebs swept' in *The Taming of the Shrew*. This passage,
in which the Welsh leader Glendower acts as interpreter
between his Welsh-speaking daughter and her English husband
Mortimer, stands alone as a beautiful lullaby.

GLENDOWER
She bids you on the wanton rushes lay you down,
And rest your gentle head upon her lap,
And she will sing the song that pleaseth you,
And on your eyelids crown the god of sleep,
Charming your blood with pleasing heaviness,
Making such difference 'twixt wake and sleep
As is the difference betwixt day and night,
The hour before the heavenly-harnessed team
Begins his golden progress in the east.

July 13 | The Two Gentlemen of Verona | Act 2 Scene 3

The Two Gentlemen of Verona is an early play and is considered by many to be Shakespeare's first. It includes the first occasion of many in Shakespeare in which a female character disguises herself as a man, and the only instance of a dog being given a large role. The dog has a name, Crab, and belongs to Proteus's clownish servant Launce. We can assume what we like about what this early experience of working with animals taught the playwright, but no animal is given such a large part again (as the Hollywood legend W.C. Fields would go on to say, 'Never work with children or animals'). That said, for the actor playing Launce, as he describes his tearful departure from his family to accompany his master to Milan, there is plenty of comic opportunity in having a real dog on stage who refuses to cry on cue.

LAUNCE
I think Crab my dog be the sourest-natured
dog that lives. My mother weeping, my father
wailing, my sister crying, our maid howling, our cat
wringing her hands, and all our house in a great
perplexity; yet did not this cruel-hearted cur shed
one tear. He is a stone, a very pebble-stone, and
has no more pity in him than a dog. A Jew would have
wept to have seen our parting. Why, my grandam,
having no eyes, look you, wept herself blind at my
parting. Nay, I'll show you the manner of it. This
shoe is my father. No, this left shoe is my father.
No, no, this left shoe is my mother. Nay, that
cannot be so neither. Yes, it is so, it is so; it
hath the worser sole. This shoe with the hole in
it is my mother, and this my father. A vengeance

on't, there 'tis. Now, sir, this staff is my
sister; for, look you, she is as white as a lily, and
as small as a wand. This hat is Nan our maid. I
am the dog. No, the dog is himself, and I am the
dog. O, the dog is me, and I am myself. Ay, so,
so. Now come I to my father: 'Father, your blessing.'
Now should not the shoe speak a word for weeping.
Now should I kiss my father; well, he weeps on. Now
come I to my mother. O, that she could speak now
like an old woman! Well, I kiss her. Why, there
'tis; here's my mother's breath up and down. Now
come I to my sister. Mark the moan she makes. Now
the dog all this while sheds not a tear, nor speaks a
word; but see how I lay the dust with my tears.

Every year, France celebrates the anniversary of the storming of the Bastille on 14 July 1789, which kickstarted the French Revolution. A French national heroine dating from an earlier time, Joan of Arc, makes a memorable appearance as Joan la Pucelle in *Henry VI, Part 1*: here she persuades Burgundy to forsake the English and join the French forces.

JOAN LA PUCELLE
Look on thy country, look on fertile France,
And see the cities and the towns defaced
By wasting ruin of the cruel foe;
As looks the mother on her lowly babe
When death doth close his tender-dying eyes,
See, see the pining malady of France;
Behold the wounds, the most unnatural wounds,
Which thou thyself hast given her woeful breast.
O, turn thy edgèd sword another way;
Strike those that hurt, and hurt not those that help!
One drop of blood drawn from thy country's bosom
Should grieve thee more than streams of foreign gore.
Return thee therefore with a flood of tears,
And wash away thy country's stainèd spots.

July 15 | Macbeth | Act 1 Scene 1

July 15 is St Swithin's Day, whose festivities featured games ranging from jousting to archery and football. Shakespeare makes no mention of the day, but it was well known enough to feature in this popular Elizabethan rhyme: 'St Swithin's day if thou dost rain / For forty days it will remain / St Swithin's day if thou be fair / For forty days will rain na mair.' Shakespeare was certainly no stranger to the prophetic power of the weather, and his new king and patron, James I, was history's most notorious royal witch-hunter. When a violent tempest impeded the King's journey across the North Sea with his wife-to-be, Anne of Denmark, he blamed witchcraft, and seventy suspects were rounded up, convicted and put to death. The Scottish King James' interest in witchcraft lies behind Shakespeare's decision to write a whole tragedy about Scotland, whose opening words are spoken by 'weird sisters'.

FIRST WITCH
When shall we three meet again?
In thunder, lightning, or in rain?

SECOND WITCH
When the hurly-burly's done,
When the battle's lost and won.

THIRD WITCH
That will be ere the set of sun.

FIRST WITCH
Where the place?

SECOND WITCH
Upon the heath.

THIRD WITCH
There to meet with Macbeth.

FIRST WITCH
I come, Gray-Malkin!

SECOND WITCH
Padock calls!

THIRD WITCH
Anon!

ALL
Fair is foul, and foul is fair.
Hover through the fog and filthy air.

July 16 | King Lear | Act 4 Scene 7

Shakespeare's elder daughter Susanna was buried near her parents in Stratford's Holy Trinity Church on 16 July 1649. She died at the ripe old age of sixty-six (pretty old for the time – there are clearly advantages to being married to a renowned doctor). Her epitaph reads:

> Witty above her sex, but that's not all, / Wise to salvation was good Mistris Hall, / Something of Shakespeare was in that, but this / Wholy of him with whom she's now in bliss. / When, Passenger, hast nere a teare, / To weepe with her that wept with all / That wept, yet set her self to chere / Them up with comforts cordiall. / Her love shall live, her mercy spread / When thou has't ner'e a teare to shed.

We know very little about Shakespeare's relationship with Susanna, but he did bequeath her the main part of his estate including his house 'the Newe Place wherein I nowe dwell,' and he also writes strong fictional father-daughter bonds in his plays. Although Cordelia is punished by Lear for refusing to prove her love to win a share of his kingdom, their bond survives intact and at the end of the play she is heartbroken to find her father senile and wretched. The tragedy's ending is so bleak that it was changed in the later seventeenth century to have Cordelia survive and the King made king once more. The original version was not restored to the stage until the mid-nineteenth century.

CORDELIA
O my dear father! Restoration hang
Thy medicine on my lips; and let this kiss
Repair those violent harms that my two sisters
Have in thy reverence made.

293

KENT
Kind and dear princess!

CORDELIA
Had you not been their father, these white flakes
Did challenge pity of them. Was this a face
To be opposed against the jarring winds?
To stand against the deep dread-bolted thunder,
In the most terrible and nimble stroke
Of quick cross lightning? To watch, poor perdu,
With this thin helm? Mine enemy's dog,
Though he had bit me, should have stood that night
Against my fire; and wast thou fain, poor father,
To hovel thee with swine, and rogues forlorn
In short and musty straw? Alack, alack!
'Tis wonder that thy life and wits at once
Had not concluded all.

Tamora, Queen of the Goths, is lying. Caught in a secret tryst with
Aaron the Moor by Bassianus and Lavinia, Tamora claims that
it was they who dragged her to the forest against her will, and
instructs her sons to take revenge. She alludes to summer only to
accentuate the shadow of death in the height of the season.

TAMORA
Have I not reason, think you, to look pale?
These two have 'ticed me hither to this place.
A barren detested vale, you see it is:
The trees, though summer, yet forlorn and lean,
O'ercome with moss and baleful mistletoe;
Here never shines the sun, here nothing breeds,
Unless the nightly owl or fatal raven.
And when they showed me this abhorrèd pit,
They told me here at dead time of the night
A thousand fiends, a thousand hissing snakes,
Ten thousand swelling toads, as many urchins,
Would make such fearful and confusèd cries
As any mortal body hearing it
Should straight fall mad, or else die suddenly.
No sooner had they told this hellish tale,
But straight they told me they would bind me here
Unto the body of a dismal yew
And leave me to this miserable death.
And then they called me foul adulteress,
Lascivious Goth, and all the bitterest terms
That ever ear did hear to such effect.
And had you not by wondrous fortune come,
This vengeance on me had they executed.
Revenge it as you love your mother's life,
Or be ye not henceforth called my children.

Like Tamora, Henry Bolingbroke alludes to the tranquil summer only to make the threat of violence more stark. Bolingbroke has offended his cousin, King Richard, by impugning the integrity of his court – for which he has been banished for ten summers and suffered the confiscation of his lands and inheritance. When Bolingbroke returns early requesting to have his property restored, and for the banishment to be repealed, he threatens that if the King does not accede to his demands he will initiate a civil war which will turn the dust of summer to bloody mud.

HENRY BOLINGBROKE
Noble lord,
Go to the rude ribs of that ancient castle,
Through brazen trumpet send the breath of parley
Into his ruined ears, and thus deliver:
Henry Bolingbroke
On both his knees doth kiss King Richard's hand,
And sends allegiance and true faith of heart
To his most royal person, hither come
Even at his feet to lay my arms and power,
Provided that my banishment repealed
And lands restored again be freely granted.
If not, I'll use the advantage of my power
And lay the summer's dust with showers of blood
Rained from the wounds of slaughtered Englishmen;
The which, how far off from the mind of Bolingbroke
It is, such crimson tempest should bedrench
The fresh green lap of fair King Richard's land
My stooping duty tenderly shall show.
Go signify as much while here we march
Upon the grassy carpet of this plain.

Let's march without the noise of threatening drum,
That from this castle's tattered battlements
Our fair appointments may be well perused.
Methinks King Richard and myself should meet
With no less terror than the elements
Of fire and water when their thundering shock
At meeting tears the cloudy cheeks of heaven.
Be he the fire, I'll be the yielding water;
The rage be his, whilst on the earth I rain
My waters – on the earth, and not on him.
March on, and mark King Richard how he looks.
[*The trumpets sound parley without, and answer within;
then a flourish. King Richard appeareth on the walls with
the Bishop of Carlisle, Aumerle, Scroop, and Salisbury*]
See, see, King Richard doth himself appear,
As doth the blushing, discontented sun
From out the fiery portal of the east
When he perceives the envious clouds are bent
To dim his glory and to stain the track
Of his bright passage to the occident.

July 19 | Sonnet 130

The poems of Italian sonneteer Francesco Petrarch (1304–74) were still a smash hit in England when Shakespeare was composing his own collection. Many of Petrarch's sonnets were pretty formulaic and revolved around complimenting each individual part of a woman in turn. Shakespeare's subversion of this convention in his sonnet to a 'dark lady' initially strikes us as distinctly unromantic. However, it does make you think, what if somebody's eyes were really as bright as the sun, or lips as red as coral while the skin is white as snow? They would look ridiculous. This poet's love is more special, he claims, because it comes from a place of honesty.

My Mistress' eyes are nothing like the Sun,
Coral is far more red, than her lips' red,
If snow be white, why then her breasts are dun:
If hairs be wires, black wires grow on her head:
I have seen roses damask'd, red and white,
But no such roses see I in her cheeks,
And in some perfumes is there more delight,
Than in the breath that from my Mistress reeks.
I love to hear her speak, yet well I know,
That Music hath a far more pleasing sound:
I grant I never saw a goddess go,
My mistress when she walks treads on the ground.
  And yet by heaven I think my love as rare,
  As any she beli'd with false compare.

July 20 | King Lear | Act 1 Scene 1

Many movies are released at this time of year, and a great
number of them have borrowed freely from Shakespeare's work,
just as Shakespeare himself borrowed from popular stories of
his time. *The Lion King* steals some of its plot from *Hamlet*;
Forbidden Planet from *The Tempest*; and there are no prizes for
guessing which play *Gnomeo and Juliet* was based on. A little
less well known is that *King Lear* inspired both Jane Smiley's *A
Thousand Acres* and the acclaimed Akira Kurosawa film *Ran*.
The plot of *King Lear* unravels from the first decision King Lear
makes: to banish his counsel and distribute his kingdom among
his daughters according to their answers to his question below.

KING LEAR
Give me the map there. Know that we have divided
In three our kingdom; and 'tis our fast intent
To shake all cares and business from our age,
Conferring them on younger strengths, while we
Unburthened crawl toward death. Our son of Cornwall –
And you, our no less loving son of Albany –
We have this hour a constant will to publish
Our daughters' several dowers, that future strife
May be prevented now. The princes, France and Burgundy,
Great rivals in our youngest daughter's love,
Long in our court have made their amorous sojourn,
And here are to be answered. Tell me, my daughters,
Since now we will divest us both of rule,
Interest of territory, cares of state,
Which of you shall we say doth love us most,
That we our largest bounty may extend
Where nature doth with merit challenge.

July 21 | Henry IV, Part 1 | Act 5 Scene 4

The Battle of Shrewsbury took place on 21 July 1403 and ended with the killing of Harry Percy, known as Hotspur. Hotspur was the leader of the rebels against Henry IV and valiant counterpart to the flippant Prince Hal, who in Shakespeare's version kills him in single combat. He was so admirably noble that the real-life King is said to have wept for his death. Here is part of his heroic final scene.

HOTSPUR
O, Harry, thou hast robbed me of my youth!
I better brook the loss of brittle life
Than those proud titles thou hast won of me.
They wound my thoughts worse than sword my flesh.
But thoughts, the slave of life, and life, time's fool,
And time, that takes survey of all the world,
Must have a stop.

Even after Hotspur's defeat at the Battle of Shrewsbury in
Henry IV, Part 1, Henry IV frets his way through the duration
of *Henry IV, Part 2*. He describes his acute insomnia as he
approaches the end of his life. In this soliloquy, Shakespeare
employs 'synecdoche', a rhetorical tool he would have learned
at school whereby a part of a thing (a head, in this case) is
substituted for the whole (the King).

KING HENRY IV
How many thousand of my poorest subjects
Are at this hour asleep! O sleep, O gentle sleep,
Nature's soft nurse, how have I frighted thee,
That thou no more wilt weigh my eyelids down
And steep my senses in forgetfulness?
Why rather, sleep, liest thou in smoky cribs,
Upon uneasy pallets stretching thee,
And hushed with buzzing night-flies to thy slumber,
Than in the perfumed chambers of the great,
Under the canopies of costly state,
And lulled with sound of sweetest melody?
O thou dull god, why liest thou with the vile
In loathsome beds, and leavest the kingly couch
A watch-case, or a common 'larum-bell?
Wilt thou upon the high and giddy mast
Seal up the ship-boy's eyes, and rock his brains
In cradle of the rude imperious surge,
And in the visitation of the winds,
Who take the ruffian billows by the top,
Curling their monstrous heads, and hanging them
With deafening clamour in the slippery clouds,
That with the hurly death itself awakes?
Canst thou, O partial sleep, give thy repose

To the wet sea-son in an hour so rude,
And in the calmest and most stillest night,
With all appliances and means to boot,
Deny it to a king? Then happy low, lie down!
Uneasy lies the head that wears a crown.

July 23 | Sonnet 30

The French writer Marcel Proust gave his sequence of
novels the title *A la recherche du temps perdu* which was
initially translated into English by C. K. Scott Moncrieff
as *Remembrance of Things Past*, a phrase taken from
Shakespeare's Sonnet 30. The quality of the translation
has been considered a masterpiece in itself, though Proust
himself was apparently unhappy with Moncrieff's choice of
a title. 'Remembrance of things past', as lovely though the
line is, misrepresented Proust's central idea of an active trawl
(recherche means search/research) through the annals of time.
The line from the sonnet suggests a much more passive act of
recall. Though clearly not enough for Proust, this poet is content
with the memory of his beloved in all of his unspoiled, perfect
sweetness. All this and not a madeleine cake in sight.

When to the sessions of sweet silent thought,
I summon up remembrance of things past,
I sigh the lack of many a thing I sought,
And with old woes new wail my dear times' waste:
Then can I drown an eye (unus'd to flow)
For precious friends hid in death's dateless night,
And weep afresh love's long-since cancell'd woe,
And moan th' expense of many a vanish'd sight.
Then can I grieve at grievances foregone,
And heavily from woe to woe tell o'er
The sad account of fore-bemoaned moan,
Which I new pay, as if not paid before.
  But if the while I think on thee (dear friend)
  All losses are restor'd, and sorrows end.

One useful indicator of Shakespeare's success is the evidence that he invested £440 in leasing half of the 'tithes of corn, grain, blade and hay' in Stratford, on 24 July 1605. Considering a household servant might expect to earn up to £5 over the course of an entire year, it is clear Shakespeare had done very well in show business. Timon in *Timon of Athens* was more profligate with his money, and fritters it away on parasitic artists and ungrateful friends, ending up miserable and impoverished. His steward Flavius has this to say.

FLAVIUS
O, the fierce wretchedness that glory brings us!
Who would not wish to be from wealth exempt,
Since riches point to misery and contempt?
Who would be so mocked with glory, or to live
But in a dream of friendship,
To have his pomp and all what state compounds
But only painted, like his varnished friends?
Poor honest lord, brought low by his own heart,
Undone by goodness! Strange, unusual blood,
When man's worst sin is he does too much good.
Who then dares to be half so kind again?
For bounty, that makes gods, does still mar men.
My dearest lord, blest to be most accursed,
Rich only to be wretched, thy great fortunes
Are made thy chief afflictions. Alas, kind lord,
He's flung in rage from this ingrateful seat
Of monstrous friends;
Nor has he with him to supply his life,
Or that which can command it.
I'll follow and inquire him out.
I'll ever serve his mind with my best will;
Whilst I have gold I'll be his steward still.

James VI of Scotland was crowned James I of England on
25 July 1603, after Elizabeth died without an heir. This was
the first time in history the two kingdoms were united, and
to celebrate the uniting of the kingdom, James had a union
flag (later known as the Union Jack) made, new coins minted,
and a Book of Common Prayer printed. He presided over
the translation known as the King James Bible, said to be
the bestselling book of all time. Shakespeare's *Cymbeline,
King of Britain*, like *King Lear*, shares James' interest in the
ancient Britain which the union of Scotland and England was
supposed to be restoring. Part of the plot of *Cymbeline* has
something in common with *The Rape of Lucrece*: Jachimo
bets Posthumus that he can seduce his wife, Imogen, of whose
chastity Posthumus has been boasting. Having tried to no avail
to seduce her, Jachimo hides in a box in her bedroom so he can
sneak out while she is asleep and look for something to help
him forge proof of her adultery.

JACHIMO
The crickets sing, and man's o'er-laboured sense
Repairs itself by rest. Our Tarquin thus
Did softly press the rushes ere he wakened
The chastity he wounded. Cytherea,
How bravely thou becom'st thy bed; fresh lily,
And whiter than the sheets. That I might touch,
But kiss, one kiss; rubies unparagoned,
How dearly they do't. 'Tis her breathing that
Perfumes the chamber thus. The flame o'th'taper
Bows toward her, and would under-peep her lids
To see th' enclosèd lights, now canopied
Under these windows, white and azure-laced
With blue of heaven's own tinct. But my design –

To note the chamber. I will write all down.
Such and such pictures; there the window; such
Th'adornment of her bed; the arras, figures,
Why, such and such; and the contents o'th'story.
Ah, but some natural notes about her body
Above ten thousand meaner moveables
Would testify, t'enrich mine inventory.
O sleep, thou ape of death, lie dull upon her,
And be her sense but as a monument,
Thus in a chapel lying. Come off, come off;
As slippery as the Gordian knot was hard.
[*He takes the bracelet from her arm*]
'Tis mine, and this will witness outwardly,
As strongly as the conscience does within,
To th'madding of her lord. On her left breast
A mole, cinque-spotted, like the crimson drops
I'th'bottom of a cowslip. Here's a voucher
Stronger than ever law could make: this secret
Will force him think I have picked the lock and ta'en
The treasure of her honour. No more. To what end?
Why should I write this down that's riveted,
Screwed to my memory? She hath been reading late
The tale of Tereus. Here the leaf's turned down
Where Philomel gave up. I have enough.
To th'trunk again, and shut the spring of it.
Swift, swift, you dragons of the night, that dawning
May bare the raven's eye! I lodge in fear;
Though this a heavenly angel, hell is here.

July 26 | Hamlet | Act 3 Scene 2

The first record of Shakespeare's play *Hamlet* dates from 26 July 1602. 'The Revenge of Hamlet Prince of Denmark' was entered for publication in the Stationers' Register (as an early form of copyright protection). In the scene when the players arrive at the palace, Hamlet is giddy with anticipation. This is during one of his excitable moods, and he assumes the job of theatre director advising them on how to act. Might this have been the advice that Shakespeare gave to his own actors?

HAMLET
Speak the speech, I pray you, as I pronounced it to
you, trippingly on the tongue. But if you mouth it
as many of your players do, I had as lief the
town crier spoke my lines. Nor do not saw the air
too much with your hand, thus. But use all gently.
For in the very torrent, tempest, and, as I may say,
the whirlwind of passion, you must acquire and beget
a temperance that may give it smoothness. O, it
offends me to the soul to hear a robustious
periwig-pated fellow tear a passion to tatters, to
very rags, to split the ears of the groundlings, who
for the most part are capable of nothing but
inexplicable dumbshows and noise. I would have such
a fellow whipped for o'erdoing Termagant. It
out-Herods Herod. Pray you avoid it.

[. . .]
Be not too tame neither. But let your own discretion
be your tutor. Suit the action to the word, the
word to the action, with this special observance, that you
o'erstep not the modesty of nature. For anything so
o'erdone is from the purpose of playing, whose end, both at

the first and now, was and is to hold, as 'twere, the
mirror up to nature, to show virtue her own feature,
scorn her own image, and the very age and body of
the time his form and pressure. Now this overdone,
or come tardy off, though it make the unskilful
laugh, cannot but make the judicious grieve; the
censure of the which one must in your allowance
o'erweigh a whole theatre of others. O, there be
players that I have seen play, and heard others
praise, and that highly, not to speak it profanely,
that, neither having th'accent of Christians nor
the gait of Christian, pagan, nor man, have so
strutted and bellowed that I have thought some of
Nature's journeymen had made men and not made them
well, they imitated humanity so abominably.

[. . .]
O, reform it altogether! And let those that play
your clowns speak no more than is set down for them.
For there be of them that will themselves laugh, to
set on some quantity of barren spectators to laugh
too, though in the meantime, some necessary
question of the play be then to be considered.
That's villanous, and shows a most pitiful ambition
in the fool that uses it.

[. . .]
Well, go make you ready.

July 27 | King John | Act 3 Scene 1

The Battle of Bouvines was fought between King John of
England and Philip II of France on 27 July 1214 and delivered
a decisive victory to the French. John's reign was full of bad
days like this, and Shakespeare dramatizes many of them. We
watch the short-lived treaty between the two nations collapse
in the context of excommunication from Rome, and the fury of
the barons at home. The megalomaniac king distributes threats
recklessly despite his weakened state: 'France' he says, 'thou
shalt rue this hour within this hour'. Poor Blanche of Castile
has loyalties on all sides: her husband, the Dauphin (or heir
apparent to the French throne) is at war with her uncle, the
King of England.

BLANCHE
The sun's o'ercast with blood; fair day, adieu!
Which is the side that I must go withal?
I am with both; each army hath a hand,
And in their rage, I having hold of both,
They whirl asunder and dismember me.
Husband, I cannot pray that thou mayst win;
Uncle, I needs must pray that thou mayst lose.
Father, I may not wish the fortune thine;
Grandam, I will not wish thy fortunes thrive.
Whoever wins, on that side shall I lose –
Assurèd loss before the match be played!

July 28 | Love's Labour's Lost | Act 5 Scene 2

The plague is the subject of many jokes throughout
Shakespeare's work, and his audiences might have appreciated
this humour in the face of danger. The theatres were closed
during major outbreaks: during the epidemic of 1592–3
Shakespeare turned to writing poems instead of plays, and
the lyricism of *Venus and Adonis* and *The Rape of Lucrece*
characterizes the first batch of plays he composed after they
reopened, including *Love's Labour's Lost*. Love is likened to
the plague when the young scholar Berowne suggests the words
'Lord have mercy on us' be written on his smitten friends, since
these same words were what was hung on the doors of plague
victims.

BEROWNE
Yet I have a trick
Of the old rage. Bear with me, I am sick;
I'll leave it by degrees. Soft, let us see:
Write 'Lord have mercy on us' on those three.
They are infected; in their hearts it lies;
They have the plague, and caught it of your eyes.
These lords are visited; you are not free,
For the Lord's tokens on you do I see.

The Spanish Armada was defeated by English naval forces (with a bit of help from an enormous storm) on 29 June 1588. The Spanish were consequently ripe for ribbing, and Armado's laughably self-dramatizing confessions of love for the country girl Jaquenetta are among many examples of Spaniard-bashing to be found in the theatres of the 1590s.

ARMADO
I do affect the very ground, which is base, where
her shoe, which is baser, guided by her foot, which
is basest, doth tread. I shall be forsworn, which
is a great argument of falsehood, if I love. And
how can that be true love which is falsely
attempted? Love is a familiar; Love is a devil;
there is no evil angel but Love. Yet was Samson so
tempted, and he had an excellent strength; yet was
Solomon so seduced, and he had a very good wit.
Cupid's butt-shaft is too hard for Hercules' club,
and therefore too much odds for a Spaniard's rapier.
The first and second cause will not serve my turn;
the passado he respects not, the duello he regards
not. His disgrace is to be called boy, but his
glory is to subdue men. Adieu, valour; rust, rapier;
be still, drum; for your manager is in love; yea,
he loveth. Assist me, some extemporal god of rhyme,
for I am sure I shall turn sonnet. Devise, wit;
write, pen; for I am for whole volumes in folio.

Stealing into the Capulets' garden at night after meeting their daughter at their party, Romeo extols the beauty of Juliet which he compares to the glorious sun. More unusually, he then goes on to envy her gloves for their privilege of being so close to her skin. This analogy would have been close at hand for Shakespeare (pardon the pun), whose father was a glove maker. This is one of Shakespeare's most celebrated speeches.

ROMEO
But soft! What light through yonder window breaks?
It is the East, and Juliet is the sun!
Arise, fair sun, and kill the envious moon,
Who is already sick and pale with grief
That thou her maid art far more fair than she.
Be not her maid, since she is envious.
Her vestal livery is but sick and green,
And none but fools do wear it. Cast it off.
It is my lady. O, it is my love!
O that she knew she were!
She speaks. Yet she says nothing. What of that?
Her eye discourses. I will answer it.
I am too bold. 'Tis not to me she speaks.
Two of the fairest stars in all the heaven,
Having some business, do entreat her eyes
To twinkle in their spheres till they return.
What if her eyes were there, they in her head?
The brightness of her cheek would shame those stars,
As daylight doth a lamp. Her eyes in heaven
Would through the airy region stream so bright
That birds would sing and think it were not night.
See how she leans her cheek upon her hand!
O that I were a glove upon that hand,
That I might touch that cheek!

July 31 | Romeo and Juliet | Act 4 Scene 5

This is Juliet's birthday, Lammas Eve, the day before what is sometimes known as 'Lamb-mass' on account of the ritual of sacrificing a young sheep on this date. The parallel between Juliet and a lamb to slaughter is obvious. The Nurse unwittingly draws the comparison to the forefront of our minds a moment before she discovers Juliet apparently dead in her bedroom. Although the Nurse's grief is premature – Juliet has only drugged herself unconscious temporarily – the quick shift from light-hearted teasing to deep-rooted sorrow is jarring and prefigures the disastrous conclusion.

NURSE
Mistress! What, mistress! Juliet! Fast, I warrant her, she.
Why, lamb! Why, lady! Fie, you slug-abed!
Why, love, I say! Madam! Sweet-heart! Why, bride!
What, not a word? You take your pennyworths now.
Sleep for a week. For the next night, I warrant,
The County Paris hath set up his rest
That you shall rest but little. God forgive me!
Marry, and amen! How sound is she asleep!
I needs must wake her. Madam, madam, madam!
Ay, let the County take you in your bed.
He'll fright you up, i'faith. Will it not be?

[*Undraws the curtains*]

What, dressed, and in your clothes, and down again?
I must needs wake you; Lady! lady! lady!
Alas, alas! Help, help! My lady's dead!
O weraday that ever I was born!
Some aqua vitae, ho! My lord! My lady!

313

August

Antony's defeat at the hands of Octavius Caesar (on 1 August 30 BCE) is devastating to his pride. He takes his own life in preference to being captured – this is how warriors should die, he thinks. Only, his suicide, triggered by false news to the effect that Cleopatra is dead, is among the clumsiest in drama – first he asks Eros to kill him, who baulks at the request and takes his own life to avoid killing his master; then he stabs himself but accidentally survives into a whole other scene in which he is reunited with Cleopatra one last time. These are the last of many intended last words.

ANTONY
The miserable change now at my end
Lament nor sorrow at, but please your thoughts
In feeding them with those my former fortunes,
Wherein I lived; the greatest prince o'th'world,
The noblest; and do now not basely die,
Not cowardly put off my helmet to
My countryman; a Roman, by a Roman
Valiantly vanquished. Now my spirit is going;
I can no more.

Friar Francis, the only man who believes in Hero's innocence, becomes instrumental in clearing her name when she is wrongly accused of adultery by Claudio. These are his wonderful words about how we do not prize what we have until after we have lost it.

FRIAR FRANCIS
For it so falls out
That what we have, we prize not to the worth
Whiles we enjoy it, but, being lacked and lost,
Why then we rack the value, then we find
The virtue that possession would not show us
Whiles it was ours. So will it fare with Claudio.
When he shall hear she died upon his words,
Th'idea of her life shall sweetly creep
Into his study of imagination,
And every organ of her life,
Shall come apparelled in more precious habit,
More moving-delicate, and full of life,
Into the eye and prospect of his soul
Than when she lived indeed.

Shakespeare stands out from his contemporaries for his attention to detail for even the lowliest of characters. During the shepherdess subplot, after Rosalind's counterproductive intervention, Phoebe cruelly asks Silvius to act as a messenger to the young 'Ganymede' despite his own heartfelt feelings for her.

PHOEBE
Think not I love him, though I ask for him.
'Tis but a peevish boy. Yet he talks well;
But what care I for words? Yet words do well
When he that speaks them pleases those that hear.
It is a pretty youth – not very pretty –
But, sure, he's proud – and yet his pride becomes him.
He'll make a proper man. The best thing in him
Is his complexion; and faster than his tongue
Did make offence, his eye did heal it up.
He is not very tall – yet for his years he's tall.
His leg is but so so – and yet 'tis well.
There was a pretty redness in his lip,
A little riper and more lusty red
Than that mixed in his cheek; 'twas just the difference
Betwixt the constant red and mingled damask.
There be some women, Silvius, had they marked him
In parcels, as I did, would have gone near
To fall in love with him; but, for my part,
I love him not nor hate him not; and yet
I have more cause to hate him than to love him,
For what had he to do to chide at me?
He said mine eyes were black and my hair black,
And, now I am remembered, scorned at me;
I marvel why I answered not again.
But that's all one; omittance is no quittance.

The Countess Olivia has fallen in love with Viola, disguised as
'Cesario', who had been sent to woo her on behalf of the Duke
Orsino. She repeats their encounter to herself and commands
her steward Malvolio, who harbours a secret love for his
mistress, to coax the young 'man' back by the use of a ring.

OLIVIA
'What is your parentage?'
'Above my fortunes, yet my state is well.
I am a gentleman.' I'll be sworn thou art.
Thy tongue, thy face, thy limbs, actions, and spirit
Do give thee fivefold blazon. Not too fast! soft, soft –
Unless the master were the man. How now?
Even so quickly may one catch the plague?
Methinks I feel this youth's perfections,
With an invisible and subtle stealth,
To creep in at mine eyes. Well, let it be!
What ho, Malvolio!

[*Re-enter* MALVOLIO]
MALVOLIO
Here, madam, at your service.

OLIVIA
Run after that same peevish messenger,
The County's man. He left this ring behind him,
Would I or not. Tell him, I'll none of it.
Desire him not to flatter with his lord,
Nor hold him up with hopes; I am not for him.
If that the youth will come this way tomorrow,
I'll give him reasons for't. Hie thee, Malvolio!

MALVOLIO
Madam, I will.

[*Exit*]

OLIVIA
I do I know not what, and fear to find
Mine eye too great a flatterer for my mind.
Fate, show thy force; ourselves we do not owe.
What is decreed must be, and be this so.

August 5 | Twelfth Night | Act 2 Scene 2

Olivia's ring duly arrives with Viola, who obviously doesn't recognize it. She cottons on to what confusion her male disguise has caused and is mortified by her conclusions. She identifies with Olivia's situation, woman to woman, as another who is suffering the pangs of an unrequited love.

VIOLA
I left no ring with her; what means this lady?
Fortune forbid my outside have not charmed her!
She made good view of me, indeed so much
That – methought – her eyes had lost her tongue,
For she did speak in starts, distractedly.
She loves me, sure, the cunning of her passion
Invites me in this churlish messenger.
None of my lord's ring? Why, he sent her none.
I am the man! If it be so – as 'tis –
Poor lady, she were better love a dream.
Disguise, I see thou art a wickedness
Wherein the pregnant enemy does much.
How easy is it for the proper false
In women's waxen hearts to set their forms.
Alas, our frailty is the cause, not we,
For such as we are made, if such we be.
How will this fadge? my master loves her dearly;
And I, poor monster, fond as much on him;
And she, mistaken, seems to dote on me.
What will become of this? As I am man,
My state is desperate for my master's love.
As I am woman – now alas the day,
What thriftless sighs shall poor Olivia breathe!
O time, thou must untangle this, not I!
It is too hard a knot for me t'untie.

320

Anne Shakespeare née Hathaway's grave bears the inscription
'Here lyeth interred the body of Anne wife of William
Shakespeare who departed this life the 6th day of August 1623
being of the age of 67 yeares'. She was a farmer's daughter
and therefore likely to have been illiterate – in which case
she would not have been able to read any of her husband's
work. Just as well, really, as the 'dark lady' to whom some
of the sonnets are addressed is, in all likelihood, not her.
In Shakespeare's will, she is left his 'second best bed', and
speculation is ablaze as to what on earth this referred to – was
the 'best bed' for guests and therefore this was their marital
bed? Or was this legacy an insult? One surviving anecdote of
Shakespeare's life relates how his star actor Richard Burbage
had arranged to meet a woman smitten with his performance
as Richard III, but Shakespeare arrived first for the
assignation, reportedly quipping that 'William the Conqueror
was before Richard the Third.' We do not know what words
were read at Anne's funeral, but many have used the elegy
spoken by Guiderius and Arviragus over the supposed pageboy
Fidele in *Cymbeline*. Somehow in the theatre the fact that we
know that Fidele is not really dead, and is really these boys'
unknown sister in disguise, does not make these words any
less poignant.

GUIDERIUS
Fear no more the heat o'th'sun,
Nor the furious winter's rages.
Thou thy worldly task hast done,
Home art gone and ta'en thy wages.
Golden lads and girls all must,
As chimney-sweepers, come to dust.

ARVIRAGUS
Fear no more the frown o'th'great,
Thou art past the tyrant's stroke.
Care no more to clothe and eat,
To thee the reed is as the oak.
The sceptre, learning, physic, must
All follow this and come to dust.

GUIDERIUS
Fear no more the lightning flash,

ARVIRAGUS
Nor th'all-dreaded thunder-stone.

GUIDERIUS
Fear not slander, censure rash.

ARVIRAGUS
Thou hast finished joy and moan.

GUIDERIUS and ARVIRAGUS
All lovers young, all lovers must
Consign to thee and come to dust.

GUIDERIUS
No exorciser harm thee,

ARVIRAGUS
Nor no witchcraft charm thee.

GUIDERIUS
Ghost unlaid forbear thee.

ARVIRAGUS
Nothing ill come near thee.

GUIDERIUS and ARVIRAGUS
Quiet consummation have,
And renownèd be thy grave.

In these famous lines, Falstaff, who has been preserving his own life by pretending to be dead, reasons himself into claiming that he slew the notorious Harry Hotspur (Sir Henry Percy), after discovering his body on the battlefield.

FALSTAFF
Counterfeit? I lie, I am no counterfeit, To die
is to be a counterfeit, for he is but the
counterfeit of a man who hath not the life of a man.
But to counterfeit dying, when a man thereby
liveth, is to be no counterfeit, but the true and
perfect image of life indeed. The better part of
valour is discretion, in the which better part I
have saved my life. Zounds, I am afraid of this
gunpowder Percy, though he be dead. How if he
should counterfeit too and rise? By my faith, I am
afraid he would prove the better counterfeit.
Therefore I'll make him sure, yea, and I'll swear I
killed him. Why may not he rise as well as I?
Nothing confutes me but eyes, and nobody sees me.
Therefore, sirrah,

[*Stabbing him*]
with a new wound in your thigh, come you along with me.

[*Takes up* HOTSPUR *on his back*]

On 8 August 1588, Elizabeth I addressed her troops at Tilbury.
They were readying themselves to repel the armies of the
Spanish Armada – which, unbeknownst to them, had already
been dispersed by fireships and gales. Her rousing words
reportedly went down a storm, and her much-quoted speech
containing the line 'I know I have the body of a weak, feeble
woman; but I have the heart and stomach of a king, and a
king of England too' is as likely as not to have been authentic.
Shakespeare's Henry V invites flattering parallels with the
Queen, especially in his power of oratory: here he rallies his
outnumbered army before the Battle of Agincourt.

KING HENRY V
What's he that wishes so?
My cousin Westmoreland? No, my fair cousin.
If we are marked to die, we are enow
To do our country loss: and if to live,
The fewer men, the greater share of honour.
God's will! I pray thee wish not one man more.
By Jove, I am not covetous for gold,
Nor care I who doth feed upon my cost;
It yearns me not if men my garments wear;
Such outward things dwell not in my desires.
But if it be a sin to covet honour,
I am the most offending soul alive.
No, faith, my coz, wish not a man from England:
God's peace! I would not lose so great an honour
As one man more methinks would share from me
For the best hope I have. O, do not wish one more!
Rather proclaim it, Westmoreland, through my host,
That he which hath no stomach to this fight,

Let him depart: his passport shall be made,
And crowns for convoy put into his purse.
We would not die in that man's company
That fears his fellowship to die with us.

August 9 | A Midsummer Night's Dream |
Act 3 Scene 1

Bottom, the asinine and now literally ass-headed amateur
thespian, here wakes Titania with his inane singing, as he tries
to lift his own spirits after being 'translated' (in his words)
into his strange present form. His absurd song is overheard by
none other than the Queen of the Fairies herself, who is under
the effects of a love potion and consequently intoxicated by
the sound. The gulf between these two characters makes the
prospect of them together marvellously comic.

BOTTOM
[*Sings*]
The ousel cock so black of hue,
With orange-tawny bill,
The throstle with his note so true,
The wren with little quill.

TITANIA
[*Wakes*] What angel wakes me from my flowery bed?

BOTTOM
[*Sings*]
The finch, the sparrow, and the lark,
The plainsong cuckoo grey,
Whose note full many a man doth mark,
And dares not answer 'Nay'
for, indeed, who would set his wit to so foolish
a bird? Who would give a bird the lie, though he cry
'cuckoo' never so?

TITANIA
I pray thee, gentle mortal, sing again!
Mine ear is much enamoured of thy note.
So is mine eye enthrallèd to thy shape,
And thy fair virtue's force perforce doth move me
On the first view to say, to swear, I love thee.

August 10 | Henry VI, Part 1 | Act 1 Scene 1

A messenger brings the account of Lord Talbot's defeat to the ears of the young Henry VI, over whom the lord had served as Lord Protector. He is describing events following the Battle of Patay on 18 June 1429, in which Talbot was captured by the French (though in the play it is moved seven years earlier to coincide with the funeral of Henry V – the date 'tenth of August' for the skirmish appears nowhere in Shakespeare's sources, and must have been given to tighten the narrative structure). Talbot was a classic English hero for schoolboys when Shakespeare was growing up, and the news of his overthrow would have struck a chord on and off stage in the first performances. A certain 'Sir John Fastolf' features in the messenger's report, acting with a familiar cowardice – but the Sir John Fastolf we know from *Henry IV* would not be written until eight years later.

MESSENGER
O, no; wherein Lord Talbot was o'erthrown.
The circumstance I'll tell you more at large.
The tenth of August last this dreadful lord,
Retiring from the siege of Orleans,
Having full scarce six thousand in his troop.
By three and twenty thousand of the French
Was round encompassèd and set upon.
No leisure had he to enrank his men;
He wanted pikes to set before his archers;
Instead whereof, sharp stakes plucked out of hedges
They pitchèd in the ground confusedly
To keep the horsemen off from breaking in.
More than three hours the fight continuèd,
Where valiant Talbot, above human thought,
Enacted wonders with his sword and lance.
Hundreds he sent to hell, and none durst stand him;

Here, there, and everywhere enraged he slew.
The French exclaimed the devil was in arms;
All the whole army stood agazed on him.
His soldiers spying his undaunted spirit,
'À Talbot! À Talbot!' crièd out amain,
And rushed into the bowels of the battle.
Here had the conquest fully been sealed up
If Sir John Fastolf had not played the coward.
He, being in the vaward, placed behind
With purpose to relieve and follow them,
Cowardly fled, not having struck one stroke.
Hence grew the general wreck and massacre;
Enclosèd were they with their enemies.
A base Walloon, to win the Dauphin's grace,
Thrust Talbot with a spear into the back,
Whom all France, with their chief assembled strength,
Durst not presume to look once in the face.

August 11 | King John | Act 3 Scene 4

Shakespeare's only son Hamnet died at the age of eleven, and
was buried on 11 August 1596. Scholars have debated how soon
after this *Hamlet* was written, but the relationship between
this play and Shakespeare's son is at best superficial, at worst
conjectural. Part of Shakespeare's artistry was to make tracing
his own experiences impossible on the evidence of his plays,
such was the unique breadth and depth of his empathy. In *King
John* (which was probably written in 1596), believing her son
Arthur, who has been taken captive by John, to be doomed,
Constance bewails her loss every bit as convincingly as if this
were Shakespeare's own grief – perhaps it is.

CONSTANCE
Grief fills the room up of my absent child,
Lies in his bed, walks up and down with me,
Puts on his pretty looks, repeats his words,
Remembers me of all his gracious parts,
Stuffs out his vacant garments with his form;
Then have I reason to be fond of grief?
Fare you well. Had you such a loss as I,
I could give better comfort than you do.
[*She unbinds her hair*]
I will not keep this form upon my head
When there is such disorder in my wit.
O Lord! My boy, my Arthur, my fair son!
My life, my joy, my food, my all the world!
My widow-comfort, and my sorrows' cure!

Antony and Cleopatra are finally united in death, and historical records tell us they were buried together though their tomb has never been found. After Antony's suicide, Cleopatra has her attendant, Charmian, dress her in royal attire before she administers a fatal asp's bite to herself. The stage directions are implicit in the speech. This was often done instead of providing separate stage directions in Shakespeare's plays, as actors would only be given their part of the script. The habit of distributing part-scripts (rolled into scrolls) to actors is where the term 'role' came from.

CLEOPATRA
Give me my robe; put on my crown; I have
Immortal longings in me. Now no more
The juice of Egypt's grape shall moist this lip.
Yare, yare, good Iras; quick – methinks I hear
Antony call. I see him rouse himself
To praise my noble act. I hear him mock
The luck of Caesar, which the gods give men
To excuse their after wrath. Husband, I come.
Now to that name my courage prove my title!
I am fire and air; my other elements
I give to baser life. So, have you done?
Come then, and take the last warmth of my lips.
Farewell, kind Charmian, Iras, long farewell.
[*Kisses them.* IRAS *falls and dies*]
Have I the aspic in my lips? Dost fall?
If thou and nature can so gently part,
The stroke of death is as a lover's pinch,
Which hurts, and is desired. Dost thou lie still?
If thus thou vanishest, thou tell'st the world
It is not worth leave-taking.

In contrast to the intense but mature love that Cleopatra
bears for Antony, Juliet's love of Romeo has all the marks
of inexperience though it is no less intense. Speaking to
Romeo from her window, Juliet talks of her 'maiden blush'
being masked by the night, though her naivety shows in her
embarrassment at her post-party confessions of love being
overheard by the very person she is talking about.

JULIET
Thou knowest the mask of night is on my face,
Else would a maiden blush bepaint my cheek
For that which thou hast heard me speak tonight.
Fain would I dwell on form – fain, fain deny
What I have spoke. But farewell compliment!
Dost thou love me? I know thou wilt say 'Ay'.
And I will take thy word. Yet, if thou swearest,
Thou mayst prove false. At lovers' perjuries,
Then say, Jove laughs. O gentle Romeo,
If thou dost love, pronounce it faithfully.
Or if thou thinkest I am too quickly won,
I'll frown, and be perverse, and say thee nay,
So thou wilt woo. But else, not for the world.
In truth, fair Montague, I am too fond,
And therefore thou mayst think my 'haviour light.
But trust me, gentleman, I'll prove more true
Than those that have more cunning to be strange.
I should have been more strange, I must confess,
But that thou overheardest, ere I was ware,
My true-love passion. Therefore pardon me,
And not impute this yielding to light love,
Which the dark night hath so discoverèd.

August 14 | Macbeth | Act 2 Scene 1

On 14 August 1040 King Duncan I of Alba (Scotland) was
slain in battle by his cousin Macbeth, at Pitgaveny near Elgin,
delivering the latter the crown. In Shakespeare's telling,
Macbeth is pricked on to cold-blooded murder by a combination
of his and his wife's ambition for him to become king. His
treasonous act is preceded by one of the most famous soliloquies
of all time.

MACBETH
Is this a dagger which I see before me,
The handle toward my hand? Come, let me clutch thee –
I have thee not and yet I see thee still!
Art thou not, fatal vision, sensible
To feeling as to sight? Or art thou but
A dagger of the mind, a false creation,
Proceeding from the heat-oppressèd brain?
I see thee yet, in form as palpable
As this which now I draw.
Thou marshall'st me the way that I was going,
And such an instrument I was to use. –
Mine eyes are made the fools o' the other senses,
Or else worth all the rest. – I see thee still;
And, on thy blade and dudgeon, gouts of blood,
Which was not so before. There's no such thing.
It is the bloody business which informs
Thus to mine eyes. Now o'er the one half-world
Nature seems dead, and wicked dreams abuse
The curtained sleep. Witchcraft celebrates
Pale Hecat's offerings; and withered murder,
Alarumed by his sentinel the wolf,
Whose howl's his watch, thus with his stealthy pace,
With Tarquin's ravishing strides, towards his design

Moves like a ghost. Thou sure and firm-set earth,
Hear not my steps, which way they walk, for fear
Thy very stones prate of my whereabout
And take the present horror from the time
Which now suits with it. – Whiles I threat, he lives:
Words to the heat of deeds too cold breath gives.
[*A bell rings*]
I go, and it is done; the bell invites me.
Hear it not, Duncan, for it is a knell
That summons thee to heaven or to hell.

August 15 | Macbeth | Act 5 Scene 6

Macbeth is encouraged in his murderous deeds by an apparition conjured by the witches, who says 'Be bloody, bold, and resolute; laugh to scorn / The power of man, for none of woman born / Shall harm Macbeth'. Well that pretty much rules out everyone – but not Macduff, whose family Macbeth had ordered unwisely to be slaughtered. As he explains in Macbeth's final moments, he was 'from his mother's womb / Untimely ripped', in other words by what we now call a caesarean section and not of woman born at all.

MACBETH
Thou losest labour.
As easy mayst thou the intrenchant air
With thy keen sword impress, as make me bleed.
Let fall thy blade on vulnerable crests,
I bear a charmèd life which must not yield
To one of woman born.

MACDUFF
Despair thy charm,
And let the angel whom thou still hast served
Tell thee Macduff was from his mother's womb
Untimely ripped.

MACBETH
Accursèd be that tongue that tells me so;
For it hath cowed my better part of man;
And be these juggling fiends no more believed
That palter with us in a double sense,
That keep the word of promise to our ear
And break it to our hope. I'll not fight with thee.

In amongst the murder, mutilations and beheadings in *Titus Andronicus*, the violence takes a turn for the ridiculous when an innocent fly is caught up in it. Titus becomes instantly furious at his brother Marcus for killing the harmless insect. This is pretty rich coming from the man who in the first scene presided over the ritual sacrifice of two of Tamora's sons – if he had shown this much empathy in those circumstances, he would not have incurred her bloody revenge on his own family. In an attempt to placate Titus, Marcus tells him to think of the fly as Aaron the Moor. Titus consequently joins in the killing, as he despises the Moor whose race he likens to the colour of the fly.

[MARCUS *strikes the dish with a knife*]
TITUS
What dost thou strike at, Marcus, with thy knife?

MARCUS
At that that I have killed, my lord – a fly.

TITUS
Out on thee, murderer! Thou kill'st my heart.
Mine eyes are cloyed with view of tyranny.
A deed of death done on the innocent
Becomes not Titus' brother. Get thee gone,
I see thou art not for my company.

MARCUS
Alas, my lord, I have but killed a fly.

TITUS
'But'? How if that fly had a father and mother?
How would he hang his slender gilded wings

And buzz lamenting doings in the air.
Poor harmless fly,
That with his pretty buzzing melody
Came here to make us merry, and thou hast killed him.

MARCUS
Pardon me, sir. It was a black ill-favored fly,
Like to the Empress' Moor. Therefore I killed him.

TITUS
 O, O, O!
Then pardon me for reprehending thee,
For thou hast done a charitable deed.
Give me thy knife. I will insult on him,
Flattering myself, as if it were the Moor
Come hither purposely to poison me.
There's for thyself, and that's for Tamora.
[*Striking the fly*] Ah, sirrah!
Yet I think we are not brought so low
But that between us we can kill a fly
That comes in likeness of a coal-black Moor.

MARCUS
Alas, poor man, grief has so wrought on him
He takes false shadows for true substances.

TITUS
Come, take away. Lavinia, go with me;
I'll to thy closet and go read with thee
Sad stories chancèd in the times of old.
Come, boy, and go with me; thy sight is young
And thou shalt read when mine begin to dazzle.

Harvest-home festival was held in mid-August and was a cause of celebration. All being well, it would mark the beginning of a time of plenty and the end of hard manual work. Workmen of the fields are honoured in these lines from the masque which Prospero conjures for his daughter Miranda's engagement, with his spirits representing goddesses who speak in couplets and language characteristic of this kind of entertainment. The idealization of pastoral life, as well as the presence of ancient deities like the water spirits known as Naiads, are mainstays of Jacobean masque conventions.

IRIS
You nymphs, called naiads, of the windring brooks,
With your sedged crowns and ever-harmless looks,
Leave your crisp channels, and on this green land
Answer your summons; Juno does command.
Come, temperate nymphs, and help to celebrate
A contract of true love. Be not too late.
[*Enter certain nymphs*]
You sunburnt sicklemen, of August weary,
Come hither from the furrow, and be merry,
Make holiday; your rye-straw hats put on,
And these fresh nymphs encounter every one
In country footing.

Richard II's gardeners give us a view of the tumultuous court
from the outside, likening the governing of a kingdom to the
maintenance of a garden. This is a compelling metaphor that
occurs more than once in Shakespeare's works, which helps the
laymen (and the audience) get a handle on the politics at play.
The gardeners' assessment of Richard's affairs is overheard by
the Queen, who is worryingly far less informed than they are.
A fine example of the wisdom of the common man – if only the
King had been as careful with his kingdom as the gardeners are
with his garden.

GARDENER
O, what pity is it
That he had not so trimmed and dressed his land
As we this garden! We at time of year
Do wound the bark, the skin of our fruit trees,
Lest being overproud in sap and blood
With too much riches it confound itself.
Had he done so to great and growing men
They might have lived to bear, and he to taste
Their fruits of duty. Superfluous branches
We lop away that bearing boughs may live.
Had he done so, himself had borne the crown
Which waste of idle hours hath quite thrown down.

Shakespeare is unafraid of recycling his ideas. The gardening allegory of *Richard II* is taken up by *Othello*. However, Iago, who we will discover is a master manipulator, more sinisterly applies the metaphor of the garden to our body and interprets our mind to be the gardener. According to the logic by which he here dissuades his dupe Roderigo from taking his own life, our mind dictates our emotions and desires: even love falls under its control. We have no reason to believe that Shakespeare ever travelled to Venice or Cyprus, the play's settings, and it seems that the nettles and herbs Iago is 'planting' are very much sourced from Shakespeare's Warwickshire roots.

IAGO
Virtue! A fig! 'Tis in ourselves that we are thus,
or thus. Our bodies are our gardens, to the which
our wills are gardeners. So that if we will plant
nettles or sow lettuce, set hyssop and weed up
thyme, supply it with one gender of herbs or
distract it with many, either to have it sterile
with idleness or manured with industry, why the
power and corrigible authority of this lies in our
wills. If the beam of our lives had not one
scale of reason to poise another of sensuality, the
blood and baseness of our natures would conduct us
to most preposterous conclusions. But we have
reason to cool our raging motions, our carnal
stings, our unbitted lusts: whereof I take this, that
you call love, to be a sect or scion.

August 20 | Richard III | Act 4 Scene 1

Richard III's command of language and incomparable
arrogance enable him to woo Lady Anne, despite the fact he is
the 'fiend' who killed both her husband and her father-in-law,
Henry VI. Astonishingly, after only a brief exchange, she agrees
to marry him. Even Lady Anne herself is dismayed at how this
came to pass.

LADY ANNE
No? Why? When he that is my husband now
Came to me as I followed Henry's corse,
When scarce the blood was well washed from his hands
Which issued from my other angel husband
And that dear saint which then I weeping followed –
O, when, I say, I looked on Richard's face,
This was my wish: 'Be thou,' quoth I, 'accursed
For making me, so young, so old a widow!
And, when thou wed'st, let sorrow haunt thy bed;
And be thy wife, if any be so mad,
More miserable by the life of thee
As thou hast made me by my dear lord's death!'
Lo, ere I can repeat this curse again,
Within so small a time, my woman's heart
Grossly grew captive to his honey words
And proved the subject of my own soul's curse,
Which ever since hath kept my eyes from rest;
For never yet one hour in his bed
Did I enjoy the golden dew of sleep,
But with his timorous dreams was still awaked.
Besides, he hates me for my father Warwick,
And will, no doubt, shortly be rid of me.

August 21 | Richard III | Act 5 Scene 3

Richard's 'honey words', which were characteristic of his
intellectual superiority and immoral nature, turn to questions
and fragments on the night before the Battle of Bosworth,
which was fought on 22 August 1485. This battle was to be his
last. Some premonition of this leaves the King divided against
himself, friendless and guilty, as the ghosts of his victims come
to haunt him.

KING RICHARD III
Give me another horse! Bind up my wounds!
Have mercy, Jesu! – Soft! I did but dream.
O coward conscience, how dost thou afflict me!
The lights burn blue. It is now dead midnight.
Cold fearful drops stand on my trembling flesh.
What do I fear? Myself? There's none else by.
Richard loves Richard: that is, I am I.
Is there a murderer here? No. Yes, I am.
Then fly. What, from myself? Great reason why –
Lest I revenge. Myself upon myself?
Alack, I love myself. Wherefore? For any good
That I myself have done unto myself?
O no! Alas, I rather hate myself
For hateful deeds committed by myself.
I am a villain. Yet I lie, I am not.
Fool, of thyself speak well. Fool, do not flatter.
My conscience hath a thousand several tongues,
And every tongue brings in a several tale,
And every tale condemns me for a villain.
Perjury, perjury, in the highest degree.
Murder, stern murder, in the direst degree,
All several sins, all used in each degree,
Throng to the bar, crying all 'Guilty! Guilty!'

I shall despair. There is no creature loves me;
And if I die, no soul shall pity me.
Nay, wherefore should they, since that I myself
Find in myself no pity to myself?
Methought the souls of all that I had murdered
Came to my tent, and every one did threat
Tomorrow's vengeance on the head of Richard.

August 22 | Richard III | Act 5 Scene 4

On 22 August 1485, Richard III was defeated at the Battle
of Bosworth by Henry, Earl of Richmond (who was crowned
Henry VII, the first Tudor monarch, destined to be grandfather
of Elizabeth I). After spending the play displaying an intricate
gift for the weight of words, and the relationship between what
is seen and what is meant, Richard loses at Bosworth Field
when Richmond disguised several decoys as himself. Desperate
to continue the fight even though he is now alone and on foot,
Richard is reduced to bargaining his whole kingdom for a horse.
These are the last words he speaks.

KING RICHARD III
A horse! A horse! My kingdom for a horse!

CATESBY
Withdraw, my lord. I'll help you to a horse.

KING RICHARD III
Slave, I have set my life upon a cast,
And I will stand the hazard of the die.
I think there be six Richmonds in the field;
Five have I slain today instead of him.
A horse! A horse! My kingdom for a horse!

Arviragus and Guiderius, Cymbeline's sons who were
kidnapped as babies, have befriended a lost boy called Fidele,
who wandered into their cave. This boy is really their sister
Imogen, who is in disguise to avoid a plot to have her killed.
'His' boyish appearance doesn't prevent the princes speaking of
'him' in the warmest of terms, and their language wouldn't be
out of place in a 'fair youth' sonnet. After Imogen takes what she
believes is a headache remedy but which turns out to be a Friar
Lawrence-style drug for simulating death, Arviragus believes
Fidele is dead, and speaks his sorrow while vowing to strew 'his'
grave with the flowers of summer, and then with the vegetation
of all the other seasons too.

ARVIRAGUS
With fairest flowers
Whilst summer lasts, and I live here, Fidele,
I'll sweeten thy sad grave. Thou shalt not lack
The flower that's like thy face, pale primrose, nor
The azured harebell, like thy veins; no, nor
The leaf of eglantine, whom not to slander,
Outsweet'ned not thy breath. The ruddock would
With charitable bill – O bill sore shaming
Those rich-left heirs that let their fathers lie
Without a monument – bring thee all this,
Yea, and furred moss besides, when flowers are none,
To winter-ground thy corpse.

St Bartholomew's Day on 24 August is the hottest of the summer according to *Henry V* and was the date for the largest and most spectacular fair in London. *Bartholomew Fair* became the title and setting of a Jacobean comedy by Shakespeare's friend Ben Jonson, who was much more inclined to set his action in the contemporary city and regularly got in trouble for doing so. The fair was established by Henry II's jester to raise money for a priory and a hospital – St Bartholomew's hospital – which still stands today. The dazzling jamboree was most renowned for its cloth sale, which probably provided costumes for the theatres, and the hodgepodge of classes and professions would have been of interest to any storyteller hungry for inspiration. A tradition of selling roasted pig at the fair became a common subject of allusion. Doll Tearsheet compares her friend Falstaff's figure to one.

FALSTAFF
[. . .] Sit on my knee, Doll.
A rascal bragging slave! The rogue fled from me
like quicksilver.

DOLL TEARSHEET
I' faith, and thou followed'st him like a church.
Thou whoreson little tidy Bartholomew boar-pig,
when wilt thou leave fighting a-days, and foining
a-nights, and begin to patch up thine old body for heaven?

[*Enter, behind,* HAL *and* POINS, *disguised as drawers*]

FALSTAFF
Peace, good Doll, do not speak like a death's-head;
do not bid me remember mine end.

The Moroccan ambassador came to London in August 1600 and was greeted with much fanfare and more than a little interest. The diarist John Chamberlain wrote that it was 'no small honour to us that nations so far remote, and every way different, should meet here to admire the glory and magnificence of our Queen'. Another chronicler reported that the ambassador and his retenue 'are strangely attired and behavioured', that they 'killed all their own meat within their house' and 'turn their faces eastward when they kill any thing; they use beads, and pray to Saints'. We know that the ambassador spent time at court and it is not impossible that Shakespeare and his company performed for him. At the very least the dramatist would have known of the visit and might have seen his portrait, the first of a Muslim known to be painted in England, which now hangs in the Shakespeare Institute in Stratford-upon-Avon. *Othello* was written shortly after the visit. Here Othello, whose language bears the marks of his wide travels, describes how Desdemona was enraptured (but not bewitched) by his tales of woe.

OTHELLO
I did consent,
And often did beguile her of her tears
When I did speak of some distressful stroke
That my youth suffered. My story being done,
She gave me for my pains a world of sighs:
She swore, in faith, 'twas strange, 'twas passing strange,
'Twas pitiful, 'twas wondrous pitiful;
She wished she had not heard it, yet she wished
That heaven had made her such a man. She thanked me,
And bade me, if I had a friend that loved her,
I should but teach him how to tell my story,

And that would woo her. Upon this hint I spake:
She loved me for the dangers I had passed,
And I loved her, that she did pity them.
This only is the witchcraft I have used.

The unravelling of Othello's trust in Desdemona, his unwaveringly virtuous wife, is heartbreaking. Iago has had Emilia swipe a special handkerchief which Othello gave Desdemona. Othello is left to suspect that his wife has made a gift of it to another man. And the stakes of that suspected betrayal are set out in no uncertain terms.

OTHELLO
That handkerchief
Did an Egyptian to my mother give:
She was a charmer, and could almost read
The thoughts of people. She told her, while she kept it,
'Twould make her amiable and subdue my father
Entirely to her love; but, if she lost it
Or made gift of it, my father's eye
Should hold her loathèd, and his spirits should hunt
After new fancies. She, dying, gave it me,
And bid me, when my fate would have me wive,
To give it her. I did so; and take heed on't:
Make it a darling, like your precious eye.
To lose' or give't away were such perdition
As nothing else could match.
A sibyl, that had numbered in the world
The sun to course to hundred compasses,
In her prophetic fury sewed the work:
The worms were hallowed that did breed the silk,
And it was dyed in mummy which the skilful
Conserved of maidens' hearts.

August 27 | The Merchant of Venice | Act 2 Scene 6

Shylock's daughter Jessica, like Desdemona, forsakes her father in pursuit of love. Disguising herself as a boy, she elopes with Lorenzo, taking her father Shylock's gold. She salts the wound by converting from Judaism to Christianity. In contrast to Othello's wife, Jessica is perceptibly uneasy about the decision love is guiding her to take. The phrase 'love is blind' first appeared in Chaucer's 'Merchant's Tale', and was propelled into common usage by Shakespeare, who uses it here.

[*Enter* JESSICA, *above, in boy's clothes*]

JESSICA
Who are you? Tell me for more certainty,
Albeit I'll swear that I do know your tongue.

LORENZO
Lorenzo, and thy love.

JESSICA
Lorenzo certain, and my love indeed,
For who love I so much? And now who knows
But you, Lorenzo, whether I am yours?

LORENZO
Heaven and thy thoughts are witness that thou art.

JESSICA
Here, catch this casket; it is worth the pains.
I am glad 'tis night, you do not look on me,
For I am much ashamed of my exchange.
But love is blind, and lovers cannot see

The pretty follies that themselves commit;
For if they could, Cupid himself would blush
To see me thus transformèd to a boy.

LORENZO
Descend, for you must be my torchbearer.

JESSICA
What, must I hold a candle to my shames?
They in themselves, good sooth, are too too light.
Why, 'tis an office of discovery, love,
And I should be obscured.

LORENZO
So are you, sweet,
Even in the lovely garnish of a boy.
But come at once,
For the close night doth play the runaway,
And we are stayed for at Bassanio's feast.

JESSICA
I will make fast the doors, and gild myself
With some more ducats, and be with you straight.

Paulina in *The Winter's Tale* boldly takes Hermione's part and stands up to the King, Leontes, when he falsely accuses his wife of adultery. Paulina hopes that her powers as a petitioner will soften the King's cold accusations, especially with the aid of the newborn princess Perdita in her arms.

PAULINA
I dare be sworn.
These dangerous, unsafe lunes i'th'King, beshrew them!
He must be told on't, and he shall. The office
Becomes a woman best. I'll take't upon me.
If I prove honey-mouthed, let my tongue blister,
And never to my red-looked anger be
The trumpet any more. Pray you, Emilia,
Commend my best obedience to the Queen.
If she dares trust me with her little babe,
I'll show't the King, and undertake to be
Her advocate to th'loud'st. We do not know
How he may soften at the sight o'th'child:
The silence often of pure innocence
Persuades when speaking fails.

August 29 | The Taming of the Shrew | Act 5 Scene 1

Petruchio consistently refers to his reluctant wife Katherine as 'Kate'. Depending on your perspective, Petruchio's insistence on using the diminutive form is either a symptom of their growing intimacy, or a belittling strategy to undermine Katherine's sense of herself. Their exchanges are often spoken in prose, unusual for high-born characters and pairs of lovers – we are being presented with either a relaxed couple bedding into a normal married life, or a very unrefined dissonance between the two.

KATHERINE
Husband, let's follow to see the end of this ado.

PETRUCHIO
First kiss me, Kate, and we will.

KATHERINE
What, in the midst of the street?

PETRUCHIO
What, art thou ashamed of me?

KATHERINE
No, sir, God forbid – but ashamed to kiss.

PETRUCHIO
Why then, let's home again. [*to Grumio*] Come, sirrah, let's away.

KATHERINE
Nay, I will give thee a kiss. [*She kisses him*] Now pray thee, love, stay.

August 30 | Sonnet 5

The sonneteer expends another effort at persuading the subject to procreate to ensure the beauty they possess survives their decline and death, symbolized in the approaching winter.

Those hours that with gentle work did frame,
The lovely gaze where every eye doth dwell
Will play the tyrants to the very same,
And that unfair which fairly doth excel:
For never resting time leads summer on,
To hideous winter and confounds him there,
Sap check'd with frost and lusty leaves quite gone,
Beauty o'ersnow'd and bareness everywhere:
Then were not summer's distillation left
A liquid prisoner pent in walls of glass,
Beauty's effect with beauty were bereft,
Nor it nor no remembrance what it was.
   But flowers distill'd though they with winter meet,
    Leese but their show, their substance still lives sweet.

August 31 | A Midsummer Night's Dream | Act 5 Scene 1

The last day of summer concludes with the final summer's night. Puck's penultimate speech conjures the midnight goings-on of the fairy world.

PUCK
Now the hungry lion roars
And the wolf behowls the moon,
Whilst the heavy ploughman snores
All with weary task fordone.
Now the wasted brands do glow
Whilst the screech-owl, screeching loud,
Puts the wretch that lies in woe
In remembrance of a shroud.
Now it is the time of night
That the graves, all gaping wide,
Every one lets forth his sprite
In the churchway paths to glide.
And we fairies, that do run
By the triple Hecate's team,
From the presence of the sun
Following darkness like a dream,
Now are frolic. Not a mouse
Shall disturb this hallowed house.
I am sent with broom before
To sweep the dust behind the door.

September

Ariel is a 'fine spirit' under the power of Prospero, who had
released him from his imprisonment in a tree. He sings of
the life he will lead once released from his bonds of servitude,
flitting like a bumble bee from flower to flower by day, and
living free with the owls and the bats by night.

ARIEL
Where the bee sucks, there suck I,
In a cowslip's bell I lie;
There I couch when owls do cry.
On the bat's back I do fly
After summer merrily.
Merrily, merrily shall I live now,
Under the blossom that hangs on the bough.

September 2 | Antony and Cleopatra | Act 4 Scene 12

The deciding battle of the Roman civil wars that followed the death of Julius Caesar was won by Octavius Caesar against the lovelorn Antony on 2 September 31 BCE, at the Gulf of Actium. Enobarbus has urged his long-time friend not to take on Octavius at sea, but Antony ignores the advice and takes to the waves together with Cleopatra's forces. Antony initially gains the advantage but when the Egyptian Queen flees, he and his forces follow, and go on to lose heavily in the subsequent battle on land at Alexandria. He becomes convinced that Egypt is in cahoots with his enemies.

ANTONY
All is lost!
This foul Egyptian hath betrayèd me.
My fleet hath yielded to the foe, and yonder
They cast their caps up and carouse together
Like friends long lost. Triple-turned whore! 'Tis thou
Hast sold me to this novice, and my heart
Makes only wars on thee. Bid them all fly;
For when I am revenged upon my charm,
I have done all. Bid them all fly, begone!
[*Exit* SCARUS]
O sun, thy uprise shall I see no more.
Fortune and Antony part here; even here
Do we shake hands. All come to this? The hearts
That spanieled me at heels, to whom I gave
Their wishes, do discandy, melt their sweets
On blossoming Caesar; and this pine is barked
That overtopped them all. Betrayed I am.
O this false soul of Egypt! This grave charm,

Whose eye becked forth my wars, and called them home,
Whose bosom was my crownet, my chief end,
Like a right gipsy hath at fast and loose
Beguiled me to the very heart of loss.

September 3 | Henry V | Act 3 Scene 1

The Second World War broke out on 3 September 1939, during the course of which Prime Minister Winston Churchill invited the legendary actor Laurence Olivier to film a version of *Henry V*. Financed by the government, it was a critical and commercial success and an ingenious piece of wartime propaganda. A play full of rousing rhetoric and patriotic gumption, Shakespeare's original 1599 production would have served a similar purpose, drumming up a sense of national pride. However, Henry's own motivations aren't so easy to discern; his 'hard-favoured rage' is a 'disguise', making honour as much an empowering principle connected with kingly duty, as it may be an empty pretence, seeming to echo John Falstaff: 'What is that word "Honour"? Air.' Here he urges his troops not to abandon their attack on Harfleur.

KING HENRY V
Once more unto the breach, dear friends, once more,
Or close the wall up with our English dead!
In peace there's nothing so becomes a man
As modest stillness and humility:
But when the blast of war blows in our ears,
Then imitate the action of the tiger;
Stiffen the sinews, conjure up the blood,
Disguise fair nature with hard-favoured rage;
Then lend the eye a terrible aspect;
Let it pry through the portage of the head
Like the brass cannon; let the brow o'erwhelm it
As fearfully as doth a gallèd rock
O'erhang and jutty his confounded base,
Swilled with the wild and wasteful ocean.
Now set the teeth, and stretch the nostril wide,
Hold hard the breath, and bend up every spirit

To his full height! On, on, you noblest English,
Whose blood is fet from fathers of war-proof! –
Fathers that, like so many Alexanders,
Have in these parts from morn till even fought,
And sheathed their swords for lack of argument.
Dishonour not your mothers; now attest
That those whom you called fathers did beget you!
Be copy now to men of grosser blood,
And teach them how to war. And you, good yeoman,
Whose limbs were made in England, show us here
The mettle of your pasture; let us swear
That you are worth your breeding – which I doubt not;
For there is none of you so mean and base
That hath not noble lustre in your eyes.
I see you stand like greyhounds in the slips,
Straining upon the start. The game's afoot!
Follow your spirit, and upon this charge
Cry, 'God for Harry, England, and Saint George!'

Shakespeare is likely to have gone to the local grammar school in Stratford, where his studies would have included Latin and the art of rhetoric. The following exchange between the schoolmaster Hugh Evans, the foolish Mistress Page and her schoolboy son William (whom Shakespeare might have named after himself) riffs on misunderstandings and common half-remembered fragments of a standard Latin textbook which would have been in circulation during Shakespeare's time. The comedy of the absurd exchange derives from its senselessness, so it should take no enjoyment away from the scene if Latin is Greek to you.

MISTRESS PAGE
Sir Hugh, my husband says my son profits nothing in the world at his book. I pray you, ask him some questions in his accidence.

SIR HUGH EVANS
Come hither, William. Hold up your head. Come.

MISTRESS PAGE
Come on, sirrah. Hold up your head. Answer your master, be not afraid.

SIR HUGH EVANS
William, how many numbers is in nouns?

WILLIAM PAGE
Two.

MISTRESS QUICKLY
Truly, I thought there had been one number more,
because they say ' 'Od's nouns'.

SIR HUGH EVANS
Peace your tattlings. What is 'fair', William?

WILLIAM PAGE
Pulcher.

MISTRESS QUICKLY
Polecats! There are fairer things than polecats, sure.

SIR HUGH EVANS
You are a very simplicity 'oman. I pray you peace.
What is *lapis,* William?

WILLIAM PAGE
A stone.

SIR HUGH EVANS
And what is 'a stone,' William?

WILLIAM PAGE
A pebble.

SIR HUGH EVANS
No, it is *lapis.* I pray you, remember in your prain.

WILLIAM PAGE
Lapis.

SIR HUGH EVANS
That is a good William. What is he, William, that
does lend articles?

WILLIAM PAGE
Articles are borrowed of the pronoun, and be thus
declined: *Singulariter, nominativo, hic, haec, hoc.*

SIR HUGH EVANS
Nominativo, hig, hag, hog. Pray you mark:
genitivo, hujus. Well, what is your accusative case?

WILLIAM PAGE
Accusativo, hinc.

SIR HUGH EVANS
I pray you have your remembrance, child.
Accusativo, hung, hang, hog.

MISTRESS QUICKLY
'Hang-hog' is Latin for bacon, I warrant you.

SIR HUGH EVANS
Leave your prabbles, 'oman. What is the focative
case, William?

WILLIAM PAGE
O – *vocativo, O.*

SIR HUGH EVANS
Remember, William. Focative is *caret.*

MISTRESS QUICKLY
And that's a good root.

Polonius gives his son Laertes a long lecture of advice as he
leaves Elsinore to return to Paris. As with most parents keen
to impart their words of wisdom, just as you think they have
finished, there is yet more to come.

POLONIUS
Yet here, Laertes? Aboard, aboard, for shame!
The wind sits in the shoulder of your sail,
And you are stay'd for. There – my blessing with thee.
And these few precepts in thy memory
Look thou character. Give thy thoughts no tongue,
Nor any unproportioned thought his act.
Be thou familiar, but by no means vulgar.
Those friends thou hast, and their adoption tried,
Grapple them to thy soul with hoops of steel.
But do not dull thy palm with entertainment
Of each new-hatched, unfledged comrade. Beware
Of entrance to a quarrel. But being in,
Bear't that th'opposèd may beware of thee.
Give every man thy ear, but few thy voice.
Take each man's censure, but reserve thy judgment.
Costly thy habit as thy purse can buy,
But not express'd in fancy; rich, not gaudy;
For the apparel oft proclaims the man,
And they in France of the best rank and station
Are of a most select and generous chief in that.
Neither a borrower nor a lender be,
For loan oft loses both itself and friend,
And borrowing dulls the edge of husbandry.
This above all: to thine ownself be true,
And it must follow, as the night the day,
Thou canst not then be false to any man.
Farewell. My blessing season this in thee!

The popular 'Porter scene' in Macbeth is one of very few light moments in an otherwise unremittingly tense play. The scene eases the tension and provides comic relief after Duncan's murder. It is likely to have been written for Robert Armin, the successor to Will Kemp as the leading comic actor in Shakespeare's company. It is a rare occasion in the play when a character from a lower class is given an extended scene.

PORTER
Here's a knocking indeed! If a
man were porter of hell-gate he should have
old turning the key.
[*Knocking within*]
Knock, knock, knock! Who's there, i'the name of
Beelzebub? Here's a farmer, that hanged
himself on the expectation of plenty. Come in
time! Have napkins enow about you; here
you'll sweat for't.
[*Knocking within*]
Knock, knock! Who's there in the other devil's
name? Faith, here's an equivocator that could
swear in both the scales against either scale,
who committed treason enough for God's sake,
yet could not equivocate to heaven. O, come
in, equivocator.
[*Knocking within*]
Knock, knock, knock! Who's there? Faith, here's an
English tailor come hither for stealing out of
a French hose. Come in, tailor; here you may
roast your goose.
[*Knocking within*]
Knock, knock! Never at quiet! What are you? But

this place is too cold for hell. I'll devil-porter
it no further. I had thought to have let in
some of all professions that go the primrose
way to the everlasting bonfire.
[*Knocking within*]
Anon, anon! I pray you remember the porter.

September 7 | Henry VIII | Act 5 Scene 5

Apart from the 'Induction' to *The Taming of the Shrew*, in which a drunk tinker is tricked into believing he is a lord with the help of some Elizabethan touring actors, Shakespeare's *Henry VIII* is the closest the dramatist came to setting a play in his own time. The birth of Henry's daughter – on 7 September 1553 – the future Queen Elizabeth, is written in predictably flattering fashion, even though she had died a decade before the play was performed.

CRANMER
This royal infant – heaven still move about her! –
Though in her cradle, yet now promises
Upon this land a thousand thousand blessings,
Which time shall bring to ripeness. She shall be –
But few now living can behold that goodness –
A pattern to all princes living with her,
And all that shall succeed.

Shakespeare's father was buried on 8 September 1601 in
Stratford-upon-Avon. John Shakespeare was a glover, and the
paraphernalia of his profession makes its way into several of
his son's plays. It is on record that he received a hefty fine for
hoarding manure on the street outside his house – though this
isn't as eccentric as it sounds, because dung could be a good
little earner when sold to farmers and builders. A world away
in *Hamlet*'s Denmark, the prince is told by the ghost of his
father to avenge his murder. This is in line with ancient Senecan
conventions, which often saw a play begin with a vengeful
ghost. Shakespeare himself is rumoured to have played the
Ghost, who surprises the prince with the revelation that 'The
serpent that did sting thy father's life / Now wears his crown'.
He cannot rest in peace until he is avenged, but the information
and the reliability of its spectral source causes Hamlet to um
and ah about what to do for much of the rest of the play.

> GHOST
> Ay, that incestuous, that adulterate beast,
> With witchcraft of his wit, with traitorous gifts –
> O wicked wit and gifts, that have the power
> So to seduce! – won to his shameful lust
> The will of my most seeming-virtuous Queen.
> O Hamlet, what a falling off was there,
> From me, whose love was of that dignity
> That it went hand in hand even with the vow
> I made to her in marriage; and to decline
> Upon a wretch whose natural gifts were poor
> To those of mine!
> But virtue as it never will be moved,
> Though lewdness court it in a shape of heaven,
> So lust, though to a radiant angel linked,

Will sate itself in a celestial bed
And prey on garbage.
But soft, methinks I scent the morning air.
Brief let me be. Sleeping within my orchard,
My custom always of the afternoon,
Upon my secure hour thy uncle stole
With juice of cursèd hebona in a vial,
And in the porches of my ears did pour
The leperous distilment; whose effect
Holds such an enmity with blood of man
That swift as quicksilver it courses through
The natural gates and alleys of the body,
And with a sudden vigour doth posset
And curd, like eager droppings into milk,
The thin and wholesome blood, So did it mine.
And a most instant tetter bark'd about,
Most lazar-like, with vile and loathsome crust
All my smooth body.
Thus was I sleeping by a brother's hand
Of life, of crown, of queen, at once dispatched,
Cut off even in the blossoms of my sin,
Unhouseled, disappointed, unaneled,
No reckoning made, but sent to my account
With all my imperfections on my head.
O, horrible! O, horrible! Most horrible!
If thou hast nature in thee, bear it not.
Let not the royal bed of Denmark be
A couch for luxury and damned incest.
But howsomever thou pursues this act,
Taint not thy mind, nor let thy soul contrive
Against thy mother aught. Leave her to heaven
And to those thorns that in her bosom lodge
To prick and sting her. Fare thee well at once.
The glow-worm shows the matin to be near
And 'gins to pale his uneffectual fire.
Adieu, adieu, adieu. Remember me.

Shakespeare's mother Mary Shakespeare (née Arden) was buried on 9 September 1608, almost exactly seven years after his father. Like his wife, Shakespeare's mother was unlikely to have been able to read, but who can say how she might have influenced his work. What we can say is that mothers, particularly in Shakespeare's history plays, are formidable women, often serving to pronounce curses or articulate grief over the deaths of their warlike sons. Queen Margaret, wife of Henry VI, is one such influential woman and mother, possessing all of the strength lacking in her weak husband. Here she denounces Henry's concession to the Yorkists, which grants them and their dynasty the throne after he dies, effectively disinheriting their son Edward.

QUEEN MARGARET
Enforced thee? Art thou king, and wilt be forced?
I shame to hear thee speak. Ah, timorous wretch,
Thou hast undone thyself, thy son, and me,
And giv'n unto the house of York such head
As thou shalt reign but by their sufferance.
To entail him and his heirs unto the crown:
What is it, but to make thy sepulchre
And creep into that far before thy time?
Warwick is chancellor and the Lord of Calais;
Stern Falconbridge commands the Narrow Seas;
The Duke is made Protector of the Realm;
And yet shalt thou be safe? Such safety finds
The trembling lamb environèd with wolves.
Had I been there, which am a seely woman,
The soldiers should have tossed me on their pikes
Before I would have granted to that Act.
But thou prefer'st thy life before thine honour.

And seeing thou dost, I here divorce myself
Both from thy table, Henry, and thy bed,
Until that act of parliament be repealed
Whereby my son is disinherited.

September 10 | Richard III | Act 1 Scene 2

The grief of Lady Anne over the deaths of Henry VI and his
only son (her husband Edward), at the hands of Richard of
Gloucester, is startling in its power. While she is mourning
over the corpse of the late king, Richard appears and Henry's
multiple stab wounds begin to bleed again – it was a common
superstition that they would do so in the presence of the
murderer. Though fragile, Lady Anne is still able to lacerate her
husband's killer with the guilty charges which will haunt him in
his final moments before Bosworth.

LADY ANNE
What, do you tremble? Are you all afraid?
Alas, I blame you not, for you are mortal,
And mortal eyes cannot endure the devil.
Avaunt, thou dreadful minister of hell!
Thou hadst but power over his mortal body;
His soul thou canst not have. Therefore, be gone.

[. . .]

LADY ANNE
Foul devil, for God's sake hence, and trouble us not,
For thou hast made the happy earth thy hell,
Filled it with cursing cries and deep exclaims.
If thou delight to view thy heinous deeds,
Behold this pattern of thy butcheries.
O gentlemen, see, see! Dead Henry's wounds
Open their congealed mouths and bleed afresh!
Blush, Blush, thou lump of foul deformity;
For 'tis thy presence that exhales this blood
From cold and empty veins where no blood dwells.
Thy deeds inhuman and unnatural

Provokes this deluge most unnatural.
O God, which this blood mad'st, revenge his death!
O earth, which this blood drink'st, revenge his death!
Either heaven with lightning strike the murderer dead;
Or earth gape open wide and eat him quick,
As thou dost swallow up this good King's blood
Which his hell-governed arm hath butcherèd!

The changing of seasons often signals a changing of gear for Shakespeare, and the transition from summer to winter brings as much foreboding as summer's return after winter brings hope. His characters and their imaginary landscape move in perfect synchronicity. Humphrey, Duke of Gloucester, muses on the transience of joy in terms of the fleeting seasons, as he prepares for his wife's departure – she has been banished for engaging in witchcraft in an attempt to put her husband on the throne.

GLOUCESTER
Thus sometimes hath the brightest day a cloud;
And after summer evermore succeeds
Barren winter, with his wrathful nipping cold;
So cares and joys abound, as seasons fleet.

The Duke of Gloucester's illegitimate son, Edmund, resents
his inferior status and plots to kill or at least disgrace his older
half-brother Edgar, in the hope of taking his place. His fury
is palpable, full of rhetorical questions and the harsh, plosive
alliteration of 'base' and 'bastardy', spits off the page.

EDMUND
Thou, Nature, art my goddess; to thy law
My services are bound. Wherefore should I
Stand in the plague of custom and permit
The curiosity of nations to deprive me,
For that I am some twelve or fourteen moonshines
Lag of a brother? Why bastard? Wherefore base?
When my dimensions are as well-compact,
My mind as generous, and my shape as true
As honest madam's issue? Why brand they us
With 'base'? with 'baseness'? 'bastardy'? 'base, base'?
Who in the lusty stealth of nature take
More composition and fierce quality
Than doth within a dull, stale, tired bed
Go to the creating a whole tribe of fops
Got 'tween asleep and wake? Well then,
Legitimate Edgar, I must have your land.
Our father's love is to the bastard Edmund
As to the legitimate. Fine word, 'legitimate'!
Well, my 'legitimate', if this letter speed
And my invention thrive, Edmund the base
Shall top the legitimate. I grow. I prosper.
Now gods stand up for bastards!

Preparing the way to engineer his daughter Miranda's
engagement to Ferdinand, the son of his enemy Alonso the King
of Naples, Prospero has his spirit Ariel sing a song to encourage
the misapprehension that Alonso died in the shipwreck that has
washed Ferdinand up on another part of the island. Ferdinand
wonders at such a chilling image sung in such a beautiful voice:
'This music crept by me upon the waters, / Allaying both their
fury and my passion / With its sweet air.'

> ARIEL
> Full fathom five thy father lies,
> Of his bones are coral made;
> Those are pearls that were his eyes;
> Nothing of him that doth fade
> But doth suffer a sea-change
> Into something rich and strange.
> Sea-nymphs hourly ring his knell.
> Hark, now I hear them, ding dong bell.

Holyrood Day – or the Feast of the Cross – is when young couples would go 'a-nutting', otherwise known as meeting up in the woods. It is also the day on which Shakespeare's Harry Hotspur and Archibald, Earl of Douglas, meet in battle.

WESTMORELAND
On Holy-rood day, the gallant Hotspur there,
Young Harry Percy, and brave Archibald,
That ever-valiant and approvèd Scot,
At Holmedon met, where they did spend
A sad and bloody hour –
As by discharge of their artillery,
And shape of likelihood, the news was told;
For he that brought them, in the very heat
And pride of their contention did take horse,
Uncertain of the issue any way.

Playwright Robert Greene died in September 1592, but not before making the first reference to young Shakespeare's writing career, in a pamphlet that was published posthumously. Greene was six years older than Shakespeare, and the best part of his career ended almost as soon as it began, which did not make him particularly well disposed to the up-and-coming star: 'There is an upstart Crow, beautified with our feathers, that with his Tygers hart wrapt in a Players hyde, supposes he is as well able to bombast out a blanke verse as the best of you: and being an absolute Johannes fac totum [jack of all trades], is in his owne conceit the onely Shake-scene in a country.' History has favoured the upstart crow. Who has heard of Robert Greene? (Except, perhaps, as the author of *Pandosto*, the romance which Shakespeare would later steal as the plot of *The Winter's Tale*.) Greene's disparagement of Shakespeare made reference to one of York's lines in *Henry VI, Part 3*, as he is taunted and killed by Queen Margaret.

YORK
O tiger's heart wrapped in a woman's hide!
How couldst thou drain the lifeblood of the child,
To bid the father wipe his eyes withal,
And yet be seen to bear a woman's face?
Women are soft, mild, pitiful, and flexible;
Thou stern, obdurate, flinty, rough, remorseless.
Biddest thou me rage? Why, now thou hast thy wish;
Wouldst have me weep? Why, now thou hast thy will;
For raging wind blows up incessant showers,
And when the rage allays, the rain begins.
These tears are my sweet Rutland's obsequies,
And every drop cries vengeance for his death
'Gainst thee, fell Clifford, and thee, false Frenchwoman.

Philip the Bastard, so called because he was the illegitimate son
of Richard I, is given most of the finest speeches in *King John*,
a play written entirely in verse. He possesses far more kingly
attributes, such as valour, bravery and diplomatic skill, than
the legitimate king he serves. He consoles John and steels the
disaster-prone monarch's resolution to face rather than appease
his persistent aggressors, the French.

BASTARD
But wherefore do you droop? Why look you sad?
Be great in act, as you have been in thought;
Let not the world see fear and sad distrust
Govern the motion of a kingly eye.
Be stirring as the time; be fire with fire;
Threaten the threatener, and outface the brow
Of bragging horror. So shall inferior eyes,
That borrow their behaviors from the great,
Grow great by your example and put on
The dauntless spirit of resolution.
Away, and glister like the god of war,
When he intendeth to become the field.
Show boldness and aspiring confidence!
What, shall they seek the lion in his den,
And fright him there? And make him tremble there?
O, let it not be said! Forage, and run
To meet displeasure farther from the doors,
And grapple with him ere he comes so nigh.

September 17 is St Lambert's Day, and the day appointed by
Richard II for combat between Mowbray and Bolingbroke
to settle a dispute: the King declares 'Be ready, as your lives
shall answer for it, / At Coventry, upon St Lambert's Day'. St
Lambert, a Dutch saint, was considered a martyr to faithful
marriage, having denounced the adultery of Pepin of Herstal
and faced death as a consequence. Richard II gets rather caught
up in his sense of himself as a martyr, and there is something
of Lambert about him when he learns that he is to be separated
from his queen as well as his crown. Touching, if a little
vainglorious.

KING RICHARD II
Doubly divorced! Bad men, you violate
A twofold marriage – 'twixt my crown and me,
And then betwixt me and my married wife.
[*To* QUEEN ISABEL]
Let me unkiss the oath 'twixt thee and me;
And yet not so; for with a kiss 'twas made.
– Part us, Northumberland: I toward the north,
Where shivering cold and sickness pines the clime;
My wife to France, from whence set forth in pomp,
She came adornèd hither like sweet May,
Sent back like Hallowmas or shortest of day.

One of Richard II's failings is that he did not realize he is subject to the same faults and vulnerabilities as other men. On giving over the crown, it seems to him as though he hands over his immortality and then expects wrinkles and scars to show instantly on his face. The whole abdication scene holds Bolingbroke and other members of the court in stunned silence, while Richard theatrically transforms himself from a king to a man.

RICHARD
Give me the glass, and therein will I read.
No deeper wrinkles yet? Hath sorrow struck
So many blows upon this face of mine
And made no deeper wounds? O, flattering glass,
Like to my followers in prosperity,
Thou dost beguile me. Was this face the face
That every day under his household roof
Did keep ten thousand men? Was this the face
That like the sun did make beholders wink?
Is this the face that faced so many follies,
And was at last outfaced by Bolingbroke?
A brittle glory shineth in this face.
As brittle as the glory is the face,
[*He throws the glass down*]
For there it is, cracked in a hundred shivers.
Mark, silent King, the moral of this sport:
How soon my sorrow hath destroyed my face.

York started out as one of Richard's staunchest supporters,
but changes allegiance to Bolingbroke. In this, he betrays
his nephew but upholds the best candidate for the English
throne: does that make him a traitor? After Richard's theatrical
abdication, York describes how the London crowd watched
Bolingbroke and Richard process through the streets, and how
they responded to Richard as though he were the anticlimactic
mediocre actor coming on before the star. The usurped
king, stripped of his royal title, is doused with dust by his
contemptuous public, whose hearts already belong to
the next act.

DUKE OF YORK
As in a theatre the eyes of men,
After a well graced actor leaves the stage,
Are idly bent on him that enters next,
Thinking his prattle to be tedious:
Even so, or with much more contempt, men's eyes
Did scowl on gentle Richard. No man cried 'God save him!'
No joyful tongue gave him his welcome home;
But dust was thrown upon his sacred head,
Which with such gentle sorrow he shook off,
His face still combating with tears and smiles,
The badges of his grief and patience,
That had not God for some strong purpose steeled
The hearts of men, they must perforce have melted,
And barbarism itself have pitied him.
But heaven hath a hand in these events,
To whose high will we bound our calm contents.
To Bolingbroke are we sworn subjects now,
Whose state and honour I for aye allow.

September 20 | Measure for Measure | Act 2 Scene 4

Isabella, a young nun in *Measure for Measure*, is a persuasive petitioner. She occupies this role when her brother Claudio is cruelly imprisoned and due to be executed for getting his wife-to-be pregnant before they were officially married (an indiscretion committed by Shakespeare himself with Anne Hathaway). The tyrannical deputy Angelo, who rules the city in the Duke's absence, offers Claudio's freedom on the condition that Isabella gives up her virginity to him. Powerfully, and perhaps surprisingly to some, Isabella resolves that her brother must die because her vow of celibacy is more important than her duty to either man.

ISABELLA
To whom should I complain? Did I tell this,
Who would believe me? O perilous mouths,
That bear in them one and the selfsame tongue,
Either of condemnation or approof,
Bidding the law make curtsy to their will,
Hooking both right and wrong to th'appetite,
To follow as it draws. I'll to my brother.
Though he hath fall'n by prompture of the blood,
Yet hath he in him such a mind of honour
That, had he twenty heads to tender down
On twenty bloody blocks, he'd yield them up,
Before his sister should her body stoop
To such abhorred pollution.
Then, Isabel, live chaste, and, brother, die.
More than our brother is our chastity.
I'll tell him yet of Angelo's request,
And fit his mind to death, for his soul's rest.

A Swiss traveller Thomas Platter visited London from Basle
and, in a difficult German dialect, wrote about one of the first
performances of *Julius Caesar* on 21 September 1599 at the
brand new Globe Theatre:

> After dinner, at about two o'clock, I went with my party across
> the water; in the straw-thatched house we saw the tragedy of
> the first Emperor Julius Caesar, very pleasingly performed, with
> approximately fifteen characters; at the end of the play they danced
> together admirably and exceedingly gracefully, two in each group
> dressed in men's and two in women's apparel . . . an excellent
> performance of the tragedy of the first emperor Julius Caesar.

The dances which Platter admired were evidently customary
at the end of most plays, even tragedies like *Julius Caesar*,
and helped the audience's transition from the fictional world
of the play to the reality of everyday life. That is not to say that
Shakespeare's Rome feels unfamiliar: everyday relationships
within the play are sketched with all the subtlety of the real
thing. Here a concerned Portia quizzes her fretful husband
Brutus on the cause of his uneasiness.

PORTIA
Nor for yours neither. Y' have ungently, Brutus,
Stole from my bed; and yesternight at supper
You suddenly arose and walked about,
Musing and sighing, with your arms across;
And when I asked you what the matter was,
You stared upon me with ungentle looks.
I urged you further; then you scratched your head,
And too impatiently stamped with your foot;
Yet I insisted, yet you answered not,
But with an angry wafture of your hand

Gave sign for me to leave you. So I did,
Fearing to strengthen that impatience
Which seemed too much enkindled, and withal
Hoping it was but an effect of humour,
Which sometime hath his hour with every man.
It will not let you eat, nor talk, nor sleep;
And could it work so much upon your shape,
As it hath much prevailed on your condition,
I should not know you Brutus. Dear my lord,
Make me acquainted with your cause of grief.

Juno and Ceres, goddesses of marriage and agriculture respectively, are conjured by Ariel to bless Miranda's wedding with the following ditty. Their song depicts an idyllic image of pastoral abundance, appropriate for this time of year as the Harvest season draws to a close.

JUNO
Honour, riches, marriage-blessing,
Long continuance and increasing,
Hourly joys be still upon you,
Juno sings her blessings upon you.

CERES
Earth's increase, foison plenty,
Barns and garners never empty,
Vines and clustr'ing bunches growing,
Plants with goodly burthen bowing;
Spring come to you at the farthest,
In the very end of harvest.
Scarcity and want shall shun you,
Ceres' blessing so is on you.

September 23 | Sonnet 73

The Harvest festival is held on the nearest Sunday to the autumn equinox, 23 September. While this was a time of celebration for Elizabethans, it marked the moment the rural population would begin to look apprehensively towards a long and uncertain winter. This sense of foreboding meant the changing of the seasons serve as common metaphors for the ageing process. In Sonnet 73, the poet reflects on his own relative decrepitude compared with his fair addressee, which he likens to the advancing seasons.

That time of year thou mayst in me behold,
When yellow leaves, or none, or few do hang
Upon those boughs which shake against the cold,
Bare ruin'd choirs, where late the sweet birds sang.
In me thou seest the twilight of such day,
As after sunset fadeth in the West,
Which by and by black night doth take away,
Death's second self, that seals up all in rest.
In me thou seest the glowing of such fire,
That on the ashes of his youth doth lie,
As the death-bed, whereon it must expire,
Consum'd with that which it was nourish'd by.
  This thou perceiv'st, which makes thy love more strong,
  To love that well, which thou must leave ere long.

Iago, like Edmund in *King Lear,* Aaron in *Titus Andronicus*
and Richard III, is a committed villain. In cultivating Othello's
unfounded jealousy, Iago pretends to ward off jealousy, the
'green-eyed monster' with one hand while coaxing it in with
the other. Shakespeare has coined other familiar terms of
expression for contradictory manoeuvres: Iago knows he can
'kill with kindness' (*The Taming of the Shrew*), especially as he
can 'smile and smile and be a villain' – though he is certainly
not being 'cruel to be kind' (both from *Hamlet).*

IAGO
O, beware, my lord, of jealousy!
It is the green-eyed monster, which doth mock
The meat it feeds on. That cuckold lives in bliss
Who, certain of his fate loves not his wronger,
But O, what damnèd minutes tells he o'er,
Who dotes yet doubts, suspects yet fondly loves!

September 25 | Othello | Act 3 Scene 3

It can be unsettling to search for a moral in *Othello*, especially
as the play's source material, 'Un Capitano Moro' contains an
explicit message about the supposed dangers of miscegenation.
However, this overlooks the play's powerful message about
the poisonous and arbitrary devastation wrought by racism,
as practised by Iago over Othello to turn the latter to self-
contempt. It is concerning how Iago, though condemned to
be tortured to death, survives the end of the play, because
through him, the spirit of racism lives on. Here, Othello begins
to believe that his race could cause Desdemona to turn away
from him.

OTHELLO
This fellow's of exceeding honesty,
And knows all qualities with a learnèd spirit,
Of human dealings. If I do prove her haggard,
Though that her jesses were my dear heart-strings,
I'd whistle her off, and let her down the wind
To pray at fortune. Haply, for I am black
And have not those soft parts of conversation
That chamberers have; or for I am declined
Into the vale of years – yet that's not much –
She's gone: I am abused, and my relief
Must be to loathe her. O, curse of marriage!
That we can call these delicate creatures ours
And not their appetites! I had rather be a toad
And live upon the vapour of a dungeon
Than keep a corner in the thing I love
For others' uses. Yet 'tis the plague of great ones;
Prerogatived are they less than the base.
'Tis destiny unshunnable, like death:
Even then this forkèd plague is fated to us

When we do quicken. Desdemona comes:
Enter DESDEMONA *and* EMILIA
If she be false, O, then heaven mocks itself!
I'll not believe't.

Jealousy snakes its way through many of Shakespeare's works, just as it was a major theme in the fables of Ovid which inspired much of his writing. The character of Othello would later bear out the words of Venus all too truly, when he becomes as forsaken, enraged and vengeful as this frustrated goddess, who curses love to be forever thus.

'For where Love reigns, disturbing Jealousy
Doth call himself Affection's sentinel;
Gives false alarms, suggesteth mutiny,
And in a peaceful hour doth cry "Kill, kill!"
Distempering gentle Love in his desire,
As air and water do abate the fire.

'This sour informer, this bate-breeding spy,
This canker that eats up Love's tender spring,
This carry-tale, dissentious Jealousy,
That sometime true news, sometime false doth bring,
Knocks at my heat, and whispers in mine ear
That if I love thee I thy death should fear.'

Leontes sees his pregnant wife Hermione fraternizing with his childhood friend Polixenes, and instantly flies into a whirlwind of jealousy. The abruptness of this change of tone is characteristic of the play as a whole, which doesn't fit comfortably into any genre, running from tragedy through pastoral comedy to the wonder of its unlikely happy ending. The absence of explicit stage directions presents a choice for performers – should Hermione and Polixenes behave as Leontes describes them, or are those behaviours the invention of a jealous mind?

LEONTES
[*Aside*] Too hot, too hot!
To mingle friendship far is mingling bloods.
I have *tremor cordis* on me: my heart dances,
But not for joy, not joy. This entertainment
May a free face put on, derive a liberty
From heartiness, from bounty, fertile bosom,
And well become the agent – 't may, I grant.
But to be paddling palms and pinching fingers,
As now they are, and making practised smiles
As in a looking glass; and then to sigh, as 'twere
The mort o'th'deer – O, that is entertainment
My bosom likes not, nor my brows!

The King of Navarre and his three companions take a vow of celibacy and exclude women from their court. However, the Princess of France has been sent on serious business by her father, and negotiates entry to the scholars' sanctuary, after which it is almost immediately clear that the aspiring scholars may come to regret their oaths.

PRINCESS
Good Lord Boyet, my beauty, though but mean,
Needs not the painted flourish of your praise.
Beauty is bought by judgement of the eye,
Not uttered by base sale of chapmen's tongues.
I am less proud to hear you tell my worth
Than you much willing to be counted wise
In spending your wit in the praise of mine.
But now to task the tasker. Good Boyet,
You are not ignorant all-telling fame
Doth noise abroad Navarre hath made a vow,
Till painful study shall outwear three years,
No woman may approach his silent court.
Therefore to's seemeth it a needful course,
Before we enter his forbidden gates,
To know his pleasure; and in that behalf,
Bold of your worthiness, we single you
As our best-moving fair solicitor.
Tell him the daughter of the King of France,
On serious business craving quick dispatch,
Importunes personal conference with his grace.
Haste, signify so much, while we attend,
Like humble-visaged suitors, his high will.

Today is the Feast of St Michael and All Angels or Michaelmas,
historically the first day of term for law schools and the law
courts. These ministries of justice are out of reach for Lucrece,
though the injustice of her situation is beyond debate. In this
powerful passage, she inveighs heavily against the idleness of
words when grief is as strong as hers, and the impotency of
lawyers to alleviate her distress.

'Out, idle words, servants to shallow fools,
Unprofitable sounds, weak arbitrators!
Busy yourselves in skill-contending schools;
Debate where leisure serves with dull debaters;
To trembling clients be you mediators:
For me, I force not argument a straw,
Since that my case is past the help of law.'

Shakespeare was born in Stratford-upon-Avon, and that is
where he died, on or very near his birthday (on 23 April).
There is also a certain circularity in Antony's death: Cleopatra
remarks, 'So it should be, that none but Antony / Should
conquer Antony; but woe 'tis so!' Many of Shakespeare's
characters express death as a form of elemental shift between
opposites, and Antony's is no different. For Cleopatra, it is as
though her 'strength is all gone into heaviness', and 'wishes'
become 'fools' when he is dying in front of her. As though
closing the circle, she summons him to die where he lived,
'quickene[d] with kissing'.

CLEOPATRA
Here's sport indeed! How heavy weighs my lord!
Our strength is all gone into heaviness,
That makes the weight. Had I great Juno's power,
The strong-winged Mercury should fetch thee up
And set thee by Jove's side. Yet come a little;
Wishes were ever fools. O, come, come, come.
[*They heave* ANTONY *aloft to* CLEOPATRA]
And welcome, welcome! Die where thou hast lived;
Quicken with kissing. Had my lips that power,
Thus would I wear them out.

October

October 1 | King Lear | Act 4 Scene 4

In the world of Shakespeare's comedies, life outside the court in the countryside is generally one of pastoral innocence and perpetual summer. In the tragedies, however, the countryside is a place of isolation fraught with danger, which often signals the loss of influence for its inhabitants. King Lear's fortunes pull him into one such desolate place.

CORDELIA
Alack, 'tis he! Why, he was met even now
As mad as the vexed sea, singing aloud,
Crowned with rank fumiter and furrow-weeds,
With hardokes, hemlock, nettles, cuckoo-flowers,
Darnel, and all the idle weeds that grow
In our sustaining corn. A century send forth;
Search every acre in the high-grown field
And bring him to our eye.
[*Exit an Officer*]
[*To Doctor*] What can man's wisdom
In the restoring his bereavèd sense?
He that helps him, take all my outward worth.

October 2 | Richard III | Act 1 Scene 1

Richard III was born on 2 October 1452. The physical and moral deformity of Shakespeare's Richard had long been thought of as anti-Plantagenet Tudor propaganda; though the astonishing discovery of his remains beneath a Leicester carpark in 2012, reignited debates about the accuracy of Shakespeare's depiction as his skeleton showed that he suffered from a severe curvature of the spine. This echoes the complex relationship between Richard's physique and his character in *Richard III*'s opening soliloquy. He is 'determined to prove a villain'– but determined by whom? By his own deformity, by the force of his villainous will, or by the Tudor poet who has to present him as such?

RICHARD
Now is the winter of our discontent
Made glorious summer by this sun of York,
And all the clouds that loured upon our house
In the deep bosom of the ocean buried.
Now are our brows bound with victorious wreaths,
Our bruisèd arms hung up for monuments,
Our stern alarums changed to merry meetings,
Our dreadful marches to delightful measures.
Grim-visaged war hath smoothed his wrinkled front,
And now, instead of mounting bardèd steeds
To fright the souls of fearful adversaries,
He capers nimbly in a lady's chamber
To the lascivious pleasing of a lute.
But I, that am not shaped for sportive tricks
Nor made to court an amorous looking-glass;
I, that am rudely stamped, and want love's majesty
To strut before a wanton ambling nymph;
I, that am curtailed of this fair proportion,
Cheated of feature by dissembling Nature,

Deformed, unfinished, sent before my time
Into this breathing world, scarce half made up,
And that so lamely and unfashionable
That dogs bark at me as I halt by them –
Why I, in this weak piping time of peace,
Have no delight to pass away the time,
Unless to spy my shadow in the sun
And descant on mine own deformity.
And therefore, since I cannot prove a lover
To entertain these fair well-spoken days,
I am determined to prove a villain
And hate the idle pleasures of these days.

Saints' days, or name days, were more celebrated than birthdays in Shakespeare's time – as they still are in many parts of the world – and consequently birthdays don't come up much in the plays. That said, Cassius remarks that 'this is my birthday; this very day' before the Battle of Philippi, which was fought on 3 October 42 BCE. Cassius dies in the battle on his birthday, and in doing so the dramatist unknowingly foreshadows the timing of his own death on or around his birthday nearly 1700 years later, on 23 April 1616.

CASSIUS
Come down; behold no more.
O, coward that I am, to live so long,
To see my best friend ta'en before my face!
[*PINDARUS descends*]
Come hither, sirrah.
In Parthia did I take thee prisoner;
And then I swore thee, saving of thy life,
That whatsoever I did bid thee do,
Thou shouldst attempt it. Come now, keep thine oath;
Now be a freeman; and with this good sword,
That ran through Caesar's bowels, search this bosom.
Stand not to answer. Here, take thou the hilts,
And when my face is covered, as 'tis now,
Guide thou the sword. –
[*PINDARUS stabs him*]
       Caesar, thou art revenged,
Even with the sword that killed thee.

October 4 | Sonnet 138

Truth to Shakespeare is many things. It might lead to dark acts or bring us to the light: while 'often-times, to win us to our harm, / The instruments of darkness tell us truths, / Win us with honest trifles, to betray's / In deepest consequence' (*Macbeth* 1.3). It is also the case that 'Time's glory is to command contending kings, / To unmask falsehood, and bring truth to light' (*The Rape of Lucrece*). He convinces us that nature is the poet's truth, 'Truth needs no colour with his colour fixed, / Beauty no pencil, beauty's truth to lay' (Sonnet 101). And although Polonius in *Hamlet* advises, 'This above all; to thine own self be true' (1.3), in Sonnet 138 the poet reasons that lovers should not be quite so honest, as relationships are most happy when lovers collude in self-deception.

When my love swears that she is made of truth,
I do believe her though I know she lies,
That she might think me some untutor'd youth,
Unlearned in the world's false subtleties.
Thus vainly thinking that she thinks me young,
Although she knows my days are past the best,
Simply I credit her false-speaking tongue,
On both sides thus is simple truth supprest:
But wherefore says she not she is unjust?
And wherefore say not I that I am old?
O love's best habit is in seeming trust,
And age in love, loves not t' have years told.
    Therefore I lie with her, and she with me,
    And in our faults by lies we flattered be.

When *The Merchant of Venice* was written, the King of Morocco was an important ally of England. Morocco had gold and the King, Sheik al Mazoor, was rich, far richer than Elizabeth. Records exist of arms deals between the monarchs, and as recently as the 1990s, shipwrecked Moroccan gold was discovered in Salcombe in Devon, probably intended as payment for a consignment of cannon balls. Predictably, the Prince of Morocco here chooses the casket made of gold and consequently fails to win Portia as his wife. The inscription inside the box is the origin of the phrase 'All that glisters [glitters] is not gold'.

MOROCCO [*Reads*]
All that glisters is not gold;
Often have you heard that told.
Many a man his life hath sold
But my outside to behold.
Gilded tombs do worms infold.
Had you been as wise as bold,
Young in limbs, in judgment old,
Your answer had not been inscrolled.
Fare you well, your suit is cold.
Cold indeed, and labour lost.
Then farewell heat, and welcome frost.
Portia, adieu, I have too grieved a heart
To take a tedious leave. Thus losers part.

Whilst Portia is anxiously awaiting Bassanio's choice of casket, she calls for music. The song has hidden advice not to trust appearances, an advantage not granted to the two other suitors, and it also rhymes heavily with the word 'lead'. Bassanio accordingly chooses the lead casket, over the silver and gold, and wins Portia's hand in marriage.

SINGER
Tell me where is fancy bred,
Or in the heart, or in the head?
How begot, how nourishèd?
Reply, reply.
It is engendered in the eyes,
With gazing fed, and fancy dies
In the cradle where it lies.
Let us all ring fancy's knell.
I'll begin it – Ding, dong, bell.

ALL
Ding, dong, bell.

Shakespeare did not reserve the full complement of his literary prowess for his male characters. Female parts are as tightly characterized, and no speech by one of Shakespeare's women could be imagined in the mouth of another. Portia speaks to Brutus as only she could.

PORTIA
Is Brutus sick? And is it physical
To walk unbracèd and suck up the humours
Of the dank morning? What, is Brutus sick?
And will he steal out of his wholesome bed
To dare the vile contagion of the night,
And tempt the rheumy and unpurgèd air,
To add unto his sickness? No, my Brutus;
You have some sick offence within your mind,
Which, by the right and virtue of my place,
I ought to know of; and, upon my knees,
I charm you, by my once-commended beauty,
By all your vows of love, and that great vow
Which did incorporate and make us one,
That you unfold to me, your self, your half,
Why you are heavy, and what men tonight
Have had to resort to you; for here have been
Some six or seven, who did hide their faces
Even from darkness.

The Two Gentlemen of Verona contains one of Shakespeare's early efforts at a visual gag. The Duke of Milan locks his daughter in a tower, but this doesn't stop Valentine from trying to elope with her. Unfortunately the Duke is tipped off by Valentine's one-time friend, now love rival, Proteus. Meeting Valentine, the Duke claims that he is himself wooing a younger woman and wonders whether Valentine can lend him a ladder and a cloak – whereupon he finds the letter in which Valentine was going to inform Silvia that their escape plan was to go into action that night.

DUKE
I pray thee, let me feel thy cloak upon me.
What letter is this same? What's here? 'To Silvia'!
And here an engine fit for my proceeding.
I'll be so bold to break the seal for once.
[*Reads*]

'My thoughts do harbour with my Silvia nightly,
And slaves they are to me, that send them flying.
O, could their master come and go as lightly,
Himself would lodge where, senseless, they are lying!
My herald thoughts in thy pure bosom rest them,
While I, their king, that hither them importune,
Do curse the grace that with such grace hath blessed them,
Because myself do want my servants' fortune.
I curse myself, for they are sent by me,
That they should harbour where their lord should be.'

What's here?
'Silvia, this night I will enfranchise thee.'

407

'Tis so; and here's the ladder for the purpose.
Why, Phaeton – for thou art Merops' son –
Wilt thou aspire to guide the heavenly car,
And with thy daring folly burn the world?
Wilt thou reach stars, because they shine on thee?
Go, base intruder, overweening slave,
Bestow thy fawning smiles on equal mates;
And think my patience, more than thy desert,
Is privilege for thy departure hence.
Thank me for this more than for all the favours
Which, all too much I have bestowed on thee.
But if thou linger in my territories
Longer than swiftest expedition
Will give thee time to leave our royal court,
By heaven, my wrath shall far exceed the love
I ever bore my daughter or thyself.
Be gone; I will not hear thy vain excuse,
But, as thou lovest thy life, make speed from hence.

Just as England has St George, France has Dennis as its patron saint whose feast day is on 9 October. England fought the French, on and off, practically since the moment the kingdoms were founded. Referencing the saint in one such war, the French King Charles says, 'St Dennis bless this happy stratagem, / And once again we'll sleep secure in Rouen', (*Henry VI, Part 1*). More touchingly, at a moment of reconciliation, Henry V says to Princess Katherine of France, 'Shall not thou and I, between St Dennis and St George, compound a boy, half French, half English . . . ?'. Henry V's campaign in France is among the most notable of the conflicts between the kingdoms and is brought to a settlement through the marriage of Princess Katherine to the victorious English king. In anticipation of an English match, Katherine tries to learn English. This dialogue provides welcome comic relief after the violent words of the preceding war scenes.

KATHERINE
Dites-moi l'anglais pour le bras.

ALICE
De arm, madame.

KATHERINE
Et le coude?

ALICE
D'elbow.

KATHERINE
D'elbow. Je m'en fais la répétition de tous les mots que vous m'avez appris dès à présent.

ALICE
Il est trop difficile, madame, comme je pense.

KATHERINE
Excusez-moi, Alice; écoutez – d'hand, de fingre,
de nailès, d'arma, de bilbow.

ALICE
D'elbow, madame.

KATHERINE
O Seigneur Dieu, je m'en oublie! D'elbow. Comment
appelez-vous le col?

ALICE
De nick, madame.

KATHERINE
De nick. Et le menton?

ALICE
De chin.

KATHERINE
De sin. Le col, de nick; le menton, de sin.

After Antony's suicide, the Romans attempt to persuade
Cleopatra into an alliance. One of Caesar's followers, Dolabella,
is sent with this embassage and, like most characters who
encounter the Egyptian Queen, is stunned into silence by the
force of her grief and her personality. Cleopatra describes her
irreplaceable vision of Antony as if she is describing a divine
dream: she likens his generosity to that of autumn.

CLEOPATRA
I dreamt there was an emperor Antony.
O, such another sleep, that I might see
But such another man!

DOLABELLA
If it might please ye –

CLEOPATRA
His face was as the heavens, and therein stuck
A sun and moon, which kept their course and lighted
The little O o'th'earth.

DOLABELLA
Most sovereign creature –

CLEOPATRA
His legs bestrid the ocean; his reared arm
Crested the world; his voice was propertied
As all the tunèd spheres, and that to friends;
But when he meant to quail and shake the orb,
He was as rattling thunder. For his bounty,
There was no winter in't; an Antony it was
That grew the more by reaping. His delights

Were dolphin-like; they showed his back above
The element they lived in. In his livery
Walked crowns and crownets; realms and islands were
As plates dropped from his pocket.

DOLABELLA
Cleopatra –

CLEOPATRA
Think you there was or might be such a man
As this I dreamt of?

DOLABELLA
Gentle madam, no.

October 11 | Pericles | Act 4 Scene 6

Today is the UN's International Day of the Girl. Girls have magical associations in some of Shakespeare's plays. Marina from *Pericles* and Perdita of *The Winter's Tale* have much in common in this regard. Both girls are royal heirs, initially banished from their state as babies but mysteriously able to thrive in a noble and virtuous fashion even in exile. Moreover, once reunited with their respective fathers, these young women are able to restore them to health and deliver a sense of redemption for past mistakes. Marina's story is the tougher: after being kidnapped by pirates from carers who were trying to have her killed anyway, she is sold into prostitution, but preserves her chastity by dissuading her would-be clients from a dishonourable life. Here she tries to talk her overseer into abandoning his profession, and negotiates a teaching job for herself instead.

MARINA
Do anything but this
Thou doest. Empty old receptacles
Or common shores of filth;
Serve by indenture to the common hangman.
Any of these ways are yet better than this,
For what thou professest, a baboon, could he speak,
Would own a name too dear. That the gods
Would safely deliver me from this place!
Here, here's gold for thee.
If that thy master would gain by me,
Proclaim that I can sing, weave, sew, and dance,
With other virtues which I'll keep from boast,
And I will undertake all these to teach.
I doubt not but this populous city will
Yield many scholars.

There was an eclipse of both the sun and the moon on 12
October 1605, which augured ill for superstitious Jacobeans.
Likewise Othello, after murdering his wife, expects some
celestial movement to ensue: 'Methinks it should be now a huge
eclipse, Of sun and moon' and that 'th'affrighted globe Should
yawn at alteration'. A little under a month after the eclipse,
Guy Fawkes would try to blow up the King and Parliament.
In apparent reference to that coincidence – or prophecy – the
Duke of Gloucester frets for the safety of himself and for Lear's
kingdom.

GLOUCESTER
These late eclipses in the sun and moon portend
no good to us. Though the wisdom of nature can
reason it thus and thus, yet nature finds itself
scourged by the sequent effects: love cools,
friendship falls off, brothers divide. In
cities, mutinies; in countries, discord; in
palaces, treason; and the bond cracked 'twixt son
and father. This villain of mine comes under the
prediction: there's son against father; the King
falls from bias of nature: there's father against
child. We have seen the best of our time.
Machinations, hollowness, treachery, and all
ruinous disorders follow us disquietly to our
graves.

Henry IV's coronation was held on 4 October 1399. Shakespeare's plays covering his reign contain some of the finest comedy to be found in the canon, particularly in the action centred around Sir John Falstaff. This rotund drunkard was originally named Oldcastle after a real knight, but his descendants complained at his portrayal and so he was renamed Falstaff. One of Falstaff's most notable speeches, however, is likely to strike a different tone in every age. His dismissal of 'honour' as justification for violence is comical to audiences who share Henry V's warlike nature, just as it is sad and prescient to anyone scarred by war. Elizabethans would have been just as ambivalent about war, and though Falstaff begins by attempting to justify his cowardice, he ends with a sobering condemnation of senseless death that will find sympathetic ears in any theatre.

FALSTAFF
Well, 'tis no matter, honour pricks
me on. Yea, but how if honour prick me off when I
come on, how then? Can honour set to a leg? No. Or
an arm? No. Or take away the grief of a wound? No.
Honour hath no skill in surgery then? No. What is
honour? A word. What is in that word honour? What
is that honour? Air. A trim reckoning! Who hath it?
He that died a'Wednesday. Doth he feel it? No.
Doth he hear it? No. 'Tis insensible, then? Yea,
to the dead. But will it not live with the living?
No. Why? Detraction will not suffer it. Therefore
I'll none of it. Honour is a mere scutcheon – and so
ends my catechism.

The Two Gentlemen of Verona is thought to be one of
Shakespeare's earliest plays, although there is no record of early
performance, and like half of Shakespeare's plays it did not
reach print until the collected Folio edition appeared in 1623.
The first mention of the play is by the clergyman and literary
critic Francis Meres, who writes in 1598 that Shakespeare is
'most excellent in' writing comedies, inviting his readers to
'witnes his Gentlemen of Verona, his Errors, his Love labors
lost, his Love labours wonne, his Midsummers night dreame
& his The Merchant of Venice'. Meres includes *Love Labours
Wonne*, but the play has never been found. This song from *The
Two Gentlemen of Verona* has been set to music many times,
most notably by the towering genius of Schubert. It is sung by
Thurio at the request of Proteus, and is unknowingly performed
in front of Proteus' forsaken lover, Julia, who has followed him
in disguise.

THURIO
Who is Silvia? What is she,
That all our swains commend her?
Holy, fair and wise is she;
The heaven such grace did lend her,
That she might admirèd be.

Is she kind as she is fair?
For beauty lives with kindness.
Love doth to her eyes repair,
To help him of his blindness;
And, being helped, inhabits there.

Then to Silvia let us sing
That Silvia is excelling;
She excels each mortal thing
Upon the dull earth dwelling.
To her let us garlands bring.

With fierce eloquence, Lucrece berates time itself for bringing
on Tarquin's despicable assault. Wracked with shame and
anger, her words resonate painfully down the ages.

'Misshapen Time, copesmate of ugly Night,
Swift subtle post, carrier of grisly care,
Eater of youth, false slave to false delight,
Base watch of woes, sin's pack-horse, virtue's snare;
Thou nursest all, and murderest all that are.
O hear me then, injurious shifting Time;
Be guilty of my death, since of my crime.

'Why hath thy servant Opportunity
Betrayed the hours thou gav'st me to repose,
Cancelled my fortunes and enchainèd me
To endless date of never-ending woes?
Time's office is to fine the hate of foes,
To eat up errors by opinion bred,
Not spend the dowry of a lawful bed.'

In the tragicomedy *The Winter's Tale*, Time itself is a character whose role is to move the action sixteen years forward to when the exiled princess Perdita is grown up. Time slides the action from the tragic events at the Sicilian court to the fair pastoral setting of Bohemia. Time recaps the action so far, and prefaces what is to come.

TIME
I that please some, try all; both joy and terror
Of good and bad; that makes and unfolds error,
Now take upon me, in the name of Time,
To use my wings. Impute it not a crime
To me or my swift passage that I slide
O'er sixteen years, and leave the growth untried
Of that wide gap, since it is in my power
To o'erthrow law and in one self-born hour
To plant and o'erwhelm custom. Let me pass
The same I am ere ancient'st order was
Or what is now received. I witness to
The times that brought them in; so shall I do
To th'freshest things now reigning, and make stale
The glistering of this present, as my tale
Now seems to it. Your patience this allowing,
I turn my glass, and give my scene such growing
As you had slept between. Leontes leaving –
Th'effects of his fond jealousies so grieving
That he shuts up himself – imagine me,
Gentle spectators, that I now may be
In fair Bohemia; and remember well,
I mentioned a son o'th'King's, which Florizel
I now name to you; and with speed so pace
To speak of Perdita, now grown in grace

Equal with wond'ring. What of her ensues
I list not prophecy; but let Time's news
Be known when 'tis brought forth. A shepherd's daughter,
And what to her adheres, which follows after,
Is th'argument of Time. Of this allow,
If ever you have spent time worse ere now;
If never, yet that Time himself doth say
He wishes earnestly you never may.

For our sonneteer, the very seasons appear differently without his beloved near. Sonnet 97 describes a 'teeming autumn', which is bereft and bleak in the lover's absence. Nature is complicit in his feelings of abandonment.

How like a Winter hath my absence been
From thee, the pleasure of the fleeting year!
What freezings have I felt, what dark days seen?
What old December's bareness everywhere?
And yet this time remov'd was summer's time,
The teeming Autumn, big with rich increase,
Bearing the wanton burthen of the prime,
Like widowed wombs after their Lords' decease:
Yet this abundant issue seem'd to me,
But hope of orphans and unfathered fruit;
For Summer and his pleasures wait on thee,
And thou away, the very birds are mute.
  Or if they sing, 'tis with so dull a cheer,
    That leaves look pale, dreading the Winter's near.

In the celebrated 'degrees' speech, Ulysses outlines the virtues of social hierarchy for the maintenance of peace and trust. His sense that government is founded on a need to repress what would otherwise be chaos, later developed in Thomas Hobbes' *Leviathan*, is still debated furiously (though not nearly so musically) in philosophy seminars and political conferences today.

ULYSSES
Troy, yet upon his basis, had been down,
And the great Hector's sword had lacked a master,
But for these instances:
The specialty of rule hath been neglected,
And look how many Grecian tents do stand
Hollow upon this plain, so many hollow factions.
When that the general is not like the hive
To whom the foragers shall all repair,
What honey is expected? Degree being vizarded,
Th'unworthiest shows as fairly in the mask.
The heavens themselves, the planets, and this centre
Observe degree, priority, and place,
Insisture, course, proportion, season, form,
Office, and custom, in all line of order.
And therefore is the glorious planet Sol
In noble eminence enthroned and sphered
Amidst the other; whose med'cinable eye
Corrects the ill aspects of planets evil,
And posts like the commandment of a king,
Sans check, to good and bad. But when the planets
In evil mixture to disorder wander,
What plagues and what portents, what mutiny,
What raging of the sea, shaking of earth,

Commotion in the winds, frights, changes, horrors,
Divert and crack, rend and deracinate
The unity and married calm of states
Quite from their fixure! O, when degree is shaked,
Which is the ladder to all high designs,
Then enterprise is sick. How could communities,
Degrees in schools and brotherhoods in cities,
Peaceful commerce from dividable shores,
The primogenitive and due of birth,
Prerogative of age, crowns, sceptres, laurels,
But by degree, stand in authentic place?
Take but degree away, untune that string,
And hark what discord follows! Each thing meets
In mere oppugnancy: the bounded waters
Should lift their bosoms higher than the shores,
And make a sop of all this solid globe;
Strength should be lord of imbecility,
And the rude son should strike his father dead;
Force should be right, or, rather, right and wrong –
Between whose endless jar justice resides –
Should lose their names, and so should justice too.
Then everything includes itself in power,
Power into will, will into appetite;
And appetite, an universal wolf,
So doubly seconded with will and power,
Must make perforce an universal prey,
And last eat up himself. Great Agamemnon,
This chaos, when degree is suffocate,
Follows the choking;
And this neglection of degree it is
That by a pace goes backward in a purpose
It hath to climb. The general's disdained
By him one step below, he by the next,
That next by him beneath: so every step,
Exampled by the first pace that is sick
Of his superior, grows to an envious fever

Of pale and bloodless emulation,
And 'tis this fever that keeps Troy on foot,
Not her own sinews. To end a tale of length,
Troy in our weakness lives, not in her strength.

October 19 | King John | Act 5 Scene 7

King John actually died of dysentery on 19 October 1216, but
Shakespeare has a disgruntled monk poison him in his play.
However, Shakespeare's history plays have made such an
impact that his dramatized version of the truth – certainly the
more appealing considering John's tyranny – is often taken as
fact.

KING JOHN
Poisoned – ill fare! Dead, forsook, cast off;
And none of you will bid the winter come
To thrust his icy fingers in my maw,
Nor let my kingdom's rivers take their course
Through my burned bosom, nor entreat the north
To make his bleak winds kiss my parchèd lips
And comfort me with cold. I do not ask you much –
I beg cold comfort; and you are so strait
And so ingrateful you deny me that.

PRINCE HENRY
O that there were some virtue in my tears
That might relieve you!

KING JOHN
The salt in them is hot.
Within me is a hell, and there the poison
Is as a fiend confined to tyrannize
On unreprievable, condemnèd blood.

October 20 | Henry VI, Part 2 | Act 2 Scene 4

On 20 October 1441, Eleanor Duchess of Gloucester appeared before the council of the Crown accused of witchcraft, 'wherof some she denyed and some she grauntid'. Shakespeare's play suggests she was tricked into practising witchcraft. Her husband Gloucester fails to protect her from banishment, despite his role as Lord Protector to young Henry VI.

DUCHESS
Ah, Gloucester, teach me to forget myself;
For whilst I think I am thy married wife,
And thou a prince, Protector of this land,
Methinks I should not thus be led along,
Mailed up in shame, with papers on my back,
And followed with a rabble that rejoice
To see my tears and hear my deep-fet groans.
The ruthless flint doth cut my tender feet,
And when I start, the envious people laugh
And bid me be advisèd how I tread.
Ah, Humphrey, can I bear this shameful yoke?
Trowest thou that e'er I'll look upon the world,
Or count them happy that enjoy the sun?
No, dark shall be my light, and night my day;
To think upon my pomp shall be my hell.
Sometime I'll say I am Duke Humphrey's wife,
And he a prince and ruler of the land;
Yet so he ruled and such a prince he was
As he stood by whilst I, his forlorn duchess,
Was made a wonder and a pointing-stock
To every idle rascal follower.
But be thou mild and blush not at my shame,
Nor stir at nothing till the axe of death
Hang over thee, as sure it shortly will;

For Suffolk, he that can do all in all
With her that hateth thee and hates us all,
And York, and impious Beaufort, that false priest,
Have all limed bushes to betray thy wings;
And fly thou how thou canst, they'll tangle thee.
But fear not thou until thy foot be snared,
Nor never seek prevention of thy foes.

October 21 | The Taming of the Shrew | Induction Scene 1

References to the fact that female parts were taken by boy actors are laced through Shakespeare's plays. For example, in the induction scenes which precede the opening of *The Taming of the Shrew*, a lord hatches a plan to bamboozle the tinker Christopher Sly by having him woken from his drink-induced nap by a pageboy dressed as a woman, who will pretend to be his wife. This lord delivers some instructions for the boy's performance in a woman's role, drawing on the sexist assumption that women's emotions are usually performances in themselves. What's more, he suggests that the boy should not only be able to play a woman well, but he should be able to play a woman as well as a woman plays a woman. This is underpinned by another much more radical assumption: gender is just a performance, even outside the context of a play.

LORD
Tell him from me – as he will win my love –
He bear himself with honourable action,
Such as he hath observed in noble ladies
Unto their lords, by them accomplishèd.
Such duty to the drunkard let him do,
With soft low tongue and lowly courtesy,
And say 'What is't your honour will command,
Wherein your lady and your humble wife
May show her duty and make known her love?'
And then with kind embracements, tempting kisses,
And with declining head into his bosom,
Bid him shed tears, as being overjoyed
To see her noble lord restored to health,
Who for this seven years hath esteemèd him
No better than a poor and loathsome beggar.

And if the boy have not a woman's gift
To rain a shower of commanded tears,
An onion will do well for such a shift,
Which in a napkin being close conveyed,
Shall in despite enforce a watery eye.

Not only did boys play the female parts (as it was illegal until the 1660s for women to act in the public theatre), but in several of the comedies, Shakespeare introduces a further gender reversal and has the female characters disguise themselves as men, right up to the reveal at the end of the play. Their secret cover is never broken and many comic moments revolve around their mistaken identities. On a more serious side, Rosalind suggests to her cousin Celia that a male disguise will lend them protection from men.

ROSALIND
Were it not better,
Because that I am more than common tall,
That I did suit me all points like a man?
A gallant curtle-axe upon my thigh,
A boar-spear in my hand, and, in my heart
Lie there what hidden woman's fear there will,
We'll have a swashing and a martial outside,
As many other mannish cowards have
That do outface it with their semblances.

October 23 | Othello | Act 5 Scene 2

In the closing moments of his life, Othello seeks to salvage some nobility for posterity by making an eloquent account of his misdeeds.

OTHELLO
Soft you; a word or two before you go.
I have done the state some service and they know't:
No more of that. I pray you in your letters
When you shall these unlucky deeds relate
Speak of me as I am: nothing extenuate,
Nor set down aught in malice. Then must you speak
Of one that loved not wisely, but too well;
Of one, not easily jealous but, being wrought,
Perplexed in the extreme; of one whose hand
Like the base Indian threw a pearl away
Richer than all his tribe; of one whose subdued eyes,
Albeit unusèd to the melting mood,
Drop tears as fast as the Arabian trees
Their med'cinable gum. Set you down this:
And say, besides, that in Aleppo once
Where a malignant and a turbaned Turk
Beat a Venetian and traduced the state,
I took by th'throat the circumcisèd dog
And smote him thus.
[*He stabs himself*]
[. . .]
OTHELLO
I kissed thee, ere I killed thee: no way but this,
Killing myself, to die upon a kiss.

There is a certain amount of playfulness to the Chorus in
Henry V, as he begs for the audience's imagination to help set
the scene. After all, there was no elaborate scenery, only the
willingness of the theatregoers to suspend their disbelief and
participate in the illusions created by the writer and his actors.
Here he calls upon our imaginations to supply a more vivid
picture of the night before the Battle of Agincourt than any
stage could set.

CHORUS
Now entertain conjecture of a time
When creeping murmur and the poring dark
Fills the wide vessel of the universe.
From camp to camp, through the foul womb of night,
The hum of either army stilly sounds,
That the fixed sentinels almost receive
The secret whispers of each other's watch.
Fire answers fire, and through their paly flames
Each battle sees the other's umbered face.
Steed threatens steed, in high and boastful neighs,
Piercing the night's dull ear; and from the tents
The armourers, accomplishing the knights,
With busy hammers closing rivets up,
Give dreadful note of preparation.
The country cocks do crow, the clocks do toll,
And the third hour of drowsy morning name.
Proud of their numbers, and secure in soul,
The confident and over-lusty French
Do the low-rated English play at dice,
And chide the cripple tardy-gaited night
Who, like a foul and ugly witch doth limp
So tediously away. The poor condemnèd English,

Like sacrifices, by their watchful fires
Sit patiently and inly ruminate
The morning's danger; and their gesture sad,
Investing lank-lean cheeks and war-worn coats,
Presenteth them unto the gazing moon
So many horrid ghosts. O now, who will behold
The royal Captain of this ruined band
Walking from watch to watch, from tent to tent,
Let him cry, 'Praise and glory on his head!'
For forth he goes and visits all his host,
Bids them good morrow with a modest smile,
And calls them brothers, friends, and countrymen.
Upon his royal face there is no note
How dread an army hath enrounded him,
Nor doth he dedicate one jot of colour
Unto the weary and all-watchèd night,
But freshly looks, and overbears attaint
With cheerful semblance and sweet majesty;
That every wretch, pining and pale before,
Beholding him, plucks comfort from his looks.
A largess universal, like the sun,
His liberal eye doth give to every one,
Thawing cold fear, that mean and gentle all
Behold, as may unworthiness define,
A little touch of Harry in the night.
And so our scene must to the battle fly;
Where – O for pity! – we shall much disgrace,
With four or five most vile and ragged foils,
Right ill-disposed in brawl ridiculous,
The name of Agincourt. Yet sit and see,
Minding true things by what their mockeries be.

October 25 | Henry V | Act 4 Scene 3

On the morning of the Battle of Agincourt, which took place
on 25 October 1415, Shakespeare's *Henry V* reflects on the
coincidence of the impending battle with St Crispin's Day.
In his oration, the battle is already envisaged as if in safe
retrospect, an occasion of triumphal national remembrance.
According to Henry, war, like festivity, elides the hierarchical
distinctions between king and countrymen, domestic festivity
and national pride. Despite these egalitarian promises, when
the list of casualties is read out after the battle nobody below
the rank of esquire is named. As well as being the day of the
Battle of Agincourt, St Crispin's Day was also the official holiday
associated with the guild of shoemakers. Thomas Dekker's
comedy *The Shoemakers' Holiday*, also premiered in 1599,
offers a rather more peace-loving account of Henry's French
wars and their consequences for London's civilians.

KING HENRY V
This day is called the Feast of Crispian:
He that outlives this day, and comes safe home,
Will stand a-tiptoe when the day is named,
And rouse him at the name of Crispian.
He that shall see this day, and live old age,
Will yearly on the vigil feast his neighbours,
And say, 'Tomorrow is Saint Crispian.'
Then will he strip his sleeve, and show his scars,
And say, 'These wounds I had on Crispin's day.'
Old men forget; yet all shall be forgot,
But he'll remember, with advantages,
What feats he did that day. Then shall our names,
Familiar in his mouth as household words,
Harry the King, Bedford and Exeter,
Warwick and Talbot, Salisbury and Gloucester,

Be in their flowing cups freshly remembered.
This story shall the good man teach his son;
And Crispin Crispian shall ne'er go by,
From this day to the ending of the world,
But we in it shall be rememberèd –
We few, we happy few, we band of brothers:
For he today that sheds his blood with me
Shall be my brother; be he ne'er so vile,
This day shall gentle his condition;
And gentlemen in England now abed
Shall think themselves accursed they were not here,
And hold their manhoods cheap, whiles any speaks
That fought with us upon Saint Crispin's day.

October 26 | Henry V | Act 4 Scene 7

The Battle of Agincourt was one of England's great victories against the odds over the French during the Hundred Years' War. Estimates as to the scale to which Henry's forces were outnumbered range between 3-1 and 30-1, which in either case suggests an impressive feat for the English. Perhaps the continuing risk of being outnumbered provides some excuse for the war crime Henry commits during the battle, when he gives orders to his men to kill their prisoners of war.

KING HENRY V
I was not angry since I came to France
Until this instant. Take a trumpet, Herald;
Ride thou unto the horsemen on yon hill.
If they will fight with us, bid them come down,
Or void the field: they do offend our sight.
If they'll do neither, we will come to them,
And make them skirr away as swift as stones
Enforcèd from the old Assyrian slings.
Besides, we'll cut the throats of those we have,
And not a man of them that we shall take
Shall taste our mercy. Go and tell them so.

October 27 | Much Ado About Nothing |
Act 2 Scene 3

Benedick and Beatrice, who have spent the play sparring in
barbed lines of prose, are about to meet again after Benedick
has been tricked into hearing that Beatrice is in love with him.
Benedick's soliloquy is one of the funniest in the canon.

BENEDICK
[*Coming forward*] This can be no trick. The
conference was sadly borne. They have the truth of
this from Hero. They seem to pity the lady; it
seems her affections have their full bent. Love me?
Why, it must be requited. I hear how I am censured:
they say I will bear myself proudly, if I perceive
the love come from her; they say too that she will
rather die than give any sign of affection. I did
never think to marry. I must not seem proud; happy
are they that hear their detractions and can put
them to mending. They say the lady is fair; 'tis a
truth, I can bear them witness; and virtuous; so,
I cannot reprove it; and wise, but for loving
me. By my troth, it is no addition to her wit, nor
no great argument of her folly, for I will be
horribly in love with her. I may chance have some
odd quirks and remnants of wit broken on me,
because I have railed so long against marriage; but
doth not the appetite alter? A man loves the meat
in his youth that he cannot endure in his age.
Shall quips and sentences and these paper bullets of
the brain awe a man from the career of his humour?
No, the world must be peopled. When I said I would
die a bachelor, I did not think I should live till I
were married. Here comes Beatrice. By this day,
she's a fair lady! I do spy some marks of love in her.

October 28 | Troilus and Cressida | Act 1 Scene 1

Sometimes two characters converse in a mixture of verse
and prose, which emphasizes their differences in both social
standing and temperament. An example of the latter can be
found in Shakespeare's ancient world, where young Troilus,
with heart aching for love of Cressida, speaks only in verse,
while her infuriatingly dilatory uncle Pandarus urges patience
in chatty prose.

TROILUS
The Greeks are strong, and skilful to their strength,
Fierce to their skill and to their fierceness valiant;
But I am weaker than a woman's tear,
Tamer than sleep, fonder than ignorance,
Less valiant than the virgin in the night,
And skilless as unpractised infancy.

PANDARUS
Well, I have told you enough of this; for my part,
I'll not meddle nor make no farther. He that will
have a cake out of the wheat must needs tarry the grinding.

TROILUS
Have I not tarried?

PANDARUS
Ay, the grinding; but you must tarry the bolting.

TROILUS
Have I not tarried?

PANDARUS
Ay, the bolting; but you must tarry the leavening.

TROILUS
Still have I tarried.

PANDARUS
Ay, to the leavening; but here's yet in the word
hereafter the kneading, the making of the cake, the
heating of the oven, and the baking. Nay, you must
stay the cooling too, or you may chance to burn your lips.

TROILUS
Patience herself, what goddess e'er she be,
Doth lesser blench at sufferance than I do.

In a play whose narrative has mainly stayed a long way from romance, Henry V meets Princess Katherine for the first time, proposes, and insists on a kiss. Given that this political alliance is one of the demands made among the victorious king's stipulations for a peace treaty, is this really a love scene? The bodies of the real couple could be visited at Westminster Abbey from around 1503 until they were eventually buried in 1778: Henry's tomb and Katherine's embalmed body could be kissed for a penny entry fee – the same price for watching the play at the Globe. The seventeenth-century diarist Samuel Pepys had the opportunity of kissing the corpse on his birthday: 'we did see . . . the body of Queen Katherine of Valois; and I had the upper part of her body in my hands, and I did kiss her mouth, reflecting upon it that I did kiss a Queen'.

KING HENRY V
Come, your answer in broken music – for thy voice is
music, and thy English broken; therefore, Queen of
all, Katherine, break thy mind to me in broken
English – wilt thou have me?

KATHERINE
Dat is as it shall please de *Roi mon père.*

KING HENRY V
Nay, it will please him well, Kate – it shall please
him, Kate.

KATHERINE
Den it sall also content me.

KING HENRY V
Upon that I kiss your hand, and I call you my Queen.

KATHERINE
Laissez, mon seigneur, laissez, laissez! Ma foi, je
ne veux point que vous abaissiez votre grandeur en
baisant la main d'une – notre Seigneur – indigne
serviteur. Excusez-moi, je vous supplie, mon
très puissant seigneur.

KING HENRY V
Then I will kiss your lips, Kate.

KATHERINE
Les dames et demoiselles pour être baisées devant
leurs noces, il n'est pas la coutume de France.

KING HENRY V
Madame my interpreter, what says she?

ALICE
Dat it is not be de fashion *pour les* ladies of
France – I cannot tell wat is *baiser en* Anglish.

KING HENRY V
To kiss.

ALICE
Your majestee *entendre* bettre *que moi.*

KING HENRY V
It is not a fashion for the maids in France to kiss
before they are married, would she say?

ALICE
Oui, vraiment.

KING HENRY V
O Kate, nice customs curtsy to great kings. Dear
Kate, you and I cannot be confined within the weak
list of a country's fashion. We are the makers of
manners, Kate, and the liberty that follows our
places stops the mouth of all find-faults – as I will
do yours for upholding the nice fashion of your
country in denying me a kiss; therefore, patiently,
and yielding.
[*Kissing her*]
You have witchcraft in your lips, Kate: there is
more eloquence in a sugar touch of them than in the
tongues of the French Council, and they should
sooner persuade Harry of England than a general
petition of monarchs.

October 30 | All's Well That Ends Well | Act 2 Scene 3

Mrs Marie Mountjoy, with whose French expatriate family Shakespeare lodged in London in the early seventeenth century, died on this date, and it is through records pertaining to a family squabble that we get to learn something more about Shakespeare's daily life. Shakespeare was called as a witness in a case of a disputed dowry. He had initially been put upon by the landlady to persuade her daughter's suitor to marry her on promise of a dowry. After the marriage, this husband brought proceedings against the Mountjoys for the non-payment of the promised amount. Perhaps as befits someone sympathetic to all sides in a drama, Shakespeare seems to have given contradictory testimony as to how much money had been promised. It's not much, but it is a relative feast of information for those seeking some account of Shakespeare's everyday circumstances in London. In *All's Well That Ends Well* a young aristocrat called Bertram is forced into a marriage by the King of France to Helena, the orphan of a mere doctor. The King promises to pay her dowry during this passage. It's possible that Shakespeare played the part of the King, as a contemporary report notes that he played 'kingly parts'.

KING
Here, take her hand,
Proud, scornful boy, unworthy this good gift,
That dost in vile misprision shackle up
My love and her desert; that canst not dream
We, poising us in her defective scale,
Shall weigh thee to the beam; that wilt not know
It is in us to plant thine honour where
We please to have it grow. Check thy contempt.
Obey our will which travails in thy good.

Believe not thy disdain, but presently
Do thine own fortunes that obedient right
Which both thy duty owes and our power claims;
Or I will throw thee from my care for ever
Into the staggers and the careless lapse
Of youth and ignorance, both my revenge and hate
Loosing upon thee in the name of justice,
Without all terms of pity. Speak. Thine answer.

BERTRAM
Pardon, my gracious lord; for I submit
My fancy to your eyes. When I consider
What great creation and what dole of honour
Flies where you bid it, I find that she, which late
Was in my nobler thoughts most base, is now
The praisèd of the King; who, so ennobled,
Is as 'twere born so.

KING
Take her by the hand
And tell her she is thine; to whom I promise
A counterpoise, if not to thy estate,
A balance more replete.

BERTRAM
I take her hand.

KING
Good fortune and the favour of the King
Smile upon this contract, whose ceremony
Shall seem expedient on the now-born brief,
And be performed tonight. The solemn feast
Shall more attend upon the coming space,
Expecting absent friends. As thou lovest her
Thy love's to me religious; else, does err.

October 31 | Macbeth | Act 4 Scene 1

Halloween is the eve of All Saints' Day, featuring a strange confluence of pagan and Christian rituals. The Elizabethan population regarded this as a night for warding off evil spirits and satanic visitations, which had a tight hold on the public imagination. Here, the unforgettable witches of *Macbeth* concoct their fiendish potion.

ALL
Double, double, toil and trouble;
Fire burn, and cauldron bubble.

SECOND WITCH
Fillet of a fenny snake
In the cauldron boil and bake;
Eye of newt, and toe of frog,
Wool of bat, and tongue of dog,
Adder's fork, and blind-worm's sting,
Lizard's leg and howlet's wing,
For a charm of powerful trouble,
Like a hell-broth, boil and bubble.

ALL
Double, double, toil and trouble;
Fire burn, and cauldron bubble.

THIRD WITCH
Scale of dragon, tooth of wolf,
Witch's mummy, maw and gulf
Of the ravined salt sea shark,
Root of hemlock digged i'the dark,
Liver of blaspheming Jew,
Gall of goat, and slips of yew

Silvered in the moon's eclipse,
Nose of Turk, and Tartar's lips,
Finger of birth-strangled babe
Ditch-delivered by a drab,
Make the gruel thick and slab.
Add thereto a tiger's chaudron,
For the ingredients of our cauldron.

ALL
Double, double, toil and trouble;
Fire burn, and cauldron bubble.

SECOND WITCH
Cool it with a baboon's blood;
Then the charm is firm and good.

November

November 1 | The Taming of the Shrew | Act 4 Scene 3

Hallowmas, or All Saints' Day, is connected with a tradition of begging and becomes closely linked with degraded dignity. Lovestruck Valentine is said to 'speak puling, like a Hallowmas beggar', while Richard II's wife 'came adorned hither like sweet May,' but when banished is 'Sent back like Hallowmas'. The shame of destitution was all too real for the four-fifths of the English population who fell below the poverty line towards the end of Elizabeth's reign. Disappointing harvests and plague outbreaks caused prices to climb as steeply as wages fell, and government assistance was meagre at best, absent at worst. The alternative relief provided by the Church often fell short of the needs of their parishes. Katherine, who is starved of sleep and food by her new husband Petruchio, compares her state to the familiar plight of the begging poor.

KATHERINE
The more my wrong, the more his spite appears.
What, did he marry me to famish me?
Beggars that come unto my father's door
Upon entreaty have a present alms,
If not, elsewhere they meet with charity.
But I, who never knew how to entreat,
Nor never needed that I should entreat,
Am starved for meat, giddy for lack of sleep,
With oaths kept waking, and with brawling fed.
And that which spites me more than all these wants,
He does it under name of perfect love,
As who should say, if I should sleep or eat,
'Twere deadly sickness or else present death.
I prithee go and get me some repast,
I care not what, so it be wholesome food.

All Souls' Day, which follows Hallowmas every year, is traditionally an opportunity to commemorate the dead. The spectacle of death formed a source of entertainment in Elizabethan England: London Bridge would have the heads of traitors hung at its southern end and public executions drew big crowds. Pamphlets containing the crimes of the convicted would be circulated before the victim would be allowed a final speech before the assembled spectators. This allowance was curtailed as some dissenters were openly criticizing the state without fear of ramification – unless, of course, they had family who could be punished on their behalf. Lord Buckingham bewails his fate at the executioner's block, after deserting Richard III and being recaptured and sentenced.

BUCKINGHAM
Why, then All Souls' Day is my body's doomsday.
This is the day which in King Edward's time
I wished might fall on me when I was found
False to his children or his wife's allies;
This is the day wherein I wished to fall
By the false faith of him whom most I trusted;
This, this All Souls' Day to my fearful soul
Is the determined respite of my wrongs.
That high All-seer that I dallied with
Hath turned my feignèd prayer on my head
And given in earnest what I begged in jest.
Thus doth He force the swords of wicked men
To turn their own points on their masters' bosoms;
Thus Margaret's curse falls heavy on my neck:
'When he,' quoth she, 'shall split thy heart with sorrow,
Remember Margaret was a prophetess.'
– Come lead me, officers, to the block of shame.
Wrong hath but wrong, and blame the due of blame.

The first Act of Supremacy was passed by Henry VIII on 3
November 1534, which made the reigning monarch the head of
the Church of England and confirmed England's schism with
Rome. The theological groundwork that would entrench the
Protestant faith as an alternative to Catholicism was pioneered
by Martin Luther, who nailed a paper containing Ninety-
five Theses – which would spark the Protestant reformation
– onto the door of Castle Church in Wittenberg, Germany.
Hamlet's determination to return to his studies at Wittenberg,
with its connotations of anti-authoritarianism, is therefore
understandably greeted with misgivings by the new king.
Interestingly enough, Shakespeare's father, in his capacity as
chamberlain of Stratford, recorded that two shillings had been
'paid for defacing images in the Chapel of the Holy Cross' – an
important job in post-Reformation England, in which any form
of idolatry was banned.

KING CLAUDIUS
'Tis sweet and commendable in your nature, Hamlet,
To give these mourning duties to your father.
But you must know your father lost a father;
That father lost, lost his; and the survivor bound
In filial obligation for some term
To do obsequious sorrow. But to persever
In obstinate condolement is a course
Of impious stubbornness. 'Tis unmanly grief.
It shows a will most incorrect to heaven,
A heart unfortified, a mind impatient,
An understanding simple and unschooled.
For what we know must be, and is as common
As any the most vulgar thing to sense,
Why should we in our peevish opposition

Take it to heart? Fie, 'tis a fault to heaven,
A fault against the dead, a fault to nature,
To reason most absurd, whose common theme
Is death of fathers, and who still hath cried,
From the first corse till he that died today,
'This must be so.' We pray you throw to earth
This unprevailing woe, and think of us
As of a father. For let the world take note,
You are the most immediate to our throne;
And with no less nobility of love
Than that which dearest father bears his son
Do I impart toward you. For your intent
In going back to school in Wittenberg,
It is most retrograde to our desire;
And, we beseech you, bend you to remain
Here in the cheer and comfort of our eye,
Our chiefest courtier, cousin, and our son.

Falstaff's various prodigious appetites often coincide. In
anticipation of his rendezvous with Mistress Ford (who has
no intention of satisfying his desires, but has tricked him into
coming to Herne's Oak so that he can be publicly shamed), his
mind drifts immediately to thoughts of 'kissing comfits', which
could sweeten his breath, and 'potatoes' and 'eringoes' (sea
holly) which were both considered aphrodisiacs. Amidst an
exchange of deer-related innuendo (deer have associations with
cuckoldry and virility), Falstaff famously beckons the sky to rain
potatoes.

MISTRESS FORD
Sir John! Art thou there, my deer, my male deer?

FALSTAFF
My doe with the black scut! Let the sky rain
potatoes. Let it thunder to the tune of 'Greensleeves',
hail kissing-comfits, and snow eringoes. Let
there come a tempest of provocation, I will shelter me here.

Macbeth was probably first performed within a year of the foiled Gunpowder Plot in 1605. There was widespread outrage that King James I of England (and VI of Scotland) – the divinely appointed monarch – was so nearly murdered by Catholic insurgents, including the infamous Guido (Guy) Fawkes. Tracing the consequences of a plot to assassinate a king, Macbeth must have resonated with the fears of its first audiences.

LADY MACBETH
. . . screw your courage to the sticking place,
And we'll not fail. When Duncan is asleep –
Whereto the rather shall his day's hard journey
Soundly invite him – his two chamberlains
Will I with wine and wassail so convince
That memory, the warder of the brain,
Shall be a-fume, and the receipt of reason
A limbeck only. When in swinish sleep
Their drenchèd natures lie as in a death,
What cannot you and I perform upon
The unguarded Duncan? What not put upon
His spongy officers, who shall bear the guilt
Of our great quell?

MACBETH
Bring forth men-children only!
For thy undaunted mettle should compose
Nothing but males. Will it not be received,
When we have marked with blood those sleepy two
Of his own chamber and used their very daggers,
That they have done't?

LADY MACBETH
Who dares receive it other,
As we shall make our griefs and clamour roar
Upon his death?

MACBETH
I am settled; and bend up
Each corporal agent to this terrible feat.
Away, and mock the time with fairest show:
False face must hide what the false heart doth know.

Tormented by having committed murder and treason, Macbeth becomes despondent and paranoid, while his wife, who started out as the more strong-willed of the two, is sent mad by guilt-ridden delusions. In the end, ambition proves to be this couple's hamartia (tragic flaw). In this chilling sleep-walking scene, Lady Macbeth betrays her part in Duncan's murder and is overheard by her doctor as she tries to scrub imaginary stains from her hands.

LADY MACBETH
Out, damned spot! Out, I say! – One: two: why
then, 'tis time to do't. – Hell is murky! – Fie, my
lord, fie! A soldier and afeard? – What need we
fear who knows it, when none can call our power to
accompt? – Yet who would have thought the old man
to have had so much blood in him?

DOCTOR
Do you mark that?

LADY MACBETH
The Thane of Fife had a wife; where is she now? –
What, will these hands ne'er be clean? – No more
o'that, my lord, no more o' that. You mar all with
this starting.

DOCTOR
Go to, go to: you have known what you should not.

GENTLEWOMAN
She has spoke what she should not, I am sure of
that. Heaven knows what she has known.

LADY MACBETH
Here's the smell of the blood still. All the
perfumes of Arabia will not sweeten this little
hand. Oh! Oh! Oh!

DOCTOR
What a sigh is there! The heart is sorely charged.

GENTLEWOMAN
I would not have such a heart in my bosom for the
dignity of the whole body.

DOCTOR
Well, well, well.

GENTLEWOMAN
Pray God it be, sir.

DOCTOR
This disease is beyond my practice; yet I have known
those which have walked in their sleep who have died
holily in their beds.

LADY MACBETH
Wash your hands; put on your nightgown; look not so
pale. I tell you yet again, Banquo's buried; he
cannot come out on's grave.

DOCTOR
Even so?

LADY MACBETH
To bed, to bed! there's knocking at the gate.
Come, come, come, come, give me your hand. What's
done cannot be undone. To bed, to bed, to bed.

November 7 | A Midsummer Night's Dream | Act 2 Scene 1

Winter's advance could be hurried on by a marital dispute in the fairy world, if *A Midsummer Night's Dream* is to be believed. The powerful King Oberon's jealousy over Titania, and their custody dispute over an Indian boy, has caused the weather to alter and turn wintry in Theseus's human kingdom.

TITANIA
These are the forgeries of jealousy;
And never since the middle summer's spring
Met we on hill, in dale, forest, or mead,
By pavèd fountain or by rushy brook,
Or in the beached margent of the sea
To dance our ringlets to the whistling wind,
But with thy brawls thou hast disturbed our sport.
Therefore the winds, piping to us in vain,
As in revenge have sucked up from the sea
Contagious fogs which, falling in the land,
Have every pelting river made so proud
That they have overborne their continents.
The ox hath therefore stretched his yoke in vain,
The ploughman lost his sweat, and the green corn
Hath rotted ere his youth attained a beard;
The fold stands empty in the drownèd field,
And crows are fatted with the murrion flock.
The nine men's morris is filled up with mud,
And the quaint mazes in the wanton green
For lack of tread are undistinguishable.
The human mortals want their winter cheer.
No night is now with hymn or carol blessed.
Therefore the moon, the governess of floods,
Pale in her anger, washes all the air,

That rheumatic diseases do abound;
And thorough this distemperature we see
The seasons alter: hoary-headed frosts
Far in the fresh lap of the crimson rose,
And on old Hiems' thin and icy crown
An odorous chaplet of sweet summer buds
Is as in mockery set. The spring, the summer,
The childing autumn, angry winter change
Their wonted liveries, and the mazèd world,
By their increase, now knows not which is which.
And this same progeny of evils
Comes from our debate, from our dissension.
We are their parents and original.

Romeo's friend Mercutio gets caught in the conflict between two noble houses, Capulet and Montague, and loses his life in a needless brawl. In this fictional Verona, just as in Elizabethan England, there were laws against fighting on the streets. Mercutio is the epitome of hot-headed masculinity: full of bravado, quickly provoked to violence, and mercurial (which shares a root with his name).

MERCUTIO
Ay, ay, a scratch, a scratch. Marry, 'tis enough.
Where is my page? Go, villain, fetch a surgeon.

[. . .]

No, 'tis not so deep as a well, nor so wide as a
church-door. But 'tis enough. 'Twill serve. Ask for
me tomorrow, and you shall find me a grave man. I
am peppered, I warrant, for this world. A plague a'both
your houses! Zounds, a dog, a rat, a mouse, a
cat, to scratch a man to death! A braggart, a
rogue, a villain, that fights by the book of
arithmetic! Why the devil came you between us? I
was hurt under your arm.

[. . .]

Help me into some house, Benvolio,
Or I shall faint. A plague a'both your houses!
They have made worms' meat of me.
I have it, and soundly too. Your houses!

November 9 | Richard III | Act 3 Scene 5

There was a bizarre custom associated with London's Lord Mayor's Day, held every 9 November, which involved the Lord Mayor's fool leaping, fully clothed, into a bowl of custard. The elderly councillor, Lafeu, makes reference to it in *All's Well That Ends Well*: 'You have made shift to run int 't, boots and spurs and all, like him that leaped into the custard.' The Lord Mayor had significant powers in the city and considerable influence over its population, so would have been an essential ally in keeping the domestic peace. Realizing this, Richard III dupes the Lord Mayor into believing he is a religious and retiring man, reluctant to take up the throne, while framing the loyal Hastings as a traitor at the same time. Notice Richard's use of 'you' instead of the informal 'thou' in the way he addresses the Mayor, calculated to show humility and respect.

LOVEL
Here is the head of that ignoble traitor,
The dangerous and unsuspected Hastings.

RICHARD
So dear I loved the man that I must weep.
I took him for the plainest harmless creature
That breathed upon this earth a Christian;
Made him my book, wherein my soul recorded
The history of all her secret thoughts.
So smooth he daubed his vice with show of virtue
That, his apparent open guilt omitted –
I mean, his conversation with Shore's wife –
He lived from all attainder of suspect.

BUCKINGHAM
Well, well, he was the covert'st sheltered traitor.

Would you imagine, or almost believe,
Were't not that by great preservation
We live to tell it, that the subtle traitor
This day had plotted, in the Council House,
To murder me and my good Lord of Gloucester?

LORD MAYOR
Had he done so?

RICHARD
What? Think you we are Turks or infidels?
Or that we would, against the form of law,
Proceed thus rashly to the villain's death
But that the extreme peril of the case,
The peace of England, and our persons' safety
Enforced us to this execution?

LORD MAYOR
Now fair befall you! He deserved his death,
And you my good lords both have well proceeded
To warn false traitors from the like attempts.

BUCKINGHAM
I never looked for better at his hands
After he once fell in with Mistress Shore.
Yet had we not determined he should die
Until your lordship came to see his end,
Which now the loving haste of these our friends,
Somewhat against our meaning, have prevented;
Because, my lord, we would have had you heard
The traitor speak, and timorously confess
The manner and the purpose of his treason,
That you might well have signified the same
Unto the citizens, who haply may
Misconstrue us in him and wail his death.

Joan of Arc, or Joan la Pucelle in the play, is one of the best rhetoricians to be found in the entire *Henry VI* trilogy. She is able, despite being a woman and of lowly birth, to persuade the Dauphin (or heir to the French throne) to allow her the command of an entire French army against the English. She does this partly by the strength of her words, but also by defeating him in single combat. She is the exemplar of political will, warlike virtue and righteous authority, against whom many leaders would pale in comparison.

JOAN LA PUCELLE
Dauphin, I am by birth a shepherd's daughter,
My wit untrained in any kind of art.
Heaven and Our Lady gracious hath it pleased
To shine on my contemptible estate.
Lo, whilst I waited on my tender lambs
And to sun's parching heat displayed my cheeks,
God's Mother deignèd to appear to me,
And in a vision full of majesty
Willed me to leave my base vocation
And free my country from calamity;
Her aid she promised and assured success.
In complete glory she revealed herself;
And whereas I was black and swart before,
With those clear rays which she infused on me
That beauty am I blessed with which you see.
Ask me what question thou canst possible,
And I will answer unpremeditated.
My courage try by combat, if thou darest,
And thou shalt find that I exceed my sex.
Resolve on this: thou shalt be fortunate
If thou receive me for thy warlike mate.

November 11 | Henry VI, Part 3 | Act 2 Scene 5

November 11 is Martinmas, a feast day held in commemoration
of St Martin who spent his life protecting the vulnerable. The
date now strikes a more ominous resonance as Armistice Day,
and we still remember the vulnerable and unprotected on
this day. Here the weakened Henry VI, a compassionate man
tormented by war, feels a crushing helplessness at the outset of
the Wars of the Roses.

KING HENRY VI
Woe above woe! Grief more than common grief!
O that my death would stay these ruthful deeds!
O pity, pity, gentle heaven, pity!
The red rose and the white are on his face,
The fatal colours of our striving houses;
The one his purple blood right well resembles;
The other his pale cheeks, methinks, presenteth.
Wither one rose, and let the other flourish;
If you contend, a thousand lives must wither.

Richard II blames himself for his loss of the throne, as he
reasons that he conceded the crown to a usurper. Not only
has he been downgraded from a king to a man, he is the worst
kind of man because he is a traitor to the rightful king he once
embodied.

KING RICHARD II
Mine eyes are full of tears. I cannot see.
And yet salt water blinds them not so much
But they can see a sort of traitors here.
Nay, if I turn mine eyes upon myself
I find myself a traitor with the rest.
For I have given here my soul's consent
To'undeck the pompous body of a king;
Made glory base, and sovereignty a slave;
Proud majesty, a subject; state, a peasant.
[. . .]
No lord of thine, thou haught, insulting man;
Nor no man's lord. I have no name, no title –
No, not that name was given me at the font –
But 'tis usurped. Alack the heavy day,
That I have worn so many winters out
And know not now what name to call myself!
O that I were a mockery king of snow,
Standing before the sun of Bolingbroke,
To melt myself away in water-drops!
Good king; great king – and yet not greatly good –
An if my word be sterling yet in England
Let it command a mirror hither straight
That it may show me what a face I have
Since it is bankrupt of his majesty.

Shakespeare stimulates every sense, giving images a smell, a sound, and a colour even when he doesn't mention those aspects explicitly. When read or heard, the language can be completely immersive, particularly in the later plays. However complex Caliban of *The Tempest* may be, what is certain is that he speaks one of the most beautiful speeches in the play. The words themselves, like the isle he talks of, hum with gentle sounds and sweet airs.

CALIBAN
Be not afeard; the isle is full of noises,
Sounds, and sweet airs, that give delight and hurt not.
Sometimes a thousand twangling instruments
Will hum about mine ears; and sometime voices,
That if I then had waked after long sleep
Will make me sleep again; and then in dreaming,
The clouds methought would open, and show riches
Ready to drop upon me, that when I waked
I cried to dream again.

The rule of three is common among artists of all kinds, often featuring in the composition of melodies and paintings in order to underpin a sense of balance and harmony. All the more jarring, then, that Lear lets out a 'howl' four times, over-spilling the ubiquitous rule of three in his unquenchable grief at the death of Cordelia, his youngest and favourite daughter. The scene is devastating, especially as Lear imagines he hears her speak even after she has been killed.

KING LEAR
Howl, howl, howl, howl! O, you are men of stones.
Had I your tongues and eyes, I'd use them so
That heaven's vault should crack. She's gone for ever.
I know when one is dead, and when one lives;
She's dead as earth. Lend me a looking-glass;
If that her breath will mist or stain the stone,
Why then she lives.
[. . .]
This feather stirs – she lives! If it be so,
It is a chance which does redeem all sorrows
That ever I have felt.
[. . .]
A plague upon you, murderers, traitors all!
I might have saved her; now she's gone for ever.
Cordelia, Cordelia, stay a little. Ha!
What is't thou sayest? Her voice was ever soft,
Gentle and low – an excellent thing in woman.
I killed the slave that was a-hanging thee.

November 15 | The Winter's Tale | Act 4 Scene 4

A pedlar's life involved travelling about, touting for business in improvised locations, much like the life of an actor. Both professions came to be regarded with suspicion at a time when harsh vagrancy laws were put in place to limit the movement of people for fear of organized rebellion. Autolycus dons a pedlar's habit and adopts many of its stereotypical ulterior motives – to con, cheat and blag a trade amongst guileless pastoral communities. The conniving character made an impression on the astrologer Simon Forman, who saw *The Winter's Tale* in 1611 and drew a moral from it, writing in his diary, 'Beware of trusting feigned beggars or fawning felons'.

AUTOLYCUS
Will you buy any tape,
Or lace for your cape,
My dainty duck, my dear-a?
Any silk, any thread,
Any toys for your head,
Of the new'st and fin'st, fin'st wear-a?
Come to the pedlar:
Money's a meddler
That doth utter all men's ware-a.

November 16 is St Edmund's Day, named after the original
patron saint of England (before St George). Edmund was an
early king of East Anglia, buried in Bury St Edmunds, which
was a town of enormous royal importance during the reign of
King John. The dying Viscount Melun warns his fellow English
nobles of the French King's plan to behead them, after Louis
has used them to gain victory over John. This duplicitous plan
was sworn upon the altar at St Edmund – the very place where
a treaty between the two nations had been broached shortly
before.

MELUN
Fly, noble English, you are bought and sold.
Unthread the rude eye of rebellion,
And welcome home again discarded faith.
Seek out King John and fall before his feet;
For if the French be lords of this loud day,
He means to recompense the pains you take
By cutting off your heads. Thus hath he sworn,
And I with him, and many more with me,
Upon the altar at Saint Edmundsbury;
Even on that altar where we swore to you
Dear amity and everlasting love.

November 17 | Love's Labour's Lost | Act 5 Scene 2

Elizabeth I succeeded to the throne on 17 November 1558 after the death of her sister, Mary I, and this day remained a national holiday – known as 'Queen Bess's Day' – well into the eighteenth century. *Love's Labour's Lost* ends with a Princess turning Queen, whose rhetoric seems to draw flattering parallels with the real Queen, and who inherits her throne without a husband. Unusually for a comedy, the play thus ends with a death rather than a marriage: postponing an answer to the King of Navarre's proposal, the Princess begins her reign by declaring a year's mourning for her deceased father.

PRINCESS
A time, methinks, too short
To make a world-without-end bargain in.
No, no, my lord, your grace is perjured much,
Full of dear guiltiness; and therefore this:
If for my love – as there is no such cause –
You will do aught, this shall you do for me:
Your oath I will not trust; but go with speed
To some forlorn and naked hermitage,
Remote from all the pleasures of the world;
There stay until the twelve celestial signs
Have brought about the annual reckoning.
If this austere insociable life
Change not your offer made in heat of blood;
If frosts and fasts, hard lodging and thin weeds,
Nip not the gaudy blossoms of your love,
But that it bear this trial, and last love;
Then, at the expiration of the year,
Come challenge me, challenge me by these deserts,
And, by this virgin palm now kissing thine,
I will be thine; and, till that instance, shut

My woeful self up in a mourning house,
Raining the tears of lamentation
For the remembrance of my father's death.
If this thou do deny, let our hands part,
Neither entitled in the other's heart.

November 18 | Othello | Act 4 Scene 1

Desdemona is just as distraught that Othello thinks she has
been unfaithful, as Othello is at thinking it. Like her husband
who is turned to self-loathing by the suspicion, she examines
herself for anything that could have given him the idea and asks
Iago for advice. Little does she know, but her choice of confidant
is sorely misjudged: Iago is the architect of her present misery.
She kneels before him in this scene, giving another example of
stage directions being incorporated into the dialogue: 'Here I
kneel'.

DESDEMONA
O good Iago,
What shall I do to win my lord again?
Good friend, go to him; for, by this light of heaven,
I know not how I lost him. Here I kneel:
If e'er my will did trespass 'gainst his love,
Either in discourse of thought or actual deed;
Or that mine eyes, mine ears, or any sense
Delighted them in any other form;
Or that I do not yet, and ever did,
And ever will – though he do shake me off
To beggarly divorcement – love him dearly,
Comfort forswear me! Unkindness may do much,
And his unkindness may defeat my life,
But never taint my love. I cannot say 'whore':
It does abhor me now I speak the word;
To do the act that might the addition earn
Not the world's mass of vanity could make me.

Hamlet's inner turmoil has every outward appearance of
insanity, which breaks Ophelia's heart. She has only five scenes,
and in each one her state of mind is connected with Hamlet's
treatment of her though she only appears onstage with him
once (unless you count his presence at her funeral). John
Everett Millais' famous painting *Ophelia* captures the loneliness
in which she bears her suffering at the moment of her 'muddy
death'; the culmination of an anguish which builds throughout
the play.

OPHELIA
O, what a noble mind is here o'erthrown!
The courtier's, soldier's, scholar's, eye, tongue, sword,
Th'expectancy and rose of the fair state,
The glass of fashion and the mould of form,
Th'observed of all observers, quite, quite down!
And I, of ladies most deject and wretched,
That sucked the honey of his music vows,
Now see that noble and most sovereign reason
Like sweet bells jangled, out of tune and harsh,
That unmatched form and feature of blown youth
Blasted with ecstasy: O, woe is me
T'have seen what I have seen, see what I see!

The Jailer's Daughter is one of the most engaging characters in
The Two Noble Kinsmen. Her hopes of requited love are cruelly
dashed when the young nobleman Palamon trots off in pursuit
of Theseus's royal sister Emilia, who is just as indifferent to
him as he is to the jailer's daughter. Her aspirational love of
the noble-born prisoner is touchingly naive, especially as she
initially tries to reason herself out of it. As always, reason holds
nothing to the course of young love, and she decides on a grand
gesture to convince him to return her affection.

DAUGHTER
Why should I love this gentleman? 'Tis odds
He never will affect me; I am base,
My father the mean keeper of his prison,
And he a prince. To marry him is hopeless;
To be his whore is witless. Out upon't!
What pushes are we wenches driven to
When fifteen once has found us! First I saw him;
I, seeing, thought he was a goodly man;
He has as much to please a woman in him –
If he please to bestow it so – as ever
These eyes yet looked on. Next, I pitied him,
And so would any young wench, o' my conscience,
That ever dreamed, or vowed her maidenhead
To a young handsome man. Then I loved him,
Extremely loved him, infinitely loved him;
And yet he had a cousin, fair as he too;
But in my heart was Palamon, and there,
Lord, what a coil he keeps! To hear him
Sing in an evening, what a heaven it is!
And yet his songs are sad ones. Fairer spoken

Was never gentleman; when I come in
To bring him water in a morning, first
He bows his noble body, then salutes me, thus:
'Fair, gentle maid, good morrow; may thy goodness
Get thee a happy husband.' Once he kissed me;
I loved my lips the better ten days after –
Would he would do so every day! He grieves much,
And me as much to see his misery.
What should I do to make him know I love him?
For I would fain enjoy him. Say I ventured
To set him free? What says the law then? Thus much
For law or kindred! I will do it;
And this night, or tomorrow, he shall love me.

The passionate sonneteer feels the chill of winter whenever his beloved turns away because the 'fair youth' is like the sun to him.

Full many a glorious morning have I seen,
Flatter the mountain-tops with sovereign eye,
Kissing with golden face the meadows green,
Gilding pale streams with heavenly alchymy;
Anon permit the basest clouds to ride,
With ugly rack on his celestial face,
And from the forlorn world his visage hide
Stealing unseen to west with this disgrace:
Even so my Sun one early morn did shine,
With all triumphant splendor on my brow,
But out alack, he was but one hour mine,
The region cloud hath mask'd him from me now.
  Yet him for this, my love no whit disdaineth,
    Suns of the world may stain when heaven's sun staineth.

St Cecilia's Day commemorates the musicians of the world
– sixteenth-century poet John Dryden paid tribute to the
occasion in a poem, which Handel would turn into a masterful
cantata. Although Shakespeare does not mention the saint,
music is everywhere in his universe. Pericles, reunited with his
daughter Marina, whom he thought dead, is taken up by such
music before any others on stage can hear it, connecting the
harmonious balance of the cosmos with the return of his long-
lost child.

PERICLES
I embrace you.
Give me my robes. I am wild in my beholding.
O, heavens bless my girl! But hark, what music?
Tell Helicanus, my Marina, tell him
O'er, point by point, for yet he seems to doubt,
How sure you are my daughter. But what music?

HELICANUS
My lord, I hear none.

PERICLES
None?
The music of the spheres! List, my Marina!

LYSIMACHUS
It is not good to cross him; give him way.

PERICLES
Rarest sounds! Do ye not hear?

LYSIMACHUS
Music, my lord?

PERICLES
I hear most heavenly music.
It nips me unto listening, and thick slumber
Hangs upon mine eyes. Let me rest.

Since ancient times, St Clement's Day celebrated the
metalworkers and blacksmiths, who would appreciate this
convenient break between Hallowmas and Christmas. While
history plays focus on the aristocrats, commoners have
an important political role and the wise king listens to the
murmurings of his population. King John was not a wise
king. Hubert brings news to John how smiths and tailors are
gossiping about young Arthur's death, and whispering omens
and prophesies. John had indirectly issued orders for his
nephew to be killed, as being the son of John's elder brother,
Arthur had a claim to the throne; he had been more popular
than John, but ultimately not wily enough to become king.

HUBERT
Old men and beldams in the streets
Do prophesy upon it dangerously.
Young Arthur's death is common in their mouths,
And when they talk of him they shake their heads
And whisper one another in the ear;
And he that speaks doth gripe the hearer's wrist,
Whilst he that hears makes fearful action,
With wrinkled brows, with nods, with rolling eyes.
I saw a smith stand with his hammer, thus,
The whilst his iron did on the anvil cool,
With open mouth swallowing a tailor's news;
Who, with his shears and measure in his hand,
Standing on slippers, which his nimble haste
Had falsely thrust upon contrary feet,
Told of a many thousand warlike French
That were embattailèd and ranked in Kent.
Another lean unwashed artificer
Cuts off his tale and talks of Arthur's death.

November 24 | The Taming of the Shrew | Act 3 Scene 1

Elizabethan playwrights would have been aware of the Italian *commedia dell'arte* tradition, which was influential through Europe at the time. These were mostly gag-packed improvised plays which used stock characters, from which Shakespeare might have borrowed the *inamorati* (lovers) who are kept apart by the *vecchi* (older generation, or 'pantaloons'), and helped to be together by the *zanni* (comic servants). We still use the term zany to refer to eccentricity in a person, though to Shakespeare the 'zanies' were much more tricksterish and quick-witted. Lucentio draws from the tradition by dressing up as a schoolmaster to outwit Baptista and gain access to the latter's younger daughter, Bianca.

BIANCA
Where left we last?

LUCENTIO
Here, madam.
[*He reads*]
'*Hic ibat Simois, hic est Sigeia tellus,
Hic steterat Priami regia celsa senis.*'

BIANCA
Construe them.

LUCENTIO
'*Hic ibat*', as I told you before – '*Simois*', I am
Lucentio – '*hic est*', son unto Vincentio of Pisa –
'*Sigeia tellus*', disguised thus to get your love –
'*Hic steterat*', and that Lucentio that comes
a-wooing – '*Priami*', is my man Tranio – '*regia*',

bearing my port – '*celsa senis*', that we might
beguile the old pantaloon.

HORTENSIO
Madam, my instrument's in tune.

BIANCA
Let's hear. [*He plays*] O fie! The treble jars.

LUCENTIO
Spit in the hole, man, and tune again.

BIANCA
Now let me see if I can construe it: '*Hic ibat
Simois*', I know you not – '*hic est Sigeia tellus*', I
trust you not – '*Hic steterat Priami*', take heed
he hear us not – '*regia*', presume not – '*celsa senis*',
despair not.

St Catherine's Day on 25 November was a festival principally for women's merrymaking. Virginia Woolf, in her widely celebrated essay *A Room of One's Own* wrote about the near absence of friendship between women in literature, who are either sisters, love rivals, or employed by one another. Yet Mistress Quickly and Doll Tearsheet have a touching friendship in amongst the quarrelsome, self-involved and often duplicitous men of *Henry IV, Part 2*. Here they are 'Catherining', a verb used to describe companionship between women at this time.

MISTRESS QUICKLY
I' faith, sweetheart, methinks now you are in an excellent good temporality. Your pulsidge beats as extraordinarily as heart would desire, and your colour, I warrant you, is as red as any rose, in good truth, la! But, i'faith, you have drunk too much canaries, and that's a marvellous searching wine, and it perfumes the blood ere one can say 'What's this?' How do you now?

DOLL TEARSHEET
Better than I was – hem!

MISTRESS QUICKLY
Why, that's well said – a good heart's worth gold.

'Eye(s)' are everywhere in *Love's Labour's Lost*, often as portals through which lovers are enchanted; communicating, like poetry, before they are understood. The irrepressible Boyet cottons on to the King's affection for the Princess and announces his suspicions with such a tripping lightness that the language of glances was never so eloquently put into words.

BOYET
Why, all his behaviours did make their retire
To the court of his eye, peeping thorough desire.
His heart, like an agate, with your print impressed,
Proud with his form, in his eye pride expressed.
His tongue, all impatient to speak and not see,
Did stumble with haste in his eyesight to be.
All senses to that sense did make their repair,
To feel only looking on fairest of fair.
Methought all his senses were locked in his eye,
As jewels in crystal for some prince to buy;
Who, tendering their own worth from where they were
   glassed,
Did point you to buy them along as you passed.
His face's own margent did quote such amazes
That all eyes saw his eyes enchanted with gazes.
I'll give you Aquitaine, and all that is his,
An you give him for my sake but one loving kiss.

November 27 | Much Ado About Nothing | Act 5 Scene 4

A marriage licence was issued for an eighteen-year-old 'Wm Shaxpere' and a twenty-six-year-old 'Annam Whateley' (a clerk's erroneous transcription of Anne Hathaway), on 27 November 1582. They married the next day away from Stratford, perhaps preferring a private service as Anne was pregnant at the time. Consistent with convention, most of Shakespeare's comedies end in a marriage, usually attended by a nobleman to reinstate order after the preceding romantic chaos. That said, the relationships in question were rarely conventional themselves; Beatrice and Benedick are reconciled to marriage after spending much of the play professing their hatred for one another.

BENEDICK
Do not you love me?

BEATRICE
Why no, no more than reason.

BENEDICK
Why, then your uncle and the Prince and Claudio
Have been deceived; they swore you did.

BEATRICE
Do not you love me?

BENEDICK
Troth no, no more than reason.

BEATRICE
Why, then my cousin, Margaret, and Ursula
Are much deceived; for they did swear you did.

BENEDICK
They swore that you were almost sick for me.

BEATRICE
They swore that you were well-nigh dead for me.

BENEDICK
'Tis no such matter. Then you do not love me?

BEATRICE
No, truly, but in friendly recompense.
[. . .]

BENEDICK
Come, I will have thee; but, by this light, I take thee for pity.

BEATRICE
I would not deny you; but, by this good day, I yield upon great persuasion; and partly to save your life, for I was told you were in a consumption.

November 28 | Sonnet 116

The episcopal registry at Worcester contains a record of a
marriage bond bearing today's date, 28 November 1582,
documenting the union of the Shakespeares' marriage. It would
be lovely to think Sonnet 116 was written with this day in mind,
but that may be wishful thinking – this legendary sonnet is
about a marriage of minds, not a literal marriage which exists in
earthy time.

Let me not to the marriage of true minds
Admit impediments, love is not love
Which alters when it alteration finds,
Or bends with the remover to remove.
O no, it is an ever-fixed mark
That looks on tempests and is never shaken;
It is the star to every wand'ring bark,
Whose worth's unknown, although his height be taken,
Love's not Time's fool, though rosy lips and cheeks
Within his bending sickle's compass come,
Love alters not with his brief hours and weeks,
But bears it out even to the edge of doom:
    If this be error and upon me proved,
    I never writ, nor no man ever loved.

November 29 | Henry VIII | Act 3 Scene 2

Cardinal Wolsey died on 29 November 1530 of a sickness which he contracted on a journey to London to answer the charge of treason. Shakespeare here dramatizes his realization that he has fallen from the King's graces, after he has failed to secure an annulment for the King's marriage to Queen Katherine of Aragon. These words are spoken in grief with the apprehension that his loyalty to the King had overridden his loyalty to God, jeopardizing the fate of his immortal soul.

CARDINAL WOLSEY
So farewell – to the little good you bear me.
Farewell, a long farewell, to all my greatness!
This is the state of man: today he puts forth
The tender leaves of hopes, tomorrow blossoms,
And bears his blushing honours thick upon him.
The third day comes a frost, a killing frost,
And when he thinks, good easy man, full surely
His greatness is a-ripening, nips his root,
And then he falls, as I do. I have ventured,
Like little wanton boys that swim on bladders,
This many summers in a sea of glory,
But far beyond my depth. My high-blown pride
At length broke under me, and now has left me
Weary, and old with service, to the mercy
Of a rude stream that must for ever hide me.
Vain pomp and glory of this world, I hate ye.
I feel my heart new opened. O, how wretched
Is that poor man that hangs on princes' favours!
There is betwixt that smile we would aspire to,
That sweet aspect of princes, and their ruin,
More pangs and fears than wars or women have;
And when he falls, he falls like Lucifer,
Never to hope again.

November 30, as all Scots know, is St Andrew's Day, in honour
of Scotland's patron saint. The festival is thought to date back
to the eleventh-century reign of Malcolm III, the son and
heir of Duncan who is personally murdered by Macbeth in
Shakespeare's play (though in reality he was killed in combat
with Macbeth's men). Macbeth, the Thane of Glamis is told
by the three witches that he will soon become the Thane of
Cawdor, a title that belongs to an as yet living nobleman. After
that, the witches foresee, he will become king.

MACBETH
Stay, you imperfect speakers! Tell me more!
By Sinell's death I know I am Thane of Glamis;
But how of Cawdor? The Thane of Cawdor lives
A prosperous gentleman. And to be king
Stands not within the prospect of belief –
No more than to be Cawdor. Say from whence
You owe this strange intelligence; or why
Upon this blasted heath you stop our way
With such prophetic greeting? Speak, I charge you!
[*Witches vanish*]

December

December 1 | Hamlet | Act 4 Scene 7

On 1 December 1597, botanist John Gerard compiled *The Herball or Generall Historie of Plantes,* which was to be the most comprehensive plant encyclopaedia ever to have been published in the English language. Gerard's scant scientific expertise led to the inclusion of some distinctly un-scientific entries compiled from myths and folklore: among the more amusing inclusions is 'the Goose Tree' on which geese were supposed to grow. Shakespeare clearly shared a penchant for botany with Gerard. Many herbs feature across his plays – some poisonous, some medicinal – but more often than not plants and flowers occur symbolically. Soon after Ophelia's mad scene, in which she hands out herbs and flowers, Gertrude brings this poignant report of her drowning, laden with grim, floral folklore imagery.

QUEEN GERTRUDE
There is a willow grows aslant a brook,
That shows his hoar leaves in the glassy stream.
Therewith fantastic garlands did she make
Of crowflowers, nettles, daisies, and long purples,
That liberal shepherds give a grosser name,
But our cold maids do dead-men's-fingers call them.
There, on the pendent boughs her crownet weeds
Clambering to hang, an envious sliver broke,
When down her weedy trophies and herself
Fell in the weeping brook. Her clothes spread wide,
And mermaid-like awhile they bore her up;
Which time she chanted snatches of old tunes,
As one incapable of her own distress,
Or like a creature native and indued
Unto that element. But long it could not be
Till that her garments, heavy with their drink,
Pulled the poor wretch from her melodious lay
To muddy death.

We know that there were some cold winters in Shakespeare's day. The Thames, before its flow was speeded up by the removal of the medieval London Bridge and the building of the Embankments, would regularly freeze over and Frost Fairs were held on the frozen river. Elizabeth I herself took to the ice to practise archery, and boys played football 'as boldly there as it had been dry land', according to Holinshed, a contemporary source. Bolingbroke uses the image of frost as he speaks of his banishment by Richard II.

HENRY BOLINGBROKE
O, who can hold a fire in his hand
By thinking on the frosty Caucasus,
Or cloy the hungry edge of appetite
By bare imagination of a feast,
Or wallow naked in December snow
By thinking on fantastic summer's heat?
O no, the apprehension of the good
Gives but the greater feeling to the worse.
Fell sorrow's tooth doth never rankle more
Than when he bites, but lanceth not the sore.

December 3 | Sonnet 127

Sonnet 127 is the first of the sonnets dedicated to the 'Dark Lady', whose identity we may never be able to confirm. One thing we do know is that she was not Shakespeare's wife, who apparently completely eluded her husband's poetic attention (though there is an argument that she might be the addressee of Sonnet 145). One candidate for the enviable muse is Emilia Bassano Lanier – though this is not widely accepted among scholars. She may have made Shakespeare's acquaintance as the mistress of Lord Hunsdon, the patron of the Chamberlain's Men. In any case Lanier would have something in common with the writer, as she was herself a gifted poet. Her collection of feminist poetry is thought to be the first book of poems published by a woman in England.

In the old age black was not counted fair,
Or if it were it bore not beauty's name:
But now is black Beauty's successive heir,
And Beauty slander'd with a bastard shame,
For since each hand hath put on Nature's power,
Fairing the foul with Art's false borrow'd face,
Sweet beauty hath no name, no holy bower,
But is profan'd, if not lives in disgrace.
Therefore my Mistress' eyes are raven black,
Her eyes so suited, and they mourners seem,
At such who not born fair no beauty lack,
Sland'ring Creation with a false esteem,
   Yet so they mourn becoming of their woe,
   That every tongue says Beauty should look so.

Kingsley Amis commented that some of Shakespeare's jokes are
'terrible', principally because they come over as dated – there
is a diminishing pleasure taken in the word-play nowadays,
especially when the references are baffling to a modern
audience. That said, much of his comedy does still work, and
Dromio of Syracuse's fear at being mistaken for the other
Dromio by a fat kitchen wench, is timeless, if a little fattist. His
idea for generating warmth in a harsh winter anyway has the
merit of being novel.

> ANTIPHOLUS OF SYRACUSE
> How dost thou mean, a fat marriage?
>
> DROMIO OF SYRACUSE
> Marry, sir, she's the kitchen wench and all grease;
> and I know not what use to put her to but to make a
> lamp of her and run from her by her own light. I
> warrant her rags and the tallow in them will burn a
> Poland winter. If she lives till doomsday,
> she'll burn a week longer than the whole world.

December 5 | The Merry Wives of Windsor | Act 4 Scene 4

Another mention of winter in a comedy comes as part of the pretext for Mistress Page's plans to spring a trick on Falstaff. The fat knight had presumed to try to seduce both her and Mistress Ford, and in retribution she intends to exploit a local legend about a ghostly hunter, and spook the philanderer once he is enticed into the forest. Falstaff, who had been the hunter, has become the hunted.

MISTRESS PAGE
There is an old tale goes that Herne the Hunter,
Sometime a keeper here in Windsor Forest,
Doth all the winter-time, at still midnight,
Walk round about an oak, with great ragg'd horns;
And there he blasts the tree, and takes the cattle,
And makes milch-kine yield blood, and shakes a chain
In a most hideous and dreadful manner.
You have heard of such a spirit, and well you know
The superstitious idle-headed eld
Received and did deliver to our age
This tale of Herne the Hunter for a truth.

[. . .]

Nan Page my daughter, and my little son,
And three or four more of their growth, we'll dress
Like urchins, ouphes, and fairies, green and white,
With rounds of waxen tapers on their heads,
And rattles in their hands. Upon a sudden,
As Falstaff, she, and I are newly met,
Let them from forth a sawpit rush at once
With some diffusèd song. Upon their sight,

We two in great amazedness will fly.
Then let them all encircle him about,
And, fairy-like, to-pinch the unclean knight,
And ask him why, that hour of fairy revel,
In their so sacred paths he dares to tread
In shape profane.

[. . .]

The truth being known,
We'll all present ourselves, dis-horn the spirit,
And mock him home to Windsor.

December 6 | Love's Labour's Lost | Act 5 Scene 2

December 6 is St Nicholas Day, and medieval England would mark the occasion by parodying religious figures and ceremonies. One tradition was dressing a boy as a bishop who would then lead church services and prayers until Holy Innocents Day on 28 December. Following the Reformation, the day's burlesque rituals were banned first by Henry VIII then again by Elizabeth (after being briefly re-allowed by Mary). The ladies of *Love's Labour's Lost,* in an appropriately subversive spirit, swap favours (handkerchiefs) before a masked ball in order to dupe the unwitting men into misidentifying them.

PRINCESS
The effect of my intent is to cross theirs.
They do it but in mocking merriment,
And mock for mock is only my intent.
Their several counsels they unbosom shall
To loves mistook, and so be mocked withal
Upon the next occasion that we meet,
With visages displayed, to talk and greet.

ROSALINE
But shall we dance if they desire us to't?

PRINCESS
No, to the death we will not move a foot;
Nor to their penned speech render we no grace,
But while 'tis spoke each turn away her face.

BOYET
Why, that contempt will kill the speaker's heart,
And quite divorce his memory from his part.

PRINCESS
Therefore I do it, and I make no doubt
The rest will ne'er come in, if he be out.
There's no such sport as sport by sport o'erthrown,
To make theirs ours, and ours none but our own.
So shall we stay, mocking intended game,
And they, well mocked, depart away with shame.

December 7 | Sonnet 60

As the year inclines towards a close, we turn to Shakespeare's
reflections on the passing of time. In Shakespeare's Sonnet
60, the poet ruminates that time is given to us in the present,
added to the past, and taken from the future. Minutes thereby
move like supplements, each one adding to and replacing the
one which preceded it, changing places yet always moving
forwards. This is a traditional English sonnet, in which the
first three quatrains each describe a different aspect of the
subject, all of which are resolved in the final couplet. True to
the supplementary motion of time, this couplet begins with
the phrase 'and yet': 'and' offering to continue the gloomy
meditations on mortality, with 'yet' preparing us for something
we haven't thought of, which could overturn the meaning of
what we have already heard. In the end, confounding time is
itself confounded; the hope embodied in the completed verse
triumphs over death.

Like as the waves make towards the pebbled shore,
So do our minutes hasten to their end,
Each changing place with that which goes before,
In sequent toil all forwards do contend.
Nativity once in the main of light,
Crawls to maturity, wherewith being crown'd,
Crooked eclipses 'gainst his glory fight,
And Time that gave, doth now his gift confound.
Time doth transfix the flourish set on youth,
And delves the parallels in beauty's brow,
Feeds on the rarities of nature's truth,
And nothing stands but for his scythe to mow.
   And yet to times in hope, my verse shall stand
   Praising thy worth, despite his cruel hand.

Within fifty years of Shakespeare's death, King Charles II issued
a warrant allowing women to act on stage. The King, who had
much enjoyed seeing professional actresses during his exile in
France and who would take several as mistresses in England,
claimed he was only permitting women to act in deference to
those Puritans who thought that having boys cross-dress was
unnatural. The early contempt for women as actors might be
detectable in Iago's vitriol, which holds women to be inconstant
by nature through the contradictory parts they play: 'you are
pictures out of doors, / bells in your parlours, wild-cats in your
kitchens, / saints in your injuries, devils being offended, /
players in your housewifery, and housewives' in your beds'. The
first recorded professional female actors took to the London
stage on 8 December 1660 at the Vere Street Theatre, in a
production of Shakespeare's *Othello*. It is ironic that this first
performance should include a heroine who declines ever to
put on airs or act a dishonest part: however, she is offset by the
more cynical, more pragmatic, Emilia.

DESDEMONA
O, these men, these men!
Dost thou in conscience think – tell me, Emilia –
That there be women do abuse their husbands
In such gross kind?

EMILIA
There be some such, no question.

DESDEMONA
Wouldst thou do such a deed for all the world?

EMILIA
Why, would not you?

DESDEMONA
No, by this heavenly light.

EMILIA
Nor I neither by this heavenly light: I might do't as well i'
the dark.

DESDEMONA
Wouldst thou do such a deed for all the world?

EMILIA
The world's a huge thing: it is a great price for a small vice.

DESDEMONA
In troth, I think thou wouldst not.

EMILIA
In troth I think I should, and undo't when I had
done it. Marry, I would not do such a thing for a
joint ring, nor for measures of lawn, nor for
gowns, petticoats, nor caps, nor any petty
exhibition. But for all the whole world! Ud's pity, who
would not make her husband a cuckold, to make him a
monarch? I should venture purgatory for't.

December 9 | Much Ado About Nothing | Act 2 Scene 3

Falstaff and Iago are both deceivers in the affairs of love. Falstaff in *The Merry Wives of Windsor* tries to gain financial advantage and romantic favours from two married women at once, while Iago deceives Othello about his wife's fidelity because – well, there's the mystery. Here, in *Much Ado About Nothing*, Don Pedro's attendant, Balthasar, sings a song about the inconstancy of men.

> BALTHASAR [*Singing*]
> Sigh no more, ladies, sigh no more,
> Men were deceivers ever,
> One foot in sea and one on shore,
> To one thing constant never:
> Then sigh not so, but let them go,
> And be you blithe and bonny,
> Converting all your sounds of woe
> Into Hey nonny, nonny.
>
> Sing no more ditties, sing no moe,
> Of dumps so dull and heavy;
> The fraud of men was ever so,
> Since summer first was leavy:
> Then sigh not so, but let them go,
> And be you blithe and bonny,
> Converting all your sounds of woe
> Into Hey nonny, nonny.

December 10 | The Merchant of Venice | Act 1 Scene 3

December 10 is Human Rights' Day, and drama is frequently concerned with the balance of justice: our sense of how happy an ending is depends on whether the good people prevail, and if wrongdoing is sufficiently punished. The plot arc of comedies traditionally takes pains to restore justice by the end. This is epitomized in the title of *Measure for Measure*, which would seem to anticipate the even distribution of just deserts at the play's conclusion, lifted from St Matthew's Gospel: 'Judge not, that you be not judged. For ... the measure you give will be the measure you get.' The doctrine of 'a measure for measure' is pushed to its limits in *The Merchant of Venice* around the conduct and fate of Shylock. Shylock is motivated by revenge, though he acts in proportion to the wrongs done unto him and the Jewish community. Here Antonio, who had previously spat at Shylock, has asked for a loan.

SHYLOCK
Signor Antonio, many a time and oft
In the Rialto you have rated me
About my moneys and my usances.
Still have I borne it with a patient shrug,
For sufferance is the badge of all our tribe.
You call me misbeliever, cut-throat dog,
And spit upon my Jewish gaberdine,
And all for use of that which is mine own.
Well then, it now appears you need my help.
Go to then. You come to me, and you say,
'Shylock, we would have moneys,' you say so,
You, that did void your rheum upon my beard
And foot me as you spurn a stranger cur
Over your threshold, moneys is your suit

What should I say to you? Should I not say,
'Hath a dog money? Is it possible
A cur can lend three thousand ducats?' Or
Shall I bend low, and in a bondman's key,
With bated breath and whispering humbleness,
Say this:
'Fair sir, you spit on me on Wednesday last,
You spurned me such a day, another time
You called me dog, and for these courtesies
I'll lend you thus much moneys'?

December 11 | Hamlet | Act 5 Scene 2

After spending nearly the whole play prevaricating between vengeance and resignation, Hamlet accepts a duel against Laertes. The ensuing events are messy: first, Gertrude toasts the fight with a goblet of poisoned wine that had been intended for Hamlet by Claudius; then Laertes, after scratching Hamlet with his poisoned blade, ends up being disarmed by Hamlet and slashed with it himself; then Laertes reconciles with the prince and reveals Claudius's foul play, and Hamlet finally kills the latter in his own dying throes. Before the fatal scuffle, Hamlet intuits his imminent demise.

HAMLET
Not a whit. We defy augury. There is special
providence in the fall of a sparrow. If it be now,
'tis not to come. If it be not to come, it will be
now. If it be not now, yet it will come. The
readiness is all. Since no man has aught of what he
leaves, what is't to leave betimes? Let be.

December 12 | All's Well That Ends Well | Act 5 Scene 3

Like *Measure for Measure*, the title of Shakespeare's comedy *All's Well That Ends Well* may not have a completely straightforward relationship to the action of the play. That 'all is well if it ends well' is hardly true in life – memories of bad times follow us and leave an impression on our experiences of the good, and the end does not always justify the means – and the play is similarly nuanced. It is true that in the end Helena gets the husband she wanted, but first she has to, among other things: fake her own death; chase after him to Italy; disguise herself as a virgin he is attempting to seduce; trick him into consummating their marriage; and then finally reveal that she is not only alive but pregnant in front of the King just when he is trying to arrange an engagement to another woman. Why would Helena take such pains to win a man who holds her in such contempt? How can we trust that Bertram loves her freely by the end? As the King (inadequately) ties up the loose ends, these questions are still nagging.

KING
Let us from point to point this story know
To make the even truth in pleasure flow.
[To Diana] If thou beest yet a fresh uncroppèd flower
Choose thou thy husband and I'll pay thy dower;
For I can guess that by thy honest aid
Thou keepest a wife herself, thyself a maid.
Of that and all the progress more and less
Resolvèdly more leisure shall express.
All yet seems well, and if it end so meet,
The bitter past, more welcome is the sweet.
[*Flourish*]

EPILOGUE [*Spoken by the King*]
The King's a beggar, now the play is done.
All is well ended if this suit be won,
That you express content; which we will pay
With strife to please you, day exceeding day.
Ours be your patience then and yours our parts;
Your gentle hands lend us and take our hearts.

Richard II envisions his own sorry fate, including his forced
abdication and imprisonment, as a kind of winter's tale, a
woeful and unlikely narrative which would make its hearers
weep. We watch him as he turns from a king into a man, then
finally into a story.

KING RICHARD II
A king of beasts indeed! If aught but beasts
I had been still a happy king of men.
Good sometime queen, prepare thee hence for France.
Think I am dead, and that even here thou takest
As from my deathbed thy last living leave.
In winter's tedious nights sit by the fire
With good old folks, and let them tell thee tales
Of woeful ages long ago betid;
And ere thou bid goodnight, to quit their griefs
Tell thou the lamentable tale of me,
And send the hearers weeping to their beds;
For why the senseless brands will sympathize
The heavy accent of thy moving tongue,
And in compassion weep the fire out;
And some will mourn in ashes, some coal-black,
For the deposing of a rightful king.

At the desperate end of *King Lear*, the king insists that, despite his catastrophic defeat, time spent in prison will be all sweetness if spent with his favourite daughter Cordelia: they could exchange tales about courtly life just as they might have done before. There is a devastating naivety to these words, some of the last Cordelia will hear, and among the last that Lear will speak.

KING LEAR
No, no, no, no! Come, let's away to prison.
We two alone will sing like birds i'the cage;
When thou dost ask me blessing I'll kneel down
And ask of thee forgiveness; so we'll live,
And pray, and sing, and tell old tales, and laugh
At gilded butterflies, and hear poor rogues
Talk of court news; and we'll talk with them too –
Who loses and who wins, who's in, who's out –
And take upon's the mystery of things
As if we were God's spies; and we'll wear out,
In a walled prison, packs and sects of great ones
That ebb and flow by the moon.

December 15 | Macbeth | Act 5 Scene 5

There is a superstition in the theatre that referring to *Macbeth* by name will bring bad luck – so the tragedy is known instead as 'The Scottish Play'. To undo the curse if the jinxed word is uttered, tradition has it that you need to exit the theatre, spin around three times, spit, swear and then knock on the theatre door to be let back in. New research reveals that this might have been a myth invented by the critic and cartoonist Max Beerbohm at the turn of the twentieth century. Nevertheless, the added fears around the play only enhance its foreboding grip. Macbeth's most harrowing, almost nihilistic speech comes after the death of his wife. The note of disjunction which infuses the whole play is held most prominently here, as the third 'tomorrow' overreaches the pentameter (takes the line from ten to an uneven eleven syllables) and unbalances the entire speech, just as his thoughts of tomorrow unsettle his yesterdays and todays with a sense of futility.

MACBETH
She should have died hereafter.
There would have been a time for such a word –
Tomorrow, and tomorrow, and tomorrow,
Creeps in this petty pace from day to day
To the last syllable of recorded time;
And all our yesterdays have lighted fools
The way to dusty death. Out, out, brief candle!
Life's but a walking shadow, a poor player
That struts and frets his hour upon the stage
And then is heard no more. It is a tale
Told by an idiot, full of sound and fury,
Signifying nothing.

December weather is seemingly no different in the ancient Britain of *Cymbeline*, where the exiled Belarius inhabits a cave with two young men he had kidnapped as babies. These young men, Arviragus and Guiderius, are Cymbeline's sons and the rightful princes of Britain, but Belarius raises them without this knowledge and teaches them to be hunters. In an exchange familiar to anybody who has ever been a teenager, the boys complain of being bored and placed under an unfair curfew when they want to explore the world beyond.

ARVIRAGUS
What should we speak of
When we are old as you? When we shall hear
The rain and wind beat dark December, how,
In this our pinching cave, shall we discourse
The freezing hours away? We have seen nothing.
We are beastly: subtle as the fox for prey,
Like warlike as the wolf for what we eat;
Our valour is to chase what flies; our cage
We make a choir, as doth the prisoned bird,
And sing our bondage freely.

December 17 | The Taming of the Shrew | Induction Scene 2

The Roman festival of Saturnalia was gradually assimilated into the Christian tradition as part of the Christmas season. It was celebrated by the appointment of the Lord of the Saturnalia, who would act as the master of revels. Masters and servants would switch roles on this feast day. This custom is echoed in the 'Induction' to *The Taming of the Shrew*. Drunken tinker Christopher Sly wakes up to be told by a mischievous lord that he is the nobleman, while the lord and servants minister to his needs.

SLY
For God's sake, a pot of small ale.

FIRST SERVANT
Will't please your lordship drink a cup of sack?

SECOND SERVANT
Will't please your honour taste of these conserves?

THIRD SERVANT
What raiment will your honour wear today?

SLY
I am Christophero Sly, call not me 'honour' nor 'lordship'. I ne'er drank sack in my life. And if you give me any conserves, give me conserves of beef. Ne'er ask me what raiment I'll wear, for I have no more doublets than backs, no more stockings than legs, nor no more shoes than feet – nay, sometimes more feet than shoes, or such shoes as my toes look through the overleather.

LORD
Heaven cease this idle humour in your honour!
O, that a mighty man of such descent,
Of such possessions, and so high esteem,
Should be infusèd with so foul a spirit!

SLY
What, would you make me mad? Am not I Christopher
Sly, old Sly's son of Burton-heath, by birth a
pedlar, by education a cardmaker, by transmutation a
bear-herd, and now by present profession a tinker?
Ask Marian Hacket, the fat ale-wife of Wincot, if
she know me not. If she say I am not fourteen pence
on the score for sheer ale, score me up for the
lyingest knave in Christendom.

Nights are longer than days at this time of year, and night
brings terror to Lucrece. She inveighs against the night time for
its role in Tarquin's assault. It is a mark of her heartbreaking
purity – and devastating innocence – that her anger is directed
at the night and not at her attacker.

'O comfort-killing Night, image of hell,
Dim register and notary of shame,
Black stage for tragedies and murders fell,
Vast sin-concealing chaos, nurse of blame!
Blind muffled bawd, dark harbour for defame,
Grim cave of death, whispering conspirator
With close-tongued treason and the ravisher!

'O hateful, vaporous, and foggy Night,
Since thou art guilty of my cureless crime,
Muster thy mists to meet the eastern light,
Make war against proportioned course of time;
Or if thou wilt permit the sun to climb
His wonted height, yet ere he go to bed
Knit poisonous clouds about his golden head.

December 19 | Hamlet | Act 5 Scene 2

Wounded by Laertes' poisoned blade, Hamlet, having finished off the already wounded Claudius by forcing him to drink the remains of the poisoned wine that killed Gertrude, at last, dies. The 'to be or not to be' question hangs over this death-scene – he neither wholly kills himself nor is wholly killed in the execution of his father's wishes. The dying prince urges Horatio to tell his story as Fontinbras' army arrives. In the Folio edition of the play, compiled from the King's Men's working scripts, the line 'the rest is silence' is followed by a further agonized 'o, o, o, o,' so it's perhaps not all as quiet as he suggests.

HAMLET
I am dead, Horatio. Wretched Queen, adieu!
You that look pale and tremble at this chance,
That are but mutes or audience to this act,
Had I but time – as this fell sergeant, Death,
Is strict in his arrest – O, I could tell you –
But let it be. Horatio, I am dead.
Thou livest. Report me and my cause aright
To the unsatisfied.

HORATIO
Never believe it.
I am more an antique Roman than a Dane.
Here's yet some liquor left.

HAMLET
As th' art a man,
Give me the cup. Let go. By heaven, I'll ha't!
O God, Horatio, what a wounded name,
Things standing thus unknown, shall live behind me!
If thou didst ever hold me in thy heart,

Absent thee from felicity awhile,
And in this harsh world draw thy breath in pain,
To tell my story.

[*A march afar off, and shout within*]

What warlike noise is this?

OSRIC
Young Fortinbras, with conquest come from Poland,
To the ambassadors of England gives
This warlike volley.

HAMLET
O, I die, Horatio!
The potent poison quite o'er-crows my spirit.
I cannot live to hear the news from England.
But I do prophesy the election lights
On Fortinbras. He has my dying voice.
So tell him, with th'occurrents, more and less,
Which have solicited – the rest is silence.
[*He dies*]

HORATIO
Now cracks a noble heart. Good night, sweet Prince,
And flights of angels sing thee to thy rest!

The winter solstice falls each year around this time, and marks the shortest day – and the longest night – of the year. Amiens, an exiled nobleman in *As You Like It*, sings this song about winter. This is unusual, as it is usually the fool who sings except in a couple of cases like Ophelia – when she is mad – and Toby Belch – when he is drunk. Amiens is neither mad nor drunk when he sings these words, which many have set to music in the absence of the original score.

AMIENS
Blow, blow, thou winter wind,
Thou art not so unkind
As man's ingratitude.
Thy tooth is not so keen,
Because thou art not seen,
Although thy breath be rude.
Hey-ho, sing hey-ho, unto the green holly,
Most friendship is feigning, most loving mere folly;
Then hey-ho, the holly.
This life is most jolly.

Freeze, freeze, thou bitter sky
That dost not bite so nigh
As benefits forgot.
Though thou the waters warp,
Thy sting is not so sharp
As friend remembered not.
Hey-ho, sing hey-ho, unto the green holly,
Most friendship is feigning, most loving mere folly;
Then hey-ho, the holly.
This life is most jolly.

December 21 is St Thomas' Day, a Christian festival held around
the solstice. On this day, the poor were permitted to beg, which
was referred to as 'Thomasing'. It is a well-established principle
of successful leadership to keep those less fortunate than you
happy – or alternatively, so weak that they can do nothing
to challenge your rule. Julius Caesar learns this at his peril.
Early in the play, Cassius gives vent to his resentment of the
burgeoning dictator, who fancies himself as a kind of god.

CASSIUS
I know that virtue to be in you, Brutus,
As well as I do know your outward favour.
Well, honour is the subject of my story.
I cannot tell what you and other men
Think of this life; but for my single self,
I had as lief not be as live to be
In awe of such a thing as I myself.
I was born free as Caesar, so were you;
We both have fed as well, and we can both
Endure the winter's cold as well as he.
For once, upon a raw and gusty day,
The troubled Tiber chafing with her shores,
Caesar said to me, 'Dar'st thou, Cassius, now
Leap in with me into this angry flood,
And swim to yonder point?' Upon the word,
Accoutrèd as I was, I plungèd in
And bade him follow; so indeed he did.
The torrent roared, and we did buffet it
With lusty sinews, throwing it aside
And stemming it with hearts of controversy.
But ere we could arrive the point proposed,
Caesar cried, 'Help me, Cassius, or I sink!'

I, as Aeneas, our great ancestor,
Did from the flames of Troy upon his shoulder
The old Anchises bear, so from the waves of Tiber
Did I the tired Caesar. And this man
Is now become a god, and Cassius is
A wretched creature, and must bend his body
If Caesar carelessly but nod on him.
He had a fever when he was in Spain,
And when the fit was on him, I did mark
How he did shake; 'tis true, this god did shake;
His coward lips did from their colour fly,
And that same eye whose bend doth awe the world
Did lose his lustre; I did hear him groan;
Ay, and that tongue of his, that bade the Romans
Mark him and write his speeches in their books,
'Alas!' it cried, 'Give me some drink, Titinius',
As a sick girl. Ye gods, it doth amaze me
A man of such a feeble temper should
So get the start of the majestic world,
And bear the palm alone.

December 22 | Sonnet 14

John Dee, a prominent mathematician, astrologer and magician, who was even consulted by Queen Elizabeth, died on 22 December 1608. We do not know if Shakespeare admired Dee but the speaker of Sonnet 14 casts aside the prophesying powers of the stars and finds truth and beauty in his lover's face, fulfilling a common Shakespearian trope to bring the cosmic in line with a human scale. The Romantic poet John Keats would later riff on this note in his celebrated 'Ode on a Grecian Urn': '"Beauty is truth, truth beauty," – that is all / Ye know on earth, and all ye need to know'.

Not from the stars do I my judgment pluck,
And yet methinks I have Astronomy,
But not to tell of good, or evil luck,
Of plagues, of dearths, or seasons' quality;
Nor can I fortune to brief minutes tell,
Pointing to each his thunder, rain and wind,
Or say with Princes if it shall go well
By oft predict that I in heaven find.
But from thine eyes my knowledge I derive,
And constant stars in them I read such art
As truth and beauty shall together thrive
If from thyself, to store thou wouldst convert:
   Or else of thee this I prognosticate,
   Thy end is Truth's and Beauty's doom and date.

December 23 | Sonnet 71

Sonnet 71 is one of the most celebrated in the collection. The speaker is a little mischievous in this one, asking the reader not to mourn after he dies but to forget him. However, in doing so, the entire poem forms a kind of *memento mori* (a work of art that serves as a 'reminder of death') in which no line can be disentangled from 'the hand that writ it'. The theme of this poem is memorably echoed in the Victorian poet Christina Rossetti's own sonnet 'Remember', which concludes with the lines 'Better by far you should forget and smile / Than that you should remember and be sad.'

No longer mourn for me when I am dead,
Then you shall hear the surly sullen bell
Give warning to the world that I am fled
From this vile world with vilest worms to dwell:
Nay if you read this line, remember not
The hand that writ it, for I love you so,
That I in your sweet thoughts would be forgot,
If thinking on me then should make you woe.
O if (I say) you look upon this verse,
When I (perhaps) compounded am with clay,
Do not so much as my poor name rehearse;
But let your love even with my life decay.
  Lest the wise world should look into your moan,
  And mock you with me after I am gone.

In Shakespeare's day, work would cease on Christmas Eve and
families would set about decorating their houses and preparing
for the 'Twelfths' – the twelve days of festivities which began
on Christmas Day. There would be baking of the 'minced pye',
a pastry made with thirteen ingredients to represent Christ
and his apostles – it even included mutton in remembrance of
the shepherds. Christmas Eve is never mentioned in the plays,
nor is there any sign of a Christmas tree or a turkey, as the
celebrations as we know them today are Victorian in origin.
Nevertheless, the Christmas Spirit is an evocative one.

BEROWNE
Well, say I am! Why should proud summer boast
Before the birds have any cause to sing?
Why should I joy in an abortive birth?
At Christmas I no more desire a rose
Than wish a snow in May's new-fangled shows,
But like of each thing that in season grows.

December 25 | Hamlet | Act 1 Scene 1

Christmas Day was laden with omens for Elizabethans concerning the year ahead. If it fell on a Sunday, this boded well; though if you returned to work on this day, it was considered very bad luck. Christmas's mixture of pagan superstition, medieval pageantry and solemn Christian remembrance means that the Christmas season is mentioned in more proverbs than any other festival in the sixteenth century calendar. For Shakespeare then, Christmas was connected as much with solemnity and foreboding as it was a byword for seasonal joy, and hopes for the future. Both associations are apparent where Marcellus describes the visit of the ghost of Hamlet's father.

MARCELLUS
It faded on the crowing of the cock.
Some say that ever 'gainst that season comes
Wherein our Saviour's birth is celebrated,
The bird of dawning singeth all night long.
And then, they say, no spirit dares stir abroad;
The nights are wholesome; then no planets strike;
No fairy tales; nor witch hath power to charm.
So hallowed and so gracious is that time.

December 26 | King Lear | Act 2 Scene 3

King Lear is known to have been performed at the court of
James I on the feast of St Stephen, 26 December 1606 – the
anniversary, if you like, of when 'good king Wenceslas looked
out' in the later carol. It is thought that Richard Burbage, the
great leading actor of Shakespeare's company, performed the
title role. Incidentally, Burbage's gravestone, now lost, is said
to have read 'Exit Burbage'. The play, which shows the dangers
of dividing up a kingdom, may have been a reassuring spectacle
for the first monarch to unite England and Scotland. However,
due to sensitivities over the mental condition of King George
III in the early nineteenth century, this play about a mad king
was kept off the stage. December 26 is now known in the UK as
Boxing Day, named after the tradition of collecting alms for the
poor on this date.

EDGAR
I heard myself proclaimed,
And by the happy hollow of a tree
Escaped the hunt. No port is free, no place
That guard and most unusual vigilance
Does not attend my taking. While I may scape
I will preserve myself, and am bethought
To take the basest and most poorest shape
That ever penury in contempt of man
Brought near to beast. My face I'll grime with filth,
Blanket my loins, elf all my hair with knots,
And with presented nakedness outface
The wind and persecution of the sky.
The country gives me proof and precedent
Of Bedlam beggars, who with roaring voices
Strike in their numbed and mortified bare arms
Pins, wooden pricks, nails, sprigs of rosemary;

And with this horrible object from low farms,
Poor pelting villages, sheep-cotes, and mills,
Sometime with lunatic bans, sometime with prayers,
Enforce their charity: 'Poor Turlygod', 'Poor Tom'.
That's something yet. Edgar I nothing am.

December 27 | Twelfth Night | Act 5 Scene 1

This is St John the Evangelist's Day, in commemoration of one of Jesus's twelve disciples and author of the Gospel According to John, which contains the immortal phrase 'God is Love' (1 John 4:8). Feste sings out the end of *Twelfth Night* after all of the couples are happily betrothed – with the exception of Malvolio, who leaves the stage sulking and alone, Antonio, whose adored Sebastian has paired off with Olivia, and Sir Andrew Aguecheek, whose unrealistic hopes of marrying Olivia are now finally dashed. The song is a little strange, and recalls a phrase that Toby Belch utters on a couple of occasions to chase away qualms and continue with mindless frivolity: 'It's all one'. Feste uses the refrain in a similar fashion, warding off niggling melancholy with a 'hey-ho' kind of attitude.

FESTE
[*Sings*]
When that I was and a little tiny boy,
With hey-ho, the wind and the rain;
A foolish thing was but a toy,
For the rain it raineth every day.

But when I came to man's estate,
With hey-ho, the wind and the rain;
'Gainst knaves and thieves men shut their gate,
For the rain it raineth every day.

But when I came, alas, to wive,
With hey-ho, the wind and the rain;
By swaggering could I never thrive,
For the rain it raineth every day.

But when I came unto my beds,
With hey-ho, the wind and the rain;
With tosspots still had drunken heads,
For the rain it raineth every day.

A great while ago the world begun,
With hey-ho, the wind and the rain;
But that's all one, our play is done,
And we'll strive to please you every day.

December 28 | The Comedy of Errors | Act 2 Scene 2

Shakespeare's shortest play, *The Comedy of Errors*, had its first recorded performance at a law students' party in Gray's Inn Hall on Holy Innocents Day, 28 December 1594. It was a popular and familiar story of mistaken identities – a hallmark of Shakespearean comedy – involving not one but two sets of twins. Adriana has been hailed as something of a proto-feminist: 'Why should their liberty than ours be more?' she asks her sister, referring to men like Antipholus, her cavorting husband. Here, she castigates Antipholus of Syracuse, not realizing, as the audience does, that she has got the wrong twin – she means to address her husband, Antipholus of Ephesus.

ADRIANA
Ay, ay, Antipholus, look strange and frown.
Some other mistress hath thy sweet aspects.
I am not Adriana, nor thy wife.
The time was once when thou unurged wouldst vow
That never words were music to thine ear,
That never object pleasing in thine eye,
That never touch well welcome to thy hand,
That never meat sweet-savoured in thy taste,
Unless I spake, or looked, or touched, or carved to thee.
How comes it now, my husband, O how comes it,
That thou art thus estrangèd from thyself?
Thyself I call it, being strange to me
That, undividable, incorporate,
Am better than thy dear self's better part.
Ah, do not tear away thyself from me;
For know, my love, as easy mayest thou fall
A drop of water in the breaking gulf,
And take unmingled that same drop again

Without addition or diminishing,
As take from me thyself, and not me too.
How dearly would it touch me to the quick
Shouldst thou but hear I were licentious,
And that this body consecrate to thee
By ruffian lust should be contaminate?
Wouldst thou not spit at me, and spurn at me,
And hurl the name of husband in my face,
And tear the stained skin off my harlot brow,
And from my false hand cut the wedding ring,
And break it with a deep-divorcing vow?
I know thou canst, and therefore see thou do it!
I am possessed with an adulterate blot.
My blood is mingled with the crime of lust;
For if we too be one, and thou play false,
I do digest the poison of thy flesh,
Being strumpeted by thy contagion.
Keep then far league and truce with thy true bed,
I live unstained, thou undishonourèd.

December 29 | Sonnet 154

Sonnet 154 was the last of *Shakespeare's Sonnets* which was first published in 1609. It rounds off the 'Dark Lady' run with the story of Cupid, whose fire-brand (or flaming torch) is so persistent that even when the nymphs attempt to cool it in the well while the god sleeps, it burns even stronger and makes the water in the well perpetually hot.

The little Love-God lying once asleep,
Laid by his side his heart-inflaming brand,
Whilst many Nymphs that vow'd chaste life to keep,
Came tripping by, but in her maiden hand,
The fairest votary took up that fire,
Which many Legions of true hearts had warm'd,
And so the General of hot desire,
Was sleeping by a Virgin hand disarm'd.
This brand she quenched in a cool Well by,
Which from Love's fire took heat perpetual,
Growing a bath and healthful remedy,
For men diseas'd: but I, my Mistress' thrall,
  Came there for cure and this by that I prove,
  Love's fire heats water, water cools not love.

The mnemonic for remembering the colours of the rainbow,
'Richard Of York Gained Battle In Vain' – Red, Orange, Yellow,
Green, Blue, Indigo, Violet – derives from the fateful Battle of
Wakefield, fought on 30 December 1460, during the Wars of
the Roses. In the aftermath of an earlier battle, Queen Margaret
aggressively mocks Richard of York, who has sought to establish
his rival dynasty on the throne, and depose her husband the
King. Not content with just having him killed, she puts a paper
crown on his head, taunts him with the blood of his freshly
killed youngest son, and berates him for his audacity.

QUEEN MARGARET
Brave warriors, Clifford and Northumberland,
Come, make him stand upon this molehill here
That raught at mountains with outstrechèd arms,
Yet parted but the shadow with his hand.
What! Was it you that would be England's king?
Was't you that revelled in our parliament
And made a preachment of your high descent?
Where are your mess of sons to back you now?
The wanton Edward, and the lusty George?
And where's that valiant crook-back prodigy,
Dicky your boy, that with his grumbling voice
Was wont to cheer his dad in mutinies?
Or, with the rest, where is your darling Rutland?
Look, York, I stained this napkin with the blood
That valiant Clifford, with his rapier's point,
Made issue from the bosom of the boy;
And if thine eyes can water for his death,
I give thee this to dry thy cheeks withal.
Alas, poor York! But that I hate thee deadly,
I should lament thy miserable state.

I prithee grieve, to make me merry, York.
What! Hath thy fiery heart so parched thine entrails
That not a tear can fall for Rutland's death?
Why art thou patient, man? Thou shouldst be mad;
And I, to make thee mad, do mock thee thus.
Stamp, rave, and fret, that I may sing and dance.
Thou wouldst be fee'd, I see, to make me sport;
York cannot speak, unless he wear a crown.
A crown for York! And, lords, bow low to him;
Hold you his hands whilst I do set it on.

[*She puts a paper crown on York's head*]

Ay, marry, sir, now looks he like a king!
Ay, this is he that took King Henry's chair;
And this is he was his adopted heir.
But how is it that great Plantagenet
Is crowned so soon, and broke his solemn oath?
As I bethink me, you should not be king
Till our King Henry had shook hands with Death.
And will you pale your head in Henry's glory,
And rob his temples of the diadem,
Now in his life, against your holy oath?
O, 'tis a fault too too unpardonable!
Off with the crown; and, with the crown, his head;
And, whilst we breathe, take time to do him dead.

December 31 | The Tempest | Act 5 Scene 1

Ben Jonson, in his preface to the 1623 Folio of Shakespeare's works, was among the first to recognize that 'He was not of an age but for all time'; a sentiment which has been transmitted through the ages. Here Prospero speaks the last words of one of Shakespeare's last plays, beseeching the audience to release him from the island by their applause. Prospero, like the mind who created him, is able to live on untethered to his island – or his stage.

EPILOGUE
PROSPERO
Now my charms are all o'erthrown,
And what strength I have's mine own,
Which is most faint. Now 'tis true
I must be here confined by you,
Or sent to Naples. Let me not,
Since I have my dukedom got
And pardoned the deceiver, dwell
In this bare island by your spell;
But release me from my bands
With the help of your good hands.
Gentle breath of yours my sails
Must fill, or else my project fails,
Which was to please. Now I want
Spirits to enforce, art to enchant,
And my ending is despair
Unless I be relieved by prayer,
Which pierces so, that it assaults
Mercy itself, and frees all faults.
As you from crimes would pardoned be,
Let your indulgence set me free.

SYNOPSES OF PLAYS

Comedies

The Tempest

Duke Prospero has long been banished to a remote desert island, along with his now grown-up daughter Miranda, directing his magical powers there over its native inhabitants: the slavish Caliban and the ethereal spirit Ariel. He now contrives a tempestuous storm that shipwrecks King Alonso's household – including his son Prince Ferdinand, and Prospero's usurping brother Antonio – onto its shores. The ship's company is dispersed, but each is reunited, reconciled, and redeemed. Ferdinand and Miranda meet, and are married; Prospero's dukedom is restored to him; Caliban and Ariel are set free.

The Two Gentlemen of Verona

Proteus loves Julia (and she him); his dear friend Valentine loves Silvia (and she him). But when Proteus meets Silvia, he falls madly in love with her, rejecting Julia and betraying his friend. After a complicated sequence of events – involving banishment, a band of forest outlaws, Julia disguising herself as a pageboy, and an attempted rape – a reconciliation of the two couples is effected, and their marriage uncomfortably promised.

The Merry Wives of Windsor

The roguish but impoverished Sir John Falstaff seeks the simultaneous favours of two rich provincial married women – who then join forces to punish his presumption.

Measure for Measure

The Duke of Vienna delegates his authority to Angelo, his disciplinarian deputy, who zealously enforces a new moral regime of zero tolerance, which has led to a death-sentence being passed on Claudio for sleeping with his girlfriend Juliet, now pregnant, before their wedding. Claudio's sister Isabella, a trainee nun, seeks mercy from Angelo – who now proves himself a corrupt hypocrite: if Isabella sleeps with him, he says, Claudio will be spared. The desperate situation is saved by the Duke, who, disguised as a friar, theatrically contrives to expose Angelo's corruption, secure Claudio's pardon, and – at last revealing his true identity – propose marriage to Isabella.

The Comedy of Errors
Two identical twins, each named Antipholus, have been separated since childhood, and each has a servant named Dromio – themselves another pair of separated twins. Their parallel lives (in neighbouring and hostile Mediterranean states) now converge in Ephesus, where a set of bewildering confusions ensues – before the Antipholuses are reunited with each other, with their father (a merchant imprisoned there at the beginning of the play), and with their mother Emilia (now an Abbess of the city).

Much Ado About Nothing
Benedick and Beatrice have history; but their implacable mutual dislike is based on the simple fact that they completely love each other, as all their friends know – and who now contrive a series of deceptions to make them realize it. Their union is played out against the more solemn story of their younger relatives, Hero and Claudio, whose intended marriage is first thwarted – and then redeemed – by another set of deceptions.

Love's Labour's Lost
King Ferdinand of Navarre and his three friends swear themselves exempt from the company of women for a period of three years, in order to devote themselves exclusively to academic study. Then the Princess of France arrives on a state visit, along with three of her young waiting-women – with each of whom the young men fall in love and pair off – while seeking to conceal the fact from their fellows. The women playfully confuse their deception, but just as the stage seems set for four weddings, a funeral is announced: a messenger arrives with news that the King of France is dead, whereupon the men are charged to renew their suit after a penitential year of more serious thought.

A Midsummer Night's Dream
Duke Theseus of Athens is to marry Hippolyta, Queen of the Amazons. At court, Hermia loves Lysander; their friend Helena loves Demetrius. But Hermia's father proposes Demetrius as a better match, so Hermia and Lysander elope, running away into the forest, closely followed by Helena and, more reluctantly, Demetrius. Meanwhile, a band of amateur actors are rehearsing a play in the forest to celebrate Theseus's wedding. And meanwhile again, Oberon and Titania, the King and Queen of the Fairies, have quarrelled, and the love-potion Oberon commands his spirit-servant Puck to administer to her generates widespread confusion among the mortals before the course of true love can once again run smooth.

533

The Merchant of Venice

The wealthy heiress Portia is forced by the terms of her late father's will to audition for a suitable husband, and falls in love with the impoverished Bassanio, whose suit has been financed by his benefactor Antonio (the 'Merchant' of the title), who has contracted with the moneylender Shylock to bridge the loan – at the outrageous risk of 'a pound of flesh'. Antonio's debt is called in, but he is successfully defended at his trial by a brilliant young lawyer – in fact Portia in disguise.

As You Like It

Rosalind lives at court with her cousin Celia, the daughter of Duke Frederick, who has banished her own father, the usurping Duke Senior, to the Forest of Arden. Rosalind meets Orlando – whose life is sought by his usurping brother Oliver – and they fall in love, but each has now to flee the court. Rosalind (disguised as the boy 'Ganymede'), Celia ('Aliena') and the court jester, Touchstone, all trek to the Forest of Arden, closely followed by the lovelorn Orlando, himself pursued by the murderous Oliver, who comes to repent of his ways when Orlando saves his life. Despite multiple confusions, the play resolves into a festival of marriage, including that of Orlando to Rosalind, and Oliver to Celia.

The Taming of the Shrew

Three suitors arrive in Padua to seek the hand of the beautiful Bianca, but she cannot marry before her elder sister Kate, the strong-willed 'shrew' of the title, whom the impoverished Petruchio now woos – and wins, partly to gain her rich dowry and partly as a challenge to 'tame' her of her fearsome reputation. Deliberately humiliating Kate on their wedding day, he variously mistreats her thereafter. Meanwhile, Bianca has made a love-match with her choice of suitors, and Petruchio and Kate attend their wedding banquet, where Kate now declares she is a changed – and newly obedient – woman.

All's Well That Ends Well

Helena, the orphaned daughter of a celebrated doctor, is now the ward of the Countess of Roussillon. In reward for curing the King of France of an ailment, she is offered the husband of her choice, and chooses Bertram, the Countess's brattish son, with whom she is in love – but who rejects her and escapes to the wars with his boastful friend Parolles. Flippantly swearing he will only marry her on condition she both accepts a ring from him, and conceives a child by him, Bertram is then tricked into doing so, thinking her another woman, and so inadvertently fulfilling his obligation – just as Parolles is tricked into revealing his own cowardice.

Twelfth Night

Twins Viola and Sebastian are shipwrecked on the shores of Illyria, each thinking the other dead. Viola disguises herself as a boy ('Cesario'), and is employed at the court of the melancholy Orsino – who is in love with his unresponsive neighbour Olivia, who is herself grieving the death of a brother. Making things doubly awkward, the disguised Viola immediately falls in love with Orsino, and then, when she is sent as a messenger to her court, Olivia falls in love with 'Cesario'. Meanwhile, Olivia's drunken uncle, Toby Belch, conspires with friends to ridicule her sanctimonious steward Malvolio, successfully deceiving him into believing that Olivia is in love with him. The confusions multiply when Sebastian finds his way to Olivia's court, and – bewilderingly to him – is welcomed as Olivia's beloved. The truth is revealed, the twins are reunited, and each finds their true love, Viola with Orsino, Sebastian with Olivia. The only jarring note is Malvolio's bitter resentment at the cruel sport made of him.

The Winter's Tale

While entertaining his childhood friend Polixenes (King of Bohemia) on an extended visit, Leontes (King of Sicilia) becomes insanely convinced that his pregnant wife, Hermione, has been conducting an adulterous affair with him, and that the baby she is carrying is his friend's. Deaf to all reason, he arraigns Hermione for treason, giving orders to abandon their newborn baby girl on the desert shore of Bohemia – where the courtier charged with this mission is eaten by a bear. To Leontes' shame, the Oracle declares that Hermione is innocent. The couple's young son Mamillius dies, apparently from grief, closely followed by news of Hermione's death. Sixteen years later, unaware of her true parentage, their grown-up daughter Perdita, who was rescued and brought up by countryfolk, is being courted by Florizel – the son of Polixenes, whose angry objections to their liaison lead the couple to flee to Sicilia, where their true identities are revealed. The action concludes, immeasurably beautifully, when what purports to be a statue of Hermione stirs to life to offer forgiveness to all.

Histories

King John

King Richard the Lionheart (Richard I) has died, and his brother, 'Bad King John' (reigned 1199–1216), is on the English throne, then extending over large parts of France. John's reign is troublesome because of two rival contenders: Falconbridge, the patriotic and defiant 'Bastard' son of Richard I and Arthur (the infant son of their dead brother Geoffrey). There follow a series of futile wars in France, excommunication from the Pope, a failed invasion by the French – and the death of young Arthur while trying to escape his execution, which John has ordered. John dies, poisoned, and his young son Henry ascends to the throne as Henry III (reigned 1216–72).

Edward III

Rescuing the pure and indomitable Countess of Salisbury from the Scottish forces besieging her castle, King Edward III (reigned 1327–77) falls in love with her, but is brought to his senses when she threatens to kill herself rather than yield to his advances. Suitably chastened, he now enforces his claim to territories in France with a series of spectacular victories at the Battles of Sluys, Crécy and Poitiers (1340–8), aided by his heroic son Edward, the so-called Black Prince.

Richard II

The Black Prince died before his father, and so it was his son, the weak and decadent King Richard II (reigned 1377–99), who inherited the throne, and who now presides over a bitter dispute between his cousin, Henry Bolingbroke, and Thomas Mowbray (accused of embezzlement and murder). Richard banishes both men, and confiscates the inheritance Bolingbroke is due from his father, the noble John of Gaunt, who dies after bitterly criticizing Richard's government. But Bolingbroke returns, leading a popular uprising against the King, who agonizingly yields to him the crown, before then being murdered in prison. Instead of rewarding him, Bolingbroke guiltily banishes the murderer.

Henry IV, Part One

Henry Bolingbroke has usurped the throne as Henry IV (reigned 1399–1413), but soon faces rebellion from his former allies, including Edmund Mortimer and the dashing young Henry Percy, known as Hotspur. Meanwhile – to his enormous sadness – his son, Prince Hal, idles away his time in the dissolute company of the fat old knight Sir John Falstaff at the Boar's Head. Hal steps up to the plate at the Battle of Shrewsbury, where he kills Hotspur, but then returns to his old ways in time for the sequel . . .

Henry IV, Part Two

King Henry's reign (1399–1413) is still beset by rebellion, this time led by the Earl of Northumberland (Hotspur's father), and Prince Hal is still consorting – increasingly uneasily – with Falstaff. When Henry's army mobilizes, Hal rallies to the flag, and Falstaff corruptly press-gangs a battalion of cannon-fodder. The rebels are defeated, after Hal's brother Prince John duplicitously reneges on his promise to negotiate with them. Visiting his dying father, Hal mistakes him for dead, and tries on the crown for size – only for the King to awake, and upbraid him. Father and son are reconciled, however, and when Hal is crowned as Henry V, he publicly banishes Falstaff from his company.

Henry V
The newly crowned King Henry V (reigned 1413–22) unites his realm by achieving a spectacular victory against the French at the celebrated Battle of Agincourt (1415), and wins the hand of the King of France's daughter.

Henry VI, Part One
The victorious Henry V has died, to be succeeded by his baby son Henry VI (reigned 1422–61 and 1470–1) – the complications of those dates being the subject of this three-part play. English territorial gains in France are disastrously reversed – the valiant English soldier John Talbot is killed in action; his counterpart and nemesis, the messianic Joan of Arc, is captured and burned at the stake (1431). Meanwhile, factionalism has deepened at court among the rival powerbases wrangling to act as regent, culminating in a violent quarrel in a London garden between representatives of the dynastic houses of York and Lancaster, who respectively pick the emblems of the white rose and red rose: the 'Wars of the Roses' have begun.

Henry VI, Part Two
While a fragile peace exists between England and France, following the young King Henry's marriage to Margaret of Anjou, domestic division deepens and accelerates. Rebellion flares in Ireland, and closer to home in Kent, where the buffoonish pretender Jack Cade leads an abortive coup. Power abhors a vacuum, and the developing chaos culminates in the Battle of St Albans (1455) – the first encounter of the Wars of the Roses, in which the forces of Henry VI (descended from John of Gaunt, Duke of Lancaster – the Black Prince's younger brother) are defeated by those of Richard Plantagenet, Duke of York (1411–60), whose claim derives from a junior line of the same family.

Henry VI, Part Three
As *de facto* ruler, following the Battle of St Albans, Richard of York demands hard terms: in exchange for remaining King, Henry VI disinherits his son Edward in favour of the Yorkist line. Henry's wife, Margaret of Anjou, furiously rejects these terms, musters an army, and at the Battle of Wakefield (1460) York's young son Rutland, and York himself, are brutally killed. York's three surviving sons fight on: Edward (later Edward IV); the deformed and villainous Gloucester (later Richard III); and George, Duke of Clarence. Events escalate, and the Earl of Warwick (the 'Kingmaker')

switches his support to Henry VI, before dying from wounds in battle, and Queen Margaret's forces are defeated at Tewkesbury (1471). Edward, Gloucester and Clarence kill the Prince of Wales; then Gloucester murders the imprisoned Henry VI. Under Edward IV (reigned 1461–70 and 1471–83), the House of York now rules.

Richard III

The villainous and charming Duke of Gloucester plots his murderous way to the throne, dispatching family members (including his brother Clarence, and his ailing brother Edward IV's legitimate heirs, the 'Princes in the Tower'), former allies, and anyone else that opposes him, in a bloody course that sees him installed as Richard III (reigned 1483–5), and which only ends with his defeat at the Battle of Bosworth (1485). The Tudor dynasty is established under the victorious Henry Richmond (Henry VII, reigned 1485–1509) – the grandfather of Elizabeth I. The Wars of the Roses are at an end.

Henry VIII (All Is True)

Following negotiations with the French by King Henry VIII (reigned 1509–47), there is gossip at court about the disproportionate influence wielded by Cardinal Wolsey; his principal opponent, Buckingham, is arrested, then executed for treason. Meanwhile, the King has met Ann Boleyn at a party, and sets Wolsey the task of questioning the legality of his marriage to his first wife, Queen Katherine (of Aragon). Wolsey is then toppled from power, charged with treason, and executed. Told of Wolsey's death, the divorced Katherine dies, after Ann Boleyn, whom Henry has secretly married, is crowned Queen. The play ends with joyful news of the birth (1533) of a royal daughter – the future Elizabeth I.

Sir Thomas More

Riots have broken out in London, directed against an influx of refugees from Europe, but the situation is calmed by the popular, wise and witty Sheriff of London, Thomas More (1478–1535), whereupon he is promoted to the post of Lord High Chancellor at the court of Henry VIII. Generous, charismatic, and – crucially – pious, More refuses to endorse the King's divorce from Queen Katherine, and thus falls from favour – tried, imprisoned, and finally executed for his honourable principles.

Tragedies

Troilus and Cressida

The Siege of Troy has reached stalemate. As the rival armies wrangle among themselves, the Trojan Prince Troilus's love for Cressida (whose father has defected to the Greek camp) is consummated, her uncle Pandarus acting as go-between. But they only enjoy one night together before Cressida is sent to join her father in an exchange of prisoners – whereupon she immediately betrays him by accepting the suit of the Greek Diomedes, plunging Troilus into despair. Meanwhile, on the battlefield, his brother Hector is dishonourably killed by Achilles, confirming the nihilistic Greek Thersites's view that human life is nothing but 'wars and lechery', and Troilus vows revenge on Achilles on the battlefield.

Coriolanus

Following food shortages and civil unrest in Rome, the heroic Caius Martius achieves a spectacular victory against the Volscians' invading army at the town of Corioli, for which he is awarded the honorific title 'Coriolanus'. Prevailed upon to stand for political office, however, his lofty contempt for the people leads to his banishment, in revenge for which he joins forces with the Volscian leader Aufidius and marches on his ungrateful home city, deaf to all pleas to spare it – except, finally, those of his son, wife, and indomitable mother Volumnia. Peace is achieved – but Coriolanus is killed by the Volscians he has betrayed.

Titus Andronicus

Returning to Rome in triumph from the wars, the great general Titus brings home prisoners, including Tamora, Queen of the Goths, her three sons, and her lover, Aaron, a Moor. One of Tamora's sons is ritually killed, to appease the souls of the many sons Titus has lost in battle. Rome is divided, however, between Bassianus (to whom Titus's daughter Lavinia is betrothed) and his brother, the corrupt Saturninus, who, as Emperor, now makes Tamora his consort. In a vicious spiral of bloody revenge, Tamora's surviving sons rape and mutilate Lavinia, cutting out her tongue, and murder Bassianus – for which crime two of Titus's sons are accused by Aaron, and executed. The deranged Titus now kills Tamora's sons, and serves up their cooked flesh in a pie to Tamora at an imperial banquet, before killing her, and his own daughter Lavinia; Saturninus kills Titus, and is in turn killed by Titus's surviving son Lucius, who is now proclaimed Emperor.

Romeo and Juliet

The city of Verona is divided by an ongoing feud between two warring dynasties – the Capulets and Montagues. Romeo Montague, in the dumps after a love affair goes wrong, is persuaded to gatecrash a party thrown by Lord and Lady Capulet, where he meets, and passionately falls in love with, Juliet, their only daughter. The couple secretly marry, but fate intervenes: in a violent brawl between the warring factions, Juliet's cousin Tybalt, and Romeo's dear friend Mercutio, are both killed. Romeo is banished, and Juliet is forced into an arranged marriage with Count Paris, which she seeks to escape by faking her death: after drinking a potion that will render her body comatose (so the plan goes), she will be laid in her tomb, there be joined on waking by Romeo, and the two of them can then elope. But Romeo never receives the letter explaining this plan, and instead, informed of her death, he returns to the Capulet family vault in Verona, kills Paris, and desperately kills himself with poison. Only then does Juliet awake: distraught, she kills herself with Romeo's dagger.

Timon of Athens

The wealthy Timon is famed for his generosity, and widely courted by friends – to the derision of the misanthropic philosopher Apemantus. After a lavish banquet entertaining the young general Alcibiades, Timon's servant Flavius discloses that he is close to bankruptcy. Seeking financial aid from his friends, however, Timon is cold-shouldered, and he arranges a final sarcastic banquet for them of warm water and stones before cursing mankind and living as a recluse in the woods outside the city – to where Alcibiades has been banished by an ungrateful senate. Digging for roots one day, Timon discovers gold – which he now scornfully gives away, including some to Alcibiades to finance a military campaign against Athens. Meeting Apemantus, the two misanthropes curse mankind – and each other. Following Alcibiades's victory, news comes that Timon has died.

Julius Caesar

Welcomed home to Rome in triumph from the civil wars, Julius Caesar's path to absolute political power seems assured – but for a growing faction of republican politicians, headed by Cassius, uneasy at the prospect of his increasingly despotic rule, and plotting his assassination. Cassius enlists the support of his friend, the scrupulous Brutus, and Caesar is stabbed to death by the conspirators on the Ides of March (44 BCE) – the very date foretold him by a Soothsayer. Brutus and Cassius address the people at Caesar's funeral, but then allow Mark Antony, Caesar's favourite, whose life they had spared, to speak. Antony gains the support of the people, and the conspirators flee, Brutus and Cassius committing suicide in the aftermath of the Battle of Philippi (42 BCE) against the army of Mark Antony and Caesar's nephew Octavius.

Macbeth

The valiant soldier Macbeth is told by three witches that he will gain the title of Thane of Cawdor, and become king, and that his friend Banquo will father a dynasty of kings, though never himself hold that title. The first of these prophecies comes true, and Macbeth is persuaded by his wife to murder good King Duncan, who is visiting them, to be sure of the second, casting blame on Duncan's sons, who flee. Banquo is murdered on the orders of the newly crowned Macbeth, but his son escapes. Haunted by Banquo's ghost, Macbeth is now reassured by the witches, who tell him he is immune from anyone 'of woman born'. Callously murdering the family of Macduff, who has joined with Duncan's son Malcolm, the forces of good close in against him. Lady Macbeth goes mad and kills herself; and Macbeth is slain in battle by Macduff – not 'of woman born' because he was 'untimely ripped' from his mother's womb: i.e. he was delivered by caesarean section. Malcolm is proclaimed King of Scotland (Malcolm III, reigned 1058–93), to be succeeded by the dynasty established by Banquo's surviving son – then thought to include King James I.

Hamlet

Amidst mounting international tension against Norway, King Hamlet of Denmark is dead: murdered, it turns out, by his brother Claudius, who has now married his widowed queen, Gertrude – which is why his ghost now approaches his son, Prince Hamlet, on the battlements of Elsinore, seeking revenge. Hamlet feigns madness, rejects his close relationship with Ophelia (the daughter of the elderly court official Polonius), and exposes Claudius's guilt during the performance of a play by a company of travelling actors. Confronting Gertrude, he mistakenly kills the lurking Polonius, and is sent abroad by Claudius, with surreptitious orders for his death. The plot fails, and Hamlet returns to discover that Ophelia has gone mad with grief and drowned herself, and that her brother Laertes seeks revenge on him. Hamlet accepts his fate – killed in a rigged dual with Laertes, during which Gertrude drinks the poison Claudius intended for him. Hamlet at last kills Claudius, and Laertes succumbs to a scratch from his own poisoned blade, which has already mortally wounded Hamlet. It is left to his best friend Horatio to tell Hamlet's story, as the invading Norwegian army arrives.

King Lear

Old King Lear abdicates in favour of his three daughters, but sets them a disastrous 'love-test' to decide the extent of their inheritance. His elder daughters, Goneril (married to Albany) and Regan (married to Cornwall), flatter him, and manoeuvre for ever more brutal power when his youngest daughter Cordelia refuses to play the game, and is banished to France, along with Lear's honest counsellor Kent, who now disguises himself in order to serve him incognito. Meanwhile, in a closely parallel plot, Kent's fellow courtier Gloucester's illegitimate and wicked son Edmund dupes him into banishing his elder half-brother Edgar, in order to usurp his inheritance. Amidst an apocalyptic storm, Lear rages against his ungrateful daughters, whose doors are shut against him, accompanied in the countryside by his loyal Fool. After encountering the disguised Kent, and Edgar (now disguised as a mad beggar), they are offered shelter by Gloucester, who arranges their conveyance to Dover – in punishment for which, his eyes are gouged out by Cornwall; despairing, he is later prevented from killing himself by the unrecognized Edgar. Following a tender reconciliation with her father, Cordelia's invading army is defeated, and she is captured with Lear. Edgar defeats Edmund in a dual – but not in time to prevent Cordelia being hanged in prison. With Goneril and Regan also dead, Lear himself dies in unbearable suffering, and the governance of the kingdom devolves to Edgar and Albany.

Othello

The celebrated general Othello has married Desdemona, the daughter of the Venetian senator Brabantio, despite prejudice against him as an African 'Moor' – including from Iago, his trusted adjutant, whose secret hatred for him engineers his downfall. Transferred to the garrison of Cyprus to repel a failed Turkish invasion, Iago now insinuates to Othello that Desdemona has been unfaithful to him with their fellow officer, Cassio, contriving to supply proof of their adultery from a handkerchief Othello once gave her, and which she has carelessly lost. Maddened with jealousy, Othello instructs Iago to kill Cassio, then murders Desdemona in her bed. Iago's wife Emilia now declares the truth – and is stabbed to death by the cornered Iago. Cassio, grievously wounded, confirms Emilia's account; Othello, bitterly remorseful, kills himself. Iago remains inscrutably silent.

Antony and Cleopatra

Following the assassination of Julius Caesar (44 BCE), Rome is ruled by triumvirate – Mark Antony, Octavius Caesar, and Lepidus – but Antony is infatuated with the beguiling Queen of Egypt, Cleopatra, whose sensuous demands have led him to neglect his sterner duties. It is this split in Antony's loyalties, between Rome and Egypt, and his ultimate loyalty to Cleopatra, that culminates in Octavius's victory over them in the Battle of Actium (31 BCE). Amidst furious arguments, Cleopatra sends out a false report of her death; desolate, Antony makes a botched attempt at suicide, and, mortally wounded, is then reunited with Cleopatra before he dies. Rather than fall captive to the Romans, Cleopatra kills herself by snakebite.

Cymbeline

The two sons of King Cymbeline of Britain have been kidnapped in childhood. His daughter, Imogen, now shares a household with him, his new wife, and her oafish son Cloten, to whom she is betrothed against her will, despite her secret marriage to her true-love, Posthumus. Now banished to Rome, Posthumus accepts a wager as to Imogen's chastity from the villainous Jachimo, who falsely persuades him he has slept with her. Posthumus orders her murder, but his servant Pisanio, convinced of her innocence, instead advises Imogen to disguise herself as a boy, and flee to Wales, pursued there by Cloten (wearing Posthumus's clothes). There she is unwittingly welcomed by her exiled brothers, who kill Cloten – whose headless corpse Imogen mistakes for Posthumus, and takes poison: in fact a sleeping potion. Awaking, she joins the invading Roman army, against which Posthumus and the two brothers victoriously fight. A lengthy scene of reunion and reconciliation ensues.

Pericles

Pericles, Prince of the Mediterranean port of Tyre, embarks on a series of seaborne adventures – solving riddles, winning tournaments, and winning the hand of Princess Thaisa. On their journey home, however, a terrible storm breaks out, and Thaisa apparently dies at sea after giving birth to their baby daughter, Marina, whom he now entrusts to foster parents at another port. Fourteen years later, the grown-up Marina is kidnapped, and sold into a brothel, where her innate purity shames her clients. By chance – or providence – she is recruited to attend to the ailing Pericles, and father, daughter, and mother (Thaisa, miraculously cured) are reunited.

The Two Noble Kinsmen

Theseus's marriage to Hippolyta is postponed until he can prevail in the wars against Creon. When Creon is finally defeated, his nephews Palamon and Arcite (the 'Kinsmen' of the title) are confined to an Athens jail, from where they see Theseus's sister Emilia, with whom they both immediately fall in rivalrous love. Arcite is released, but remains, disguised, in Athens; Palamon is helped to escape by the unnamed Jailer's Daughter, whose unrequited love for him later drives her mad. The action culminates in a tournament between the cousins, arranged by Theseus to decide which of them shall marry Emilia. Arcite defeats Palamon – but is then fatally thrown from his horse, with his dying breath bequeathing his right to Emilia's hand to his noble kinsman Palamon.

Narrative Poems

Venus and Adonis
The beautiful youth Adonis is out hunting one day when his charms are spied – and then ardently pursued – by Venus, the goddess of Love. Adonis resists her advances, however, and the next morning she grievously discovers his body, gored to death by a boar.

The Rape of Lucrece
The Roman prince Tarquin is tormented by his lust for the fair and chaste Lucrece, the high-born wife of his fellow officer Collatine, and rapes her. Appalled, disgraced, yet resolute, Lucrece kills herself – eliciting from her family a solemn vow of revenge on Tarquin.

A Lover's Complaint
A distraught and unnamed woman is overheard lamenting her woes by a riverside: wooed by a beautiful young man whom she well knows to be feckless, she nevertheless allows herself to be seduced, and has now been abandoned.

TIMELINE

While external contemporary sources and internal illusions to current events provide good evidence for the dating of most of Shakespeare's works, scholars differ over the precise chronology of his canon: this timeline, however, represents a widespread consensus view.

c. 1557 **John Shakespeare (father) of Stratford-upon-Avon marries Mary Arden (mother).**

1558 JULY Birth of Robert Greene and George Peele. NOVEMBER Elizabeth I accedes to the English throne; birth of Thomas Kyd.

1559 JANUARY Coronation of Elizabeth I. Acts of Uniformity and Supremacy passed, rejecting papal authority and declaring Elizabeth I Supreme Head of the Church of England.

1560 Publication of the 'Geneva' Bible; Jean Nicot introduces tobacco to France.

1561 Rebellion breaks out in Ireland.

1562 Thomas Norton and Thomas Sackville's tragedy *Gorboduc* performed at court. John Hawkins transports a shipment of 300 enslaved people from the West Coast of Africa to the Caribbean: English participation in the slave trade begins.

1563 Publication of John Foxe's *Acts and Monuments*, detailing the history of Protestant martyrdom.

1564 FEBRUARY Birth of Christopher Marlowe; birth of Galileo; death of Michelangelo. 26 APRIL *'Gulielmus filius Johannes Shakspere'* **baptized at Holy Trinity, Stratford.** DECEMBER The Thames freezes over.

1565 The Ottoman Siege of Malta is repulsed. NOVEMBER Birth of Robert Devereux (later Earl of Essex).

1566 SEPTEMBER Birth of the actor Edward Alleyn. OCTOBER **Birth of Gilbert Shakespeare (brother).**

1567   Nobunaga initiates centralized government in Japan. JULY The
        infant James VI is crowned King of Scotland, following the forced
        abdication of his mother, Mary, Queen of Scots. NOVEMBER
        Birth of Thomas Nashe.

1568   Enslaved Africans are transported to the (since 1542) Spanish-
        occupied Philippines. Publication of Arthur Golding's translation
        of Ovid's *Metamorphoses* (a favourite source). SUMMER Birth of
        Richard Burbage. SEPTEMBER **John Shakespeare (father)
        elected bailiff at Stratford.**

1569   Final performances in England of the York Cycle of mystery
        plays; Don John of Austria suppresses Moorish rebellion in
        Granada; Gerard Mercator publishes navigational map of the
        world.

1570   The Mediterranean island of Cyprus is invaded by Ottoman
        forces; Gaspar Yanga leads a successful slave revolt against
        their Spanish oppressors in Mexico; John Dee publishes a
        'Mathematical Preface' to a translation of Euclid; publication
        of the first modern atlas, Abraham Ortelius's *Theatrum Orbis
        Terrarum*.

1571   AUGUST Titian's painting of *Tarquin and Lucretia* completed.
        OCTOBER Catholic (Christian) forces prevail against the
        Ottoman (Muslim) navy at the Battle of Lepanto.

1572   Dutch wars of independence begin. JANUARY Birth of John
        Donne. JUNE Birth of Ben Jonson; 'common players' classed
        as 'vagabonds and sturdy beggars' by Act of Parliament.
        SEPTEMBER Wan-Li (1563–1620) accedes to the throne as the
        14th Emperor of the declining Ming dynasty.

1573   OCTOBER Birth of his later patron, Henry Wriothesley
        (subsequently Earl of Southampton).

1574   MARCH **Birth of Richard Shakespeare (brother) in
        Stratford.** MAY Royal Patent granted for the Earl of Leicester's
        Players. DECEMBER Regulation of theatrical performances in
        London.

1575   Nicholas Hilliard paints the miniature 'Phoenix Portrait' of the

Queen; Paulo Dias de Novais of Portugal founds the port and city of Luanda, Angola. JULY Probably attends the spectacular public pageants laid on by the Earl of Leicester, the Queen's close adviser, to entertain her household at Kenilworth Castle (twelve miles from Stratford).

1576   Last performance of Wakefield cycle of mystery plays. James Burbage builds the Theater in Shoreditch; first Blackfriars theatre built. OCTOBER Rudolf II becomes Holy Roman Emperor. NOVEMBER Spanish troops, under the charge of Philip II of Spain's half-brother Don John, sack the Dutch city of Antwerp.

1577   Construction of the Curtain playhouse, Shoreditch; Elizabeth I grants the monopoly rights on whaling to the Muscovy Company. DECEMBER Francis Drake embarks on his circumnavigation of the globe aboard the *Pelican*.

1578   Martin Frobisher embarks on his third expedition, making landfall in Canada.

1579   Publication of Thomas North's translation of Plutarch's *Lives of the Noble Grecians and Romans* (a favourite source); and of Edmund Spenser's *Shepheardes Calendar*. OCTOBER Thomas Stephens (an English Catholic missionary) arrives in Goa – traditionally the first Englishman to set foot in India. DECEMBER Birth of John Fletcher.

1580   APRIL Birth of Thomas Middleton. JUNE Spanish forces invade Portugal. SEPTEMBER Francis Drake returns to Plymouth in the *Pelican* – now renamed the *Golden Hind* – after circumnavigating the globe.

1581   Publication of translations of Seneca's *Tenne Tragedies*. APRIL Francis Drake is knighted by the Queen. OCTOBER Henry Wriothesley becomes the 3rd Earl of Southampton. DECEMBER Edmund Tilney (died 1610) appointed Master of the Revels to Elizabeth's court, to license and censor all 'Comedies, Tragedies, Enterludes, or what ever such shows'.

1582   Jesuit mission founded in China. NOVEMBER **Marries Anne Hathaway at Shottery. Perhaps composes what is later (1609) published as Sonnet 145.**

1583 **MAY Susanna Shakespeare (daughter) born at Stratford.**

1584 Birth of Francis Beaumont; Walter Raleigh founds the colony of Virginia (named after Elizabeth I, the Virgin Queen). MARCH Death of Tsar Ivan IV of Russia ('Ivan the Terrible').

1585 MAY **Judith and Hamnet Shakespeare (twin children) born at Stratford (the last documented reference to the playwright by name until 1594).** AUGUST Queen Elizabeth commits military aid to the Dutch states against Spain. (The European wars drag on until 1604.)

1586 JULY The Babington Plot to assassinate Queen Elizabeth is exposed; Mary, Queen of Scots is arrested. OCTOBER Sir Philip Sidney dies of wounds at the Battle of Zutphen in Holland.

1587 Publication of *Holinshed's Chronicles* (a favourite source); Christopher Marlowe's *Tamburlaine* and Thomas Kyd's *Spanish Tragedy* first performed. JANUARY Construction of the Rose playhouse on Bankside. FEBRUARY Mary, Queen of Scots executed. JUNE William Knell, a member of the Queen's Men, is killed in a tavern brawl at Thame, Oxfordshire, during a provincial tour. SUMMER Short of a man, the Queen's Men perform at Stratford. (The company's repertoire includes versions of stories later retold in *Henry V* and *King Lear*.)

1588 Publication of Robert Greene's *Pandosto* (a later source for ***The Winter's Tale***) AUGUST The Queen addresses her troops at Tilbury; the Spanish Armada is defeated and scattered off the English coast. SEPTEMBER Death of Richard Tarlton, the greatest comedian of the age (later identified with the dead jester Yorick in *Hamlet*.)

1589 **Approximate arrival in London after the 'Lost Years' (since 1585), as an actor and textual 'fixer'. Possibly contributes to *Arden of Faversham*.** AUGUST Amidst ongoing civil war, Henry of Navarre succeeds the assassinated Henry III as King of France. SEPTEMBER The voyage to Scotland of Anne of Denmark, James VI's wife-to-be, is disrupted by storms.

1590   **Probably established in London; perhaps composing**
       The Taming of the Shrew*, and contributing to *Edward
       ***III*.** Publication of Thomas Lodge's prose novella *Rosalynde*
       (a source for ***As You Like It***), and of Books I–III of Edmund
       Spenser's *The Faerie Queene*.

1591   **Co-writes *Henry VI, Parts Two* and *Three***; publication of
       The Troublesome Reign of King John (a source for ***King John***);
       composing The Two Gentlemen of Verona (perhaps
       later revised to include Will Kemp's part as Lance).
       Marlowe and Kyd recorded as sharing London digs, and 'writing
       in one chamber'.

1592   John III of Sweden is succeeded by Sigismund III of Poland.
       MARCH–JUNE ***Henry VI, Part One* performed at the**
       Rose. JUNE–DECEMBER Plague closes down London theatres.
       SEPTEMBER **Mocked in print as an 'upstart crow'**; death
       of Robert Greene; **John Shakespeare (father) named in**
       Stratford as a possible 'recusant' (i.e. a non-attendee at
       church and perhaps an obstinate Catholic); composing
       with (or revising) George Peele's *Titus Andronicus*.
       OCTOBER Edward Alleyn marries Henslowe's stepdaughter Joan
       Woodward.

1593   **Composing *Richard III*.** FEBRUARY–DECEMBER Plague
       closes London theatres. APRIL **Completes *Venus and***
       ***Adonis*, dedicated to the Earl of Southampton: a**
       bestseller, regularly reprinted for the rest of his life.
       MAY Christopher Marlowe is stabbed to death in a Deptford
       tavern. DECEMBER theatres re-open. **Begins writing *Love's***
       Labour's Lost*; continues composing the *Sonnets
       (famous by 1598, two published 1599, all 154 published
       in 1609).

1594   JANUARY–FEBRUARY ***Titus Andronicus* performed at**
       the Rose, and submitted for publication. Plague revisits
       London, closing down the theatres. MAY **completes *The***
       ***Rape of Lucrece*, again dedicated to Southampton.**
       JUNE Theatres reopen. **Begins composing *Romeo and***
       ***Juliet*; recorded as a founder member of the Lord**
       Chamberlain's Men (along with leading actor Richard

Burbage and clown Will Kemp). Execution in London of Roderigo Lopez, a Jewish physician accused of plotting to poison the Queen. AUGUST Death of Thomas Kyd. SEPTEMBER Marlowe's *Tamburlaine, Doctor Faustus,* and *The Jew of Malta* all performed at the Rose (with Edward Alleyn in the title roles). DECEMBER *The Comedy of Errors* **performed at Gray's Inn; composing (or revising)** *King John.*

1595 Publication of Samuel Daniel's *Civil Wars* (a source for the Histories); Walter Raleigh explores the River Orinoco in South America. JANUARY **Possible early performance of** *A Midsummer Night's Dream.* FEBRUARY Execution in London of the Catholic poet and missionary Robert Southwell. MARCH **Paid for performing at court.** SUMMER The Swan playhouse opens on Bankside. AUGUST Spanish forces raid the coast of Cornwall. **Composing** *Richard II.* OCTOBER **John Shakespeare (father) applies for coat of arms.**

1596 Publication of Books IV–VI of Spenser's *Faerie Queene.* **Composing** *Henry IV, Part One.* Peace terms are negotiated between China and Japan. JUNE The Earl of Essex captures the Spanish ship *San Andres* (or *St Andrew*) on his daring raid, with Walter Raleigh, on the Spanish harbour of Cádiz. SUMMER Another invasion scare in London. AUGUST **Hamnet Shakespeare (son) buried at Stratford, aged eleven; composing** *The Merchant of Venice.* OCTOBER **Granted a coat of arms by the College of Heralds.** NOVEMBER Death of George Peele.

1597 **Composing** *Henry IV, Part Two.* Publication of John Gerard's *Herball, or Generall Historie of Plantes.* APRIL **Possible early performance of** *The Merry Wives of Windsor.* MAY **Purchases New Place in Stratford.** JUNE The Earl of Essex and Walter Raleigh command an unsuccessful armed expedition (including John Donne) to the Spanish Azores; the Dutch explorer William Barentsz dies returning from his third Arctic expedition. JULY–OCTOBER London theatres shut down, following the performance in AUGUST of *The Isle of Dogs* (a scandalous satirical play, now lost, by Ben Jonson and Thomas Nashe). NOVEMBER **Resident at St Helen's, Bishopsgate.** CHRISTMAS *Love's Labour's Lost* **performed at court.**

1598 **Paperback 'Quarto' editions of his plays begin to feature his name as their author as a selling-point on their titlepages.** Publication of the first part of Chapman's translation of Homer's *Iliad* (a source for ***Troilus and Cressida***). FEBRUARY **Prosecuted for hoarding malt in Stratford.** MAY The Treaty of Vervins ends the French civil wars. SEPTEMBER **Listed as householder in Stratford;** the actor Gabriel Spencer killed in a fight with Ben Jonson in Shoreditch. Death of Philip II of Spain. OCTOBER **Approached for a loan by Richard Quiney of Stratford; praised by Francis Meres as 'most excellent' for the 'fine filed phrase' of his comedies and tragedies, and for his 'sugar'd sonnets'; performs in Ben Jonson's *Every Man In His Humour*; composing *Much Ado About Nothing*; publication of *The Passionate Pilgrim* (featuring two of his unpublished sonnets).** *The First Part of the Civil Wars in France* (by Michael Drayton and Thomas Dekker) performed at the Rose. DECEMBER Dismantling of the Theater in Shoreditch.

1599 JANUARY Death and burial (in Westminster Abbey) of Edmund Spenser. FEBRUARY **Leaseholder of and shareholder of the Globe playhouse, built from the timbers of the 1576 Theater, and completed by MAY. Composing *As You Like It* and *Henry V*.** MARCH The Earl of Essex heads an army to Ireland to suppress rebellion. AUTUMN Thomas Dekker's *The Shoemakers' Holiday* performed (at the Rose). SEPTEMBER Essex returns in disgrace from Ireland; ***Julius Caesar*** and Ben Jonson's *Every Man Out of His Humour* are performed at the Globe. **Will Kemp, the company clown, leaves the Lord Chamberlain's Men.**

1600 JANUARY Henslowe and Alleyn contract to build the Fortune playhouse in Clerkenwell. FEBRUARY The cosmologist Giordano Bruno is burned at the stake in Rome for heresy. AUGUST Abd al-Wahid, the Moroccan Ambassador, begins a six-month residence in London. **The publication of *As You Like It*, *Much Ado About Nothing*, and *Henry V* (perhaps *Henry IV, Part Two*) is 'stayed';** publication of Morley's music to 'It Was a Lover and His Lass'. **Composition and first performances of *Hamlet*. Robert Armin replaces Kemp as the company's clown.** NOVEMBER Birth of Prince Charles – the future Charles I.

1601   FEBRUARY **Supporters of the Earl of Essex (including Southampton) commission a performance of *Richard II* at the Globe on the eve of his failed rebellion; Essex is executed, Southampton imprisoned; the company is later interrogated and exonerated.** JUNE Publication of *The Phoenix and the Turtle* (among poems by Jonson, Marston and Chapman). JULY ***Hamlet* registered for publication as 'lately acted'.** Spanish forces lay siege to the Dutch town of Ostend: a 'New Troy', it finally surrenders in June 1604. SEPTEMBER **Death of John Shakespeare (father).**

1602   FEBRUARY ***Twelfth Night* performed at Middle Temple, London.** MAY–SEPTEMBER **Purchases land and property in Stratford.** WINTER **Composing *Troilus and Cressida*.**

1603   Publication of John Florio's translation of Montaigne's *Essays* (a favourite source); **and of the first (illicit) Quarto edition of *Hamlet*.** MARCH Elizabeth I dies; James VI of Scotland accedes to the English throne. APRIL Southampton released from prison. MAY **Named in the warrant by which the Lord Chamberlain's Men became the King's Men;** plague closes the London theatres (until APRIL 1604). JULY Walter Raleigh imprisoned (until 1617) for plotting against the new King. AUGUST ***Love's Labour's Won*, praised by Meres in 1598, is included in a bookseller's catalogue (possibly an alternative title for *Much Ado About Nothing*). Performs in Ben Jonson's *Sejanus*; contributes to a revised version of *Sir Thomas More*. Composing *Othello* and *Measure for Measure*.**

1604   JANUARY James I convenes the Hampton Court Conference to propose a new English translation of the Bible. MARCH James I is ceremonially welcomed to London via Jonson and Dekker's elaborate pageant, *The Magnificent Entertainment*. MAY **Granted scarlet cloth for his livery as a member of the King's Men; bequeathed a gold ring in the will of his fellow player Augustine Phillips.** AUGUST James I concludes a European peace with Spain. AUTUMN **Sues a Stratford neighbour for an unpaid debt.** NOVEMBER Alleyn and Henslowe gain the Mastership of the King's Bears, Bulls, and Mastiff Dogs. NOVEMBER–DECEMBER *Othello* and *Measure for Measure* performed at court; resident at Silver Street, Cripplegate.

1605 **Composing *All's Well That Ends Well*.** JANUARY Publication in Madrid of the first part of Cervantes' *Don Quixote*; Ben Jonson begins a twenty-five-year collaboration with Inigo Jones on the court entertainments known as 'masques'. FEBRUARY ***The Merchant of Venice* twice performed at court.** JULY **Invests in land in Stratford.** AUGUST Ben Jonson and others are briefly imprisoned for offending the King in *Eastward Hoe*. SEPTEMBER–OCTOBER **Composing *King Lear*;** astronomical observation of both lunar and solar eclipses. NOVEMBER The 'Gunpowder Plot', to destroy England's government, is thwarted. **Begins co-writing *Timon of Athens* (with Thomas Middleton).**

1606 JANUARY **Composing *Macbeth*.** APRIL King James grants a royal charter to the Virginia Company. MAY Parliamentary Act passed to forbid actors 'in stage plays [to] jestingly of profanely speak or use the Holy Name of God'. DECEMBER ***King Lear* performed at court.**

1607 The dramatists Francis Beaumont and John Fletcher begin their writing partnership; the Virginia settlement of Jamestown (named after James I) is founded. APRIL Riots against food shortages flare up in the English Midlands. ***Antony and Cleopatra* performed.** JUNE **Susanna Shakespeare (daughter) marries Dr John Hall at Stratford.** DECEMBER The River Thames freezes over; **death of Edmund Shakespeare (his youngest brother: 'a player') and his burial at St Saviour; completes (with Middleton) *Timon of Athens*.**

1608 SPRING **Composing *Coriolanus*;** SUMMER **Writes *Pericles* (with George Wilkins): a smash hit at the Globe.** AUGUST **Sues another Stratford neighbour for unpaid debt; shareholder in lease at the Blackfriars theatre.** SEPTEMBER **Death of Mary Shakespeare (mother).**

1609 Gaspar Yanga resists Spanish assaults on his settlement of fugitive slaves at Veracruz. SUMMER Theatres close because of plague; the *Sea Venture* is wrecked on the coast of Bermuda, their scattered crew eventually making their way to Virginia. AUGUST Jonas Poole's Greenland expedition returns to London, presenting two captured polar-bear cubs to Alleyn and Henslowe's Beargarden. AUTUMN **The King's Men begin playing at Blackfriars. Publication of *Shake-speares Sonnets* and (in the same volume) *A Lover's Complaint*.** DECEMBER Galileo observes the moons of Jupiter.

1610   The estimated outset of the 'Anthropocene' geological era. **Revising *King Lear*.** JULY Publication in Venice of Claudio Monteverdi's *Vespers*; death of Caravaggio. AUGUST George Buck succeeds Edmund Tilney as Master of Revels. SEPTEMBER William Strachey's eye-witness account of the *Sea Venture* reaches London, a source for ***The Tempest***. NOVEMBER **Begins writing *The Winter's Tale*.**

1611   Publication in London of the Authorized ('King James') Version of the Bible; Epenow, a Native American, is kidnapped in Massachusetts, to be later 'exhibited' in London; work begins on the Masjid-i-Shah (the Shah Mosque) in Isfahan. JANUARY Jonson's *Masque of Oberon* (featuring shepherds and bears) performed at court. APRIL–MAY ***Macbeth, Cymbeline*, and *The Winter's Tale* performed at the Globe.** SEPTEMBER **Contributes to road repairs in Stratford;** the astrologer-doctor and play-goer Simon Forman dies in London – on the day he predicted he would. OCTOBER Gustavus Adolphus accedes to the Swedish throne. NOVEMBER ***The Tempest* and *The Winter's Tale* performed at court.**

1612   JANUARY Death of Rudolf II; publication of Thomas Shelton's translation of Cervantes' *Don Quixote*. FEBRUARY **Death of Gilbert Shakespeare (brother) in Stratford.** SUMMER **Testifies in a lawsuit in the Court of Requests.** NOVEMBER Prince Henry dies of typhoid. DECEMBER A minor sea-battle against Portuguese forces at Suvali, in the seas off Gujarat, consolidates a British presence in India.

1613   The Native American princess, Pocahontas, is held captive in Jamestown, Virginia. FEBRUARY **Death of Richard Shakespeare (brother) at Stratford;** Princess Elizabeth marries Elector Frederick (their wedding delayed following the death of Prince Henry); Michael I (the first of the Romanovs) elected Tsar of Russia. ***The Tempest* performed at court. MARCH Commissioned to write a heraldic motto for the Earl of Rutland; purchases the Blackfriars Gatehouse near the Blackfriars theatre.** SUMMER *Cardenio* **(now lost, written with Fletcher, based on Cervantes' *Don Quixote*) performed at court.** JUNE **Fire destroys the Globe during a performance of *Henry VIII* (written with Fletcher);** AUGUST Henslowe contracts to build the Hope, a combined playhouse and beargarden, on Bankside. AUTUMN **Composing *The Two Noble Kinsmen* (written with Fletcher).**

1614   Publication in Edinburgh of John Napier's work on logarithms and trigonometry; Epenow contrives his escape back to Massachusetts; **the second Globe is built, in tiles and brick, on the site of the first.** APRIL Death of the painter El Greco. AUTUMN **Involved in litigation in Stratford.** OCTOBER Ben Jonson's comedy *Bartholomew Fair* performed at the Hope playhouse.

1615   Death of Robert Armin. Galileo's work on astronomy challenged by papal authorities.

1616   Publication of *The Workes of Benjamin Jonson* (the first ever collected works of a living playwright). JANUARY Death of Philip Henslowe. FEBRUARY **Judith Shakespeare (daughter) marries Thomas Quiney (later tried for fornication) at Stratford.** MARCH Death of Francis Beaumont. 25 MARCH **Draws up his will.** 23 APRIL **Dies at Stratford;** 25 APRIL **Buried in Holy Trinity Church.** Death of Cervantes.

1617   Pardoned by the King, Walter Raleigh embarks on a disastrous expedition to South America, in search of 'El Dorado'.

1618   MARCH Death of Richard Burbage. MAY The catastrophe of the pan-European Thirty Years War (1618–48) begins. JULY Ben Jonson embarks on a walk to Scotland. OCTOBER Walter Raleigh executed at Westminster.

1619   MAY **The King's Men lodge an injunction against a series of reprinted editions of Shakespeare's plays being printed by Thomas Pavier – pending their own**

publication of the First Folio collection. SEPTEMBER
Edward Alleyn founds his College of God's Gift at Dulwich.

1620 NOVEMBER The 'Pilgrim Fathers' land at Massachusetts aboard
the *Mayflower.*

1621 NOVEMBER John Donne ordained as Dean of St Paul's
Cathedral. DECEMBER The Fortune playhouse burns down.

1622 JANUARY Birth of the French playwright Molière. JUNE Fellow
actor John Heminge dines with Edward Alleyn, possibly in
connection with Heminge and Condell's editing of Shakespeare's
works.

1623 JULY Death of the composer William Byrd. AUGUST **Death
of Anne Shakespeare (wife).** NOVEMBER **Publication
of *Mr. William Shakespeares Comedies, Histories, &
Tragedies* (the 'First Folio').** DECEMBER Following the
death of his first wife Joan in JUNE, Edward Alleyn (d. 1626)
marries Constance, the daughter of John Donne (d. 1631).

1624 Frans Hals paints *The Laughing Cavalier.* AUGUST
Performances of the 'scandalous comedy' of Middleton's *A
Game at Chess* at the Globe lead to a warrant for his arrest.
NOVEMBER Death of the Earl of Southampton.

1625 MARCH Death of James I; succeeded by his son, Charles I. JUNE
Death of the composer Orlando Gibbons. AUGUST Death of John
Fletcher.

Index of Works

Sources and Further Reading

Books:

Bate, Jonathan, *Soul of the Age* (London: Penguin, 2008)

Bate, Jonathan and Thornton, Dora, *Shakespeare: Staging the World* (London : British Museum Press, 2012)

Blackburn, Bonnie and Holford-Strevens, Leofranc, *The Oxford Companion to the Year* (Oxford: Oxford University Press, 1999)

Bloom, Harold, *The Invention of the Human* (London: Fourth Estate, 1999)

de Somogyi, Nick, *Shakespeare on Theatre* (London: Nick Hern Books, 2012)

Dobson, Michael and Wells, Stanley, *The Oxford Companion to Shakespeare* (Oxford: Oxford University Press, 2001)

Doran, Gregory, *The Shakespeare Almanac* (London: Hutchinson, 2009)

Hall, Peter, Shakespeare's Advice to the Players (London: Oberon, 2004)

Hazlitt, William, *Characters of Shakespeare's Plays* edited by J. H. Lobban (Cambridge: Cambridge University Press, 2009)

Holden, Anthony, *William Shakespeare: His Life and Work* (London: Abacus, 2016)

Hughes, Ted, *A Choice of Shakespeare's Verse* (London: Faber and Faber, 1971)

Jardine, Lisa, *Reading Shakespeare Historically* (London: Routledge, 1996)

Kermode, Frank, *Shakespeare's Language* (London: Allen Lane, 2000)

Laroque, François, *Shakespeare's Festive World: Elizabethan Seasonal Entertainment and the Professional Stage*, trans. by Janet Lloyd (Cambridge: Cambridge University Press, 1999)

Nicholl, Charles, *The Lodger on Silver Street* (London: Allen Lane, 2007)

Paterson, Don, *101 Sonnets: From Shakespeare to Heaney* (London: Faber and Faber, 2012)

Paterson, Don, *Reading Shakespeare's Sonnets: A New Commentary* (London: Faber and Faber, 2010)

Shakespeare, William and Rylands, George. *The Ages of Man: Shakespeare's Image of Man and Nature* (London: Heinemann, 1939)

Shakespeare, William; Bate, Jonathan; Héloïse, Sénéchal, and Rasmussen, Eric, *The RSC Shakespeare: William Shakespeare Complete Works* (Basingstoke : Macmillan, 2007)

Shapiro, James, *1599: A Year in the Life of William Shakespeare* (London: Faber and Faber, 2005)

Shapiro, James, *1606: William Shakespeare and the Year of Lear* (London: Faber and Faber, 2015)

Tanner, Tony, *Prefaces to Shakespeare* (Cambridge, Mass.: Belknap, 2010)

Tilley, Morris Palmer, *A Dictionary of the Proverbs in England in the Sixteenth and Seventeenth Centuries: A Collection of the Proverbs Found in English Literature and the Dictionaries of the Period* (Ann Arbor: U. of Michigan, 1950)

Tillyard, E. M. W., *The Elizabethan World Picture* (London: Harmondsworth, 1986)

Wells, Stanley, *Shakespeare on Page and Stage: Selected Essays*, ed. by Paul Edmondson (Oxford: Oxford University Press, 2016)

Willes, Margaret, *A Shakespearean Botanical* (Oxford: Bodleian, 2015)

During research I consulted *The First Folio Shakespeare* individual volumes (Harrap & co, 1906) that I bought in a second-hand bookshop in Hay-on-Wye when I was touring with the English Shakespeare Company in the late 1980s, *The Royal Shakespeare Company William Shakespeare Complete Works* (Macmillan, 2007), *The Royal Shakespeare Company William Shakespeare* individual volumes (Macmillan, 2010), Pelican Shakespeare individual editions (Penguin Random House, 2016) and Penguin single volumes (Penguin Classics, 1968, various), Folger Shakespeare library online editions, Arden Shakespeare individual editions (The Arden Shakespeare Third Series).

Podcasts:

MacGregor, Neil, *Shakespeare's Restless World* (BBC Podcasts, 2012) <https://www.bbc.co.uk/programmes/b017gm45/episodes/downloads> [accessed 05/12/2018]

Smith, Emma, *Approaching Shakespeare* (University of Oxford Podcasts, 2012-17) <https://podcasts.ox.ac.uk/series/approaching-shakespeare> [accessed 05/12/2018]

Various contributors, *Shakespeare Unlimited* (Folger Shakespeare Library Podcasts) <https://www.folger.edu/shakespeare-unlimited> [accessed 05/12/2018]

Online articles consulted include:

Brotton, Jerry, 'Is this the real model for Othello?', *Guardian*, www.theguardian.com/culture/2016/mar/19/moroccan-ambassador-london-1600-real-othello-shakespeare

'Globe', Bookanista, www.bookanista.com/globe/

'Triumphes and Mirth', Zoe Wanamaker Official Website www.
zoewanamaker.com/stage.php?name=Triumphes_and_Mirth

Websites consulted include:
BBC Shakespeare 2016, https://www.bbc.co.uk/programmes/p03fv1wr
The British Library, <www.bl.uk>
Folger Shakespeare Library, <www.folger.edu>
The Oxford English Dictionary Online, <www.oed.com>
Shakespeare Birthplace Trust, https://www.shakespeare.org.uk
Shakespeare's Globe, <www.shakespearesglobe.com

Acknowledgements

It is my great fortune that Professor Michael Dobson, Director of the Shakespeare Institute in Stratford-upon-Avon and Professor of Shakespeare Studies at the University of Birmingham, agreed to read the book at manuscript stage. All mistakes are, of course, my own. Any clever bits are most likely his suggestions.

Readers
I am most grateful, too, to Nick de Somogyi, for his expert suggestions and superlative work on the endmatter and Karen Harker at the Shakespeare Institute for her meticulous work checking all of the Shakespeare extracts.

At Macmillan
Gaby Morgan, for commissioning and championing it all, Venetia Gosling, Belinda Rasmussen, Alyx Price, Emma Quick, Kat McKenna, Simran Sandhu, The Dimpse and Sue Mason.

Research work
Dan Einav and Lana Crowe who helped at the beginning and Liam Etheridge who helped from midway to the end.

At C&W literary agency
Allison de Frees for leading me to the Ted Hughes anthology and my incomparable agent, Clare Conville, for everything.

And in America
Thank you to Patrick Nolan, Matthew Klise and the entire team at Penguin, and to Elda Rotor at Penguin Classics.

At FMcM
Annabel Robinson, Sophie Goodfellow, Fiona McMorrough.

At Fane
Alex Fane, James Albrecht and the team.

Actors, friends and family
Huge thanks to the actors, friends and family who have performed poems and Shakespeare for me in the past, or given me ideas along the way: Sarah Alexander, Ronni Ancona, Adjoa Andoh, Alexander Armstrong, Sheila Atim, Annette Badland, Maiken Baird, Morwenna Banks, Gina

Bellman, Pippa Bennett-Warner, Elena Bonham Carter, Helena Bonham Carter, Sanjeev Bhaskar, Kathryn Buscall, Venetia Butterfield, Olly Cairns, Tara Cairns, Clare Clarke, Dad, Penny Downie, Kate Duchêne, Beatie Edney, Harry Enfield, Jane Epstein, Eliza Esiri, Henrietta Esiri, Jack Esiri, Mark Esiri, Rosie Esiri, Kirsten Fear, Kate Fleetwood, Peter Forbes, Juliet Garmoyle, Tamsin Greig, Susannah Herbert, Tom Hiddleston, Chris Holifield, Caroline Hutton, Derek Jacobi, Toby Jones, Richard Kay, Rory Kinnear, Anton Lesser, Damian Lewis, Ophelia Lovibond, Damian Lynch, Tif Loehnis, Joanna Lumley, Lisa Makin, Stephen Mangan, Tobias Menzies, Ben Miller, Hattie Morahan, Helen McCrory, Alexandra Mousavizadeh, Mum, Tracy Ann Oberman, Nathaniel Parker, Poetry Summit Members, Andrea Reese, Chris Riddell, Tony Robinson, Hugh Ross, Simon Russell Beale, James Sherwood, Melanie Sherwood, Alison Steadman, Imogen Stubbs, Giles Terera, Sophie Turner, Indira Varma, Sarah Vine, Laura Wade, Zoe Wanamaker, Samuel West and Emma Wilkins.